Palgrave Executive

Today's complex and changing business environment brings with it a number of pressing challenges. To be successful, business professionals are increasingly required to leverage and spot future trends, be masters of strategy, all while leading responsibly, inspiring others, mastering financial techniques and driving innovation.

Palgrave Executive Essentials empowers you to take your skills to the next level. Offering a suite of resources to support you on your executive journey and written by renowned experts from top business schools, the series is designed to support professionals as they embark on executive education courses, but it is equally applicable to practicing leaders and managers. Each book brings you in-depth case studies, accompanying video resources, reflective questions, practical tools and core concepts that can be easily applied to your organisation, all written in an engaging, easy to read style.

More information about this series at
https://link.springer.com/bookseries/16879

John Colley • Dimitrios Spyridonidis

Unprecedented Leadership

Learning to Lead in Turbulent Times

palgrave
macmillan

John Colley
Warwick Business School
University of Warwick
Coventry, UK

Dimitrios Spyridonidis
Warwick Business School
University of Warwick
Coventry, UK

ISSN 2731-5614   ISSN 2731-5622   (electronic)
Palgrave Executive Essentials
ISBN 978-3-030-93485-9   ISBN 978-3-030-93486-6   (eBook)
https://doi.org/10.1007/978-3-030-93486-6

This Palgrave Macmillan imprint is published by the registered company Springer Nature Switzerland AG.
The registered company address is: Gewerbestrasse 11, 6330 Cham, Switzerland

Preface

Many books rely heavily on the experience and knowledge of their authors, and this book—*Unprecedented Leadership: Learning to Lead in Turbulent Times*—is no exception. It adopts a multi-perspective view founded on years of expertise from its main authors and augmented further by the valuable insights of guest contributors.

John Colley is Professor of Practice and Associate Dean at Warwick Business School. He has 30 years' experience in board director roles, 26 years of which involved chairing different organisations. His approach has been much admired by both publicly listed and privately owned organisations alike, including a FTSE 100 business and French CAC 40 business. In the last fourteen years, his doctorate research has led to the development of a dual position that balances teaching executives and leadership roles in university business schools, whilst concurrently chairing commercial businesses.

His perspective reflects valuable diversity in the discussion of theory and practice. Students are encouraged to question and reflect on their response to certain scenarios that, with their backbone of theory, will be widely applicable in the honing of leadership skills. Areas such as leading during crises, making difficult decisions, and negotiating complex situations all include ethical and value-based challenges that now come upon leaders with greater rapidity and magnitude than ever previously known.

His writing speaks specifically (but not exclusively) to developing leaders. Although most successful leaders will admit that it is broadly time and experience that have shaped their ability, this is an ongoing process for leaders and learners alike, and therefore a text that accelerates development is valuable to leaders at all stages of their career.

From a plethora of theoretical diagrams, Professor Colley's chapters reflect and summarises prominent lines of research, selecting the most helpful and relevant models to reinforce his arguments. To these he applies the filter of a practitioner with the constructive, though daunting advice that good leadership can be a 'be cruel to be kind' approach. These chapters are supported by numerous examples, posing questions that reveal the complex and ambiguous nature of decision making. Although these cases are described and discussed, for some the author has deliberately concealed their solutions. Many therefore have no clear-cut conclusion and rely on the developing leaders to consider their own approach to resolving the situation. Professor Colley has written the first four chapters in this book.

Dimitrios Spyridonidis began his working career as a veterinary surgeon before becoming an academic both researching and teaching leadership to executives. Having previously taught and researched at Henley Business School and Imperial College Business School, he has offered courses on leadership and leadership development around the globe, including the UK, Ireland, Finland, Denmark, South Africa, Malaysia, and Hong Kong.

Dimitrios is now an Associate Professor at Warwick Business School where he is the Programme Director of the Executive MBA and the Executive Diploma in Strategic Leadership. He has extensive experience working with executives to develop their capabilities, as well as contributing diverse academic perspectives. Like John, Dimitrios has developed his own practical insights for contextualised by a background of philosophical and intellectual thought, addressing key advice for leading the self, as well as strategic, responsible, and distributed leadership. Dimitrios has contributed the next three chapters (5, 6 and 7)

Together, these two main authors have developed the form and content of most of the materials presented and have very much 'practiced what they preach' in the collaborative essence of the publication. In the final section, three further authors have been invited to contribute individual chapters reflecting on their particular expertise.

Bob Thomson, also a Professor of Practice at Warwick Business School, has written several successful books on coaching, including *How to Coach* (2020). He teaches executives and MBA students and upholds his reputation as a well-known expertise in his field. He is accredited as both coach and supervisor of coaching by the European Mentoring and Coaching Council. Thomson's chapter draws on these skills in a discussion of how coaching can be a valuable means of developing both team members and senior executives.

Tim Wray is also a Professor of Practice and has held Director of Executive Education roles at Warwick Business School and previously Nottingham University Business School. He has over 30 years of experience as a practitioner, consultant, and executive educator, specialising in strategic change, leadership, organisational communication, and employee engagement. Tim leads the 'Executive Diploma in Organisational Change' offered by Warwick Business School. He has worked with senior leaders across both the public and private sectors, including several leading global companies.

Prior to entering the world of executive education, Tim spent over a decade as Director of Internal Communications at a large, publicly owned utility, including a period in which the organisation underwent major transformation. He has contributed a chapter on leadership communication within organisations, integrating communications, behavioural science, and network theory. Through this chapter, he offers a new perspective on how leaders can fully harness the power of communication as a leadership tool.

Alan Matcham is an Executive Fellow and Associate Professor at Warwick Business School. Like Professor Colley, his career spans over 30 years as a practitioner in industry, including senior international roles within the Oracle Corporation and The Thomas Cook Group. Most notably, he navigated Thomas Cook through the unprecedented and life-changing turmoil of Chinese social unrest whilst in the role of general manager in Hong Kong and China.

Having experienced great breadth of leadership approaches, styles, and contexts, Alan pursued an academic career, and for over a decade has dedicated himself to helping leaders navigate and thrive in culturally complex situations. He has worked with organisations all around the world, often on behalf of some of Europe's leading business schools. This includes being the first Executive Director of the Management Innovation Laboratory at London Business School and a Programme Director at Oxford Said and Henley Business Schools. Alan's work is deliberately intended to challenge popular myths and unhelpful orthodoxies in regard to how organisations are led and managed and, in doing so, encourages leaders to reflect on and reconsider their own approach. He contributes a different perspective again by considering various paradoxes of leadership in his chapter 'Crises, Collaboration and Hierarchy: When Does Executive Education Help?'

Coventry, UK   John Colley
Coventry, UK   Dimitrios Spyridonidis

Acknowledgements

This book is the product of many years of class-based discussion to compile the key leadership issues which really matter to our executive students. Indeed, this book was inspired by our many interactions, which helped to identify what is really important to aspiring leaders as they progress in their responsibilities and leadership capabilities. From their experiences, we have attempted to synthesise common mistakes, and reflect on what might be done differently using the models and approaches outlined in this book. Whilst there is often significant agreement on many subjects within a class, the area which produces the most debate and typically ends without accord, is that of ethics and values. An international audience rarely holds the same opinions, and we are delighted to have the privilege of assisting such a diverse body of students in the progression of their careers as they make decisions about the future of their businesses.

As the practical advice in this book is based on theory, we are indebted to the academics and practitioners who have helped identify paths forward. We have attempted to build upon and interpret their theory when analysing and deciding what to do in common practical situations.

We are also sincerely grateful to Warwick Business School for creating a learning environment in which ideas can flourish, and offering the opportunity to meet with so many talented academics and students, whose differing perspectives are ideal for challenge and development of thought.

We particularly wish to thank our guest authors Tim Wray, Alan Matcham, and Bob Thomson for their specialist knowledge and willingness to contribute a chapter each on their particular areas of expertise.

We would like to thank Rosemary Morrison for her great professionalism and patience in helping to manage this project forward to completion. In particular, her work as a developmental editor provided valuable input on the conceptual framing of the book in its early stages. We would also like to extend our appreciation to Lauren Colley for her careful editorial work in the final stages of the project. Special thanks also go to Rylee Mathis for assistance with the diagrams, the support of Palgrave Macmillan, particularly that of Liz Barlow and Srishti Gupta for their rapid responses to our questions and in helping to bring this project to fruition.

John: I would in particular like to thank my family for their unwavering support and helpful challenge. My wife Jackie has always provided great support in all I do.

Dimitrios: It goes without saying that I would like to thank my family, my father, Ioannis Spyridonidis, and my mother Vasiliki Spyridonidou, who always support and challenge me in everything I do. I would also like to thank Andrew Vaid and David McLeod who rather selflessly shared their ideas with me and allowed me to use some of their work to inform the chapter on leading change.

We do hope and anticipate that our future readers will benefit from the accumulated knowledge and experience which this book attempts to convey.

How to Use This Book

This book is designed to assist you in gaining a greater understanding of what constitutes effective leadership, particularly during turbulent times, and how you can work to become such a leader.

We consider the development of effective leadership to be an on-going process that requires many abilities including awareness, flexibility, reflection, resilience, hard work, and the courage to grow, to name a few. There is never a point at which your work is done. This becomes especially apparent when the environment in which you lead is in continual flex and challenges existing orthodoxies, assumptions, and belief systems.

Within such a setting, it has become increasingly important for leaders to find the time to stop and think, challenge their existing ways of acting as a leader, reflect on how they are defining and fulfilling their own roles and how they are working with others. Those willing to engage with this process will improve their effectiveness as a leader and be better equipped to lead during turbulent times.

To that end, this book offers several tools that you can continue to draw from in order to engage in reflective practice as you work to become a more effective leader. They include the following.

Open-Ended Real-Life Case Studies

You will find real-life case studies embedded within most chapters of this book. These are examples of organisations that went through a crisis or a difficult situation with variable degrees of success. They provide fertile ground for debate, improved problem-solving skills and critical thinking. Engagement with case studies will help readers to reflect on their decision making skills and manage complicated situations. Readers are advised to stop and think about how they would have engaged with the key issues and dilemmas within each case study

Reflection Points

As with the case studies, Reflection points suggest a time for readers to stop and think. The points are embedded in each chapter to encourage readers to exercise critical thinking and reflective practice to challenge how they think. The main aim here is to help readers grow more self-aware and in the habit of regularly reflecting on projects in which you are involved.

Journaling Opportunities

As readers go through this book, they are encouraged to keep a journal, that is, a summary of their thoughts, lessons learned, and action plans for leadership. In order to prepare for the responsibilities of leadership, it is essential to begin with personal development. Over time, readers can reflect on what they have written and capture emerging patterns that will offer insights into their behaviour or leadership practice.

Our hope is that this volume and aforementioned tools will offer opportunities for leadership development and growth. Good luck and happy reading!

Contents

Part I   Introduction   1

1   Unprecedented Times: Why a New Kind of Leadership Is
     Needed   3

Part II   Crisis from the Ground Up   23

2   Crises Global and Local: When Leadership Becomes Critical   25

3   Making Decisions in a Volatile, Uncertain World   41

4   Ethics and Values: Negotiating a Complex Minefield   65

Part III   Philosophical Underpinnings and New Directions   93

5   Leading Change in Turbulent Times   95

6   Creating the Capacity for Strategic Leadership   119

7   Responsible Leadership and Sustainability   139

Part IV   Communication, Education, and Coaching—Tools for
          Leading During Crisis   161

  8 The Purpose and Power of Leadership Communication   163

  9 Paradoxes in Executive Development   185

 10 Coaching for Leadership   219

Part V   Conclusion   235

 11 Conclusion: Unprecedented Leadership for Unprecedented
     Times   237

Index   243

List of Figures

Fig. 1.1 Main barriers to effective delegation   14
Fig. 1.2 Key elements of strategic leadership   18
Fig. 1.3 Demonstrating authenticity when communicating   20
Fig. 2.1 Leading in crisis   29
Fig. 2.2 Elements of crisis leadership   34
Fig. 3.1 Key elements of effective decision making   45
Fig. 3.2 Decision making distortion through personality influences   46
Fig. 3.3 When to involve the team   49
Fig. 3.4 Business performance before and after CEO change   55
Fig. 3.5 How to appoint the right CEO   56
Fig. 3.6 Improving your organisation's decision making   59
Fig. 4.1 Key characteristics associated with ethical decision making   74
Fig. 4.2 Creating an ethical culture   85
Fig. 4.3 Signs of a poor ethical culture (adapted from Marianne
          Jennings 'Seven Signs of Ethical Collapse')   86
Fig. 5.1 Forces for and against major change   108
Fig. 5.2 Ingredients of success. An adaptation from the work of
          Kotters' and Knoster (1991)   113
Fig. 9.1 Old and new design rules   189
Fig. 9.2 Role profile for senior executive   191
Fig. 9.3 Business as usual/business as unusual   192
Fig. 9.4 Tensions and trade-offs   193
Fig. 9.5 Formulaic approach to leadership and its development   195
Fig. 9.6 Rebalancing the executive development effort   197
Fig. 9.7 Beliefs and orthodoxies come in many flavours   208
Fig. 9.8 Discovery learning experiences   210

Part I

Introduction

1

Unprecedented Times: Why a New Kind of Leadership Is Needed

Ours is essentially a tragic age, so we refuse to take it tragically. The cataclysm has happened, we are among the ruins, we start to build up new little habitats, to have new little hopes. It is rather hard work: there is now no smooth road into the future; but we go round, or scramble over the obstacles. We've got to live, no matter how many skies have fallen. D. H. Lawrence, *Lady Chatterley's Lover* (1928)

Unbeknownst to him at the time of writing, D. H. Lawrence would be poignantly accurate when it comes to the numerous crises that have punctuated the century to come, events that for all of us have been in some way life changing.

In the context of business, a literary quote may seem misplaced. However, there are few other arenas in which decision making, mobilising and motivating a team are so pivotal to an organisation's survival. How a leader is to manage these events is the premise for this book. By assembling perspectives from both practitioners and academics, it considers how today's emerging leaders must learn to adapt and respond to crises in the face of uncertainty.

The twenty-first century has experienced a frequency and level of crises never before seen. For many years, the acceleration in climate change has been at the forefront of concerns, demanding a complete rethink by governments and organisations, not only in terms of investment in new energy sources but also in how we travel, produce, and package goods and provide services.

Exacting a more immediate and complete reaction, however, has been COVID-19, the pandemic from which few of us have emerged untouched. If not bereavement and illness, anxiety levels have left many with a poorer

© The Author(s), under exclusive license to Springer Nature Switzerland AG 2022
J. Colley, D. Spyridonidis, *Unprecedented Leadership*, Palgrave Executive Essentials,
https://doi.org/10.1007/978-3-030-93486-6_1

quality of life. Firms and organisations have struggled for survival, many have disappeared altogether, and mental health is suffering as a direct consequence of lockdowns. Some economic consequences may be addressed rapidly once the pandemic abates, but mental health issues may persist for many years, blighting people's lives.

Organisations are having to adapt at short notice to a very different future in which town centres, communication, and trade undergo or have already instigated major change. The days of the office commute seem numbered, or at least vastly diminished. In addition, a trend towards economic isolation and protectionism has had significant implications for the UK. Although sudden changes in trading partners may have severely damaged trade in some sectors, they may also create opportunities in the future.

From these apparently bleak circumstances, there are lessons to be learnt, particularly when it comes to leadership. As crises arise, accelerate, and change the face of business, leaders must learn to adapt; the need for different approaches is now unprecedented.

Crises, major change, and ethical dilemmas demand a level of leadership for which few have previously been prepared. Seizing opportunities and anticipating and responding to events require a level of capability which is not developed overnight. Agile leadership is needed in which leaders move with pace and purpose, whilst enlisting commitment and support from their team; this is when true leadership prevails.

How Crises Provide a Critical Test of Leadership Capability

Crises and significant change initiatives test any leader. Indeed, this is where many learn what leadership is really about. Relationships within a team are key to rapid and effective mobilisation, whilst still aligning efforts towards achieving the organisation's objectives.

It is at this time that leadership means motivating followers; indeed, leadership is nothing without followers. The more capable the team, the better the chances of a successful outcome. Previous team development and team involvement in decision making will be rewarded by overall motivation and commitment; practice makes perfect, or at least it certainly improves performance.

Leaders need to feel confident and secure in their team members' ability to manage even the most robust challenges. They need to build a team willing to contribute, work together, and instate better decisions and plans. Ultimately, those which do none of these things will contribute far less. Often at this stage leaders make the mistake of avoiding challenge by recruiting people with whom they feel comfortable, instead of those prepared to introduce new ideas. This is usually the way to create an underperforming team.

Teams acclimatised to working together are far more likely to achieve objectives and manage crises than those which do not. In addition, the climate of mutual support and tight focus improves the wellbeing of team members that, in times of crisis, is vital.

In the first throes of the COVID-19 pandemic the UK was not alone in being slow to make decisions and take action. The government and its departments initially failed to recognise the scale of the problem, before internal bureaucracy slowed the response to urgent needs, such as procuring Personal Protective Equipment (PPE) for medical staff and care workers. In addition, tightening border controls on travel and beginning widespread testing were unnecessarily delayed as the government awaited better data. However, as the pandemic progressed, the ability and speed of the government to decide and mobilise vastly increased, culminating in a highly successful vaccine roll out.

It has been clear from an early stage that COVID-19 presented major challenges to businesses. Most faced the need to coordinate employees working from home, others to downsize their organisation in the face of diminished demand. Closing sites, relocating operations, and often permanent geographic dispersal are major change initiatives which can, and often do, go badly wrong; often it is the quality of leadership that dictates this outcome.

A team relying alone on digital communication already contains the risk of discontentment, anxiety, and unsettled staff. Once the novelty of working at home wears off, the consequences become abundantly clear. Evidence is slowly emerging to suggest that home working slows personal development and discourages innovation. In the workplace, contact with colleagues motivates new ideas and developments. It is likely that in the future many organisations will opt for a hybrid model founded on both home and office working. This will hopefully increase staff satisfaction and reduce commuting whilst still providing the necessary environment for informal interaction and development. Once again, the nature and implementation of this fall to the leader.

Crisis management therefore means leading under conditions of sustained stress, during which they face challenges of an unknown, volatile, and constantly changing nature. These may permit little time in which to make decisions and mobilise their team. These same basic skills for leading underpin internal and external crisis management, and we can be assured of one thing: crises will continue to arise and leaders need to be prepared.

Being on the Same Side: Exploring the Leadership Relationship Between Self, Teams, and Organisations

An essential intention of this book is to explore the interrelationship between self, team, and organisation. This is a complex, often delicate dynamic in which the capable leader is a facilitator, aligning team performance with organisational needs. Getting the best out of the team begins with the self and one's own behaviour.

If we take the analogy of football, we can see that teamwork, alignment, and mutual support will often beat a team of far better individual players. Time and time again international country teams perform well below the combined qualities of the individual players. This is principally because they all play for different clubs and only occasionally meet to represent their country. In 2016, Leicester City won the English Premier League with a team paid a fraction of the other major clubs and with players who cost little to assemble. This was a victory for teamwork and by players who had developed together over the previous three years. Many clubs, pressured by fans, attempt to buy success in the form of top players; however, few succeed until the players learn to play as a team. It is no different for teams in any organisation and the key lies in development and working together. There are many ways that leaders can help accelerate this development. We also know that a team made up of the best players which are used to playing together may be virtually unbeatable. So too is it within an organisation—getting the best people on your team and developing your team so that they work together will make them difficult to beat.

In leadership, there are few rules which fit all contexts, nor any formula or 'one size fits all' approach. Team members are often motivated in quite different ways. The leader's job is to determine what works both for individuals and the team. We do know that some approaches are more likely to be effective than others, and that the role of the leader is very different from that of a team member. Exploring the differences will be more than helpful for newly appointed leaders and those with experience who wish to progress further and become effective in their roles.

Differing cultures react more positively to certain leadership approaches and may have widely varying expectations. Knowledge workers, or those with high levels of expertise in their area, are less likely to follow new initiatives unless they have a significant input to policy or project formulation. Whilst in some manufacturing environments, there is an expectation of clear 'orders' from management. You may hear 'just tell us what you want us to do' but that does not mean that there isn't a challenge from the workforce to follow which may well subsequently modify the original demand. To some extent, this direct approach may be necessitated by the high levels of coordination required, for example in manufacturing, which relies on specific jobs being repeatedly completed without error. Differing cultures, approaches, and expectations may be found within the same organisation: sales, marketing, finance, manufacturing, information services, human resources, and research and development can all require varying leadership approaches to be effective. Regardless of what approach is chosen, there are still common elements: leaders are expected to set the objectives, motivate, communicate, accept, and discuss challenges and lead decision making. In this book, we will discuss how readers can effectively develop each of these elements.

Leadership training is often diverse, ill focussed, and irrelevant, to the effect that individuals may have transitioned into leadership positions whilst being unprepared for its realities. Indeed, the criterion for selecting leaders is often competence at a technical role or level which does not necessarily translate to the very different skills and qualities needed to lead a team.

What we do know is that many people study to become better leaders as an academic pursuit, rather than through developing philosophical and experience-based understanding of the subject. This book is intended to help readers improve their practical leadership skills. It combines theory with numerous examples and mini-case studies to produce useful, pragmatic advice which will help equip readers to become better leaders.

Translating Theory into Leadership

Learning from Other Leaders

Whilst there is debate as to the extent with which leadership skills can be taught, there is little doubt that people can improve their skill sets under the right circumstances. For some, this may not always be a positive experience, some may entail encountering leaders demonstrating behaviours which you really do not want to adopt. Good or bad, it is part of the development process and there is a school of thought that believes when developing your career, you should pick jobs with leaders from whom you wish to learn. There is little doubt that previous leaders are highly influential when it comes to your style and approach.

Case Study: Learning from Leaders: What We Do and Do Not Want to Be

From my earlier career, I specifically recall learning much from one particular leader who was both dynamic and driven. Counter intuitively, he was the ultimate change agent with a leadership ethos of 'If you won't do it, I will find someone who will'. He could be quite threatening and directive, yet his sheer drive and clarity of objectives provided the motivation for managers to produce novel approaches and imaginative ideas. He could make things happen in a business no matter what.

A particularly memorable meeting with the heads of finance departments encapsulates his leadership technique. The matter in dispute concerned centralisation of the finance department, and interjecting several dissenting opinions, he simply stated, 'I'm starting to wonder whether I have the right team. I'll be back in ten minutes, when you've had time to consider the matter', before standing and leaving the room. Needless to say, the rest of the meeting was much more positive.

As employees we were far too reasonable when his demands went way beyond reason, and he often did not know when to stop in his drive to cut costs and develop the business. However, he took us well beyond what we thought possible and succeeded in turning a major loss-making business into a highly profitable concern.

In many ways, he was an enigma, as threats always wear thin with time; however, for the period in which I was under his leadership, he created a driven environment in which people were able to thrive. In all situations, you must take from your leaders those styles you wish to emulate, be wary of extremes and, most importantly, put your skills into practice.

A quote often attributed to George Bernard Shaw observes that 'The world was never changed by reasonable people. When you accept reason, you accept failure. Deadlines go back, targets are lowered whilst unreasonable expectations spur outperformance'. George Bernard Shaw was one of many to observe that a reasonable person adapts themselves to the world, whilst an unreasonable person adapts the world to their own wishes. For developing leaders, the challenge is to decide the style you wish to exhibit and avoid the elements you feel less comfortable with. The leader in the example above could never be described as reasonable, however he developed a clear vision and used his uncomfortable behaviour to drive the team on, far beyond their own expectations. The ideas *did* flow and change *did* occur albeit at a frantic pace. There was never any doubt that we would get there. As Napoleon Bonaparte said, 'A leader is a dealer in hope'.

Defining Leadership

Henry Kissinger said, 'The task of the leader is to get his people from where they are to where they have not been'. Certainly, this is a reasonable starting point for a definition of leadership. Many approaches to leadership are driven by identifying specific behaviours or characteristics such as charisma, confidence, persuasiveness, drive, and communication skills; others rely on developing behavioural skills and varying their leadership style depending on the challenge. In reality, context is critical to effective leadership. Context not just in terms of the industry and type of business, but business size, and the nature and culture of its employees. Whilst relevant, we favour definitions which focus on the outputs as well as the means of getting there.

Any definition of leadership is likely to identify that the leader's job is not just to align the team's efforts with the objectives of the organisation but to create conditions in which team members can work collaboratively so as to achieve far more as a team than as individuals.

This surprisingly simple view contends that leadership is principally leading teams of people in the pursuit of clearly established and agreed objectives. There are more subtle elements to consider however, such as actively encouraging coordination and integration within the team, more often than not creating higher and more sustainable levels of motivation.

Whilst there may be many different approaches to leadership, there are also recurrent strands, which may include the following: providing clarity of objectives in what you are trying to achieve; creating motivation, optimism, and hope; supporting high levels of communication; leading decision making within the team; developing members both as a team and individually; and providing emotional support when required. Each in turn means developing a very different skill set. We will explore these individual factors further in later chapters.

Exploring the Leadership Relationship Between Self, Teams, and Organisations

Typically, technically proficient people are often selected for promotion to leadership positions. Initially they may offer advice to team members, usually of a technical nature, allocate work and check quality, undertake the annual development interview with team members, and take on the more difficult jobs. However, this is not leadership and is unlikely to produce exceptional performance. So, what *should* leaders do?

Leadership training can be sporadic and somewhat peripheral when focussing on the necessary requirements of a business. It may provide an interesting experience, but does it create long-term improvement of an individual's leadership? Indeed, leadership development is usually amongst the first activities to be cut when finances tighten. Does this reflect corporate priorities, and what does this say about corporate belief in the effectiveness of leadership training?

Leadership research, training, and guidance literature often describes the world the way people would like it to be, rather than the way it is. In fact, leadership means dealing with the harsh realities of difficult environments, people, and high expectations from their seniors. Much of what is decided and implemented is a pragmatic compromise between 'getting things done' and complying with the stated higher demands. Many situations simply do not fit the rules, instructions, and models, all of which leave significant scope for interpretation. That is the real job of the leader.

Regrettably, some leaders do what is best for them, not the team or the organisation. They pursue their own career at the expense of others. Teams all too often function less like teams and more like individuals fighting their own corner. This can be particularly evident at boards where members avoid challenging others, simply to avoid reprisals in a 'I'll stay out of your area if you stay out of mine' manner.

What Does a Leader Actually Do?

A leader is best when people barely know he exists. When his work is done, his aim fulfilled, they will say 'we did it ourselves'. LAO TZU

Teams need a clear sense of purpose, direction, and hope. They need to know they are contributing to something worthwhile and meaningful. A priority is identifying the right objectives to benefit the organisation, followed by motivating and developing the team to become more effective. This means developing relations with sponsors to ensure the team both enjoys an effective profile and produces output which supports the organisation. The leader needs to take a high profile in any change initiative to convince others of its importance. After all, many view 'showing up' as the most important part of leadership. If the leader is absent from important meetings others may take this as a sign of the relative importance with which they view the subject. Teams watch what a leader does for signs of commitment rather more than what they say. Does the leader 'walk the talk'? As responsibilities increase then being an agent for change matters more and more.

How Team and Individual Development Form the Bedrock of Leadership

In my 13 years teaching leadership to executive MBA students, a recurring question of much interest is the challenge and importance of delegation. What I contribute to this debate comes from having chaired businesses for 25 years, studied what makes leaders effective and honed my own leadership practice according to my experience.

You may ask why so many leaders, particularly those at a crucial time in their career development, find delegation so difficult. Typically aged between early to late thirties, students may soon be encountering significant leadership responsibilities for the first time and leading increasingly large teams. Unless they can effectively delegate, they become overwhelmed by work and fail in their primary role—to lead.

Simply working harder than the team is not leadership and fails to allow for the necessary consideration a managerial role demands. Leadership is about extending your influence through the team as a whole. It requires the ability to identify what is really needed, set objectives, and communicate effectively, the core skills that will lead your team to be more effective than they would be as individuals. There is little chance of successfully leading new initiatives and projects without the perspective and time to lead.

So Why Is Delegation So Hard?

Firstly, due to a strong work ethic that says we can only earn our salary premium by working harder than others, it goes against the grain to ask team members to do our work. The team may well think this, but does that matter? Leadership is a completely different job to being a team member, and it is a job that demands delegation regardless of the push back that may come.

A second key reason leaders may not delegate is insecurity. New leaders may not trust team members to do the job as well as you could. The old mantra 'if you want a job done well, then do it yourself' might sometimes be true but will prevent you developing both your team and your career. You have to learn to trust the team and accept that not everything will be perfect. Indeed, I have usually found that team members often make a better job of delegated work than I might.

A further inhibitor is having enough people to delegate to. If this is an issue, which at some stage it almost certainly will be, you might have to make a case for more resources to support your work. If you do, make absolutely certain you have eliminated low-value work first. This is because a primary objection from senior management may be that you struggle to prioritise, so be decisive in establishing which work is essential to ensure they are not correct in their objection.

How Do You Go About Delegating?

A natural response I have repeatedly observed is for team members to delegate work back to you. You may well hear 'but I'm not trained', 'I'm already overstretched', or 'your predecessor did this'. If they require further training, then arrange it. If a review of their workload proves it to be excessive, then establish a plan to stream-line or re-distribute tasks. Ultimately, they will develop the capability to do more complex and interesting work. Each employee review must end by making clear their job, responsibilities within the team, and their next review date.

Perhaps most importantly, team members need to understand that the future is not the same as the past, and organisations must constantly develop and evolve to maintain standards. Your role in leading a team is to ascertain how your team can better advance the organisation's vision. Unless you can demonstrate effectiveness on a wider scale, then you are unlikely to progress further in leadership.

Regularly reviewing employee progress is a means of deterring the need for open door policies. Yes, a supportive work environment is important, but being *too* accessible only encourages team members to avoid making any real decisions. They will not develop unless they learn to make decisions for themselves and draw confidence from that process. Clear review dates and times help people to do their own thinking, and not take the easy option of trying to push work and decisions back to their bosses.

The role of the leader is to prevent their team from being overwhelmed with work. In modern matrix organisations, initiatives abound to the point of being overwhelming, and an overwhelmed team will not perform well. This is particularly notable in regard to any work that is perceived as being low value and not worth doing. Ultimately, this will only act to destroy morale and motivation—the cornerstones of any successful business.

Most aspiring leaders want to be positive, keen, and willing to please; however, discussion of priorities is essential. Team leadership often entails saying 'no' to people: 'No' to team members who prefer to do what interests them rather than what the organisation needs, 'no' to sponsors and 'no' to senior managers requesting low-value work when the team needs to focus on what really matters to the organisation. We all like to be popular but leaders have to accept that decisions are often unpopular in some quarters; if you want to lead, you can't be everyone's friend all the time.

Ultimately, you will never become a leader unless you can effectively delegate. You simply will not have the requisite time to think and lead. Many an intelligent individual and promising career has foundered on this fundamental obstacle. Don't let yours go the same way. To quote Andrew Carnegie 'No man will make a great leader who wants to do it all himself or to get all the credit for doing it'. (Fig. 1.1)

Case Study: 'Sink or Swim' and Learning to Delegate

In my first major job as Director of Finance to a large subsidiary, part of a multi-national business, I had a team of over 50 people reporting to me. This not only included various accounting roles but Information Systems, Legal, and Estates. In previous positions, I had perhaps six or seven reports. I was completely overwhelmed by the new job. Huge amounts of work arrived and I attempted to take on far too much of it. In reality, the rest of my team could leave at 5.00 pm whilst I was there most of the evening. The 'penny eventually dropped' and I realised that I must trust the team and delegate almost everything controlling the quality. This required a daily discipline and determination to delegate as it is a different way of working. As I discovered, they were talented people and quite capable of running the place themselves with clear direction and motivation. Learning to lead taught me some harsh lessons that every morning the job is to delegate and through frequent section leader meetings get them to work together as a team. Good quality people will rise to the challenge.

Many team leaders spend far too much time looking upwards and trying to convince their seniors of what a great job they are doing. Whilst some upwards awareness and management is necessary, too much irritates everyone. Let the team do the talking. Their achievements will be seen as the leader's achievements without proclaiming your own role. Give the team the credit, it costs you nothing and encourages and motivates the team.

Reflection

How good are you at delegation? Could you be better? If so, what changes could you make?
What sort of a leader do you want to be?

Once a leader has created the time to lead, the next question becomes 'What sort of a leader do they want to be?' What approach do they want to take to their new leadership role? Personal and team wellbeing will be a high priority as mental health and resilience by necessity become much higher

MAIN BARRIERS TO EFFECTIVE DELEGETION
And remedial behaviours and actions

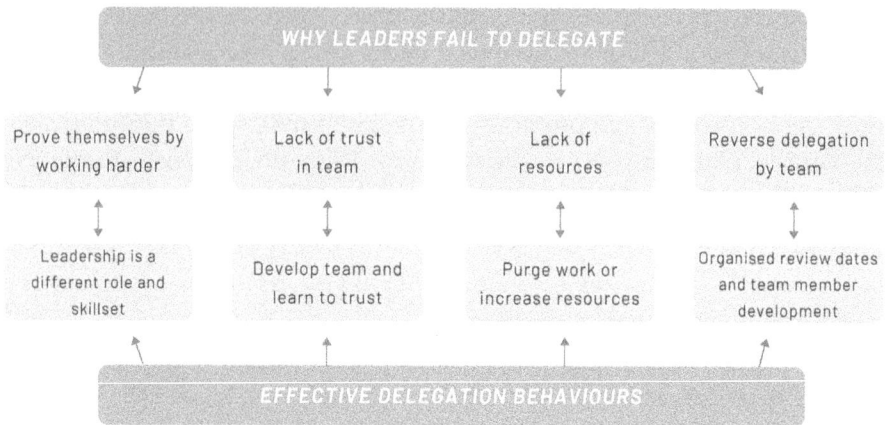

Fig. 1.1 Main barriers to effective delegation

priorities, both the leader's own and the team. Poor decision making is predominantly a consequence of personality rather than lack of data or inexperience. For example, experienced leaders often become overconfident and take excessive risks or worse engage in 'bet the house' deals. We will explore the impact of personality on decision making in the chapter 'Decision Making'.

Views from Practice: Responsibility, Accountability, and Power

Some years ago, I was fortunate to have the opportunity to interview Willie Walsh, CEO of British Airways Ltd (BA) (2005-10) and then CEO of the parent International Consolidated Airlines Group (IAG) (2011-20). IAG owned not only BA Ltd but also Iberian, Aer Lingus, and Vueling Ltd with a combined turnover of £23 bn in 2019. BA in particular had, prior to Willie Walsh, been viewed by many as a 'basket case' with a high cost base, intransigent unions, bureaucratic processes, and overstaffed at almost every level. Previous CEOs had not effectively addressed many of the key issues despite marginal and intermittent profitability. Willie Walsh certainly faced these challenges although the repercussions in terms of reputational damage from a saga of disputes linger on.

Willie's view of leadership is quite clear as being about accepting responsibility and accountability and not about seeking power or control. Many see leadership roles as about gaining power rather than accepting responsibility for all the many stakeholders to a major organisation. Ultimately, responsibility is passed to one's successor with relief. In Willie's view, accountability is being willing to present bad news to stakeholders. Most senior people are very keen to announce good news but when it comes to facing customers, staff, or shareholders with bad news then few are so keen. During the disastrous teething problems when commissioning Heathrow's new Terminal 5 in 2008, when 42,000 pieces of luggage were parted from their owners and 500 flights were cancelled over 10 days, Willie Walsh was there at the terminal apologising to customers and listening to their grievances.

I myself have witnessed many board meetings when there seems to be an unwritten rule that only good news can be presented. Unfortunately, this inevitably results in the 'real' issues not being discussed and, as a consequence, they may not be addressed.

Leadership inevitably involves taking risks when facing key challenges and some will turn out badly. Without an appetite for risk, then progress is likely to be limited indeed. Decision making inevitably involves risk and the bigger the decision then the greater the risk. Indeed, Willie also points out that leaders have to live with criticism—if you take a leadership role your decisions are at times bound to attract criticism. Being unduly 'thin skinned' will make the job very difficult indeed, few practicing leaders will tell you otherwise. One has to be willing to take on difficult challenges that many may avoid in order to reduce their chance of failure.

Overview of Unprecedented Leadership

This book is organised into three major sections. The first, 'Crisis from the Ground Up' is authored by Professor John Colley and includes the following chapters:

Crises Global and Local: When Leadership Becomes Critical

The key leadership question arising during crises is how it differs from leadership decision making in more normal times. There are differences during crises in that the level of fear and prolonged pressure for the leader and the team can be 'off the scale', to the extent that activity almost comes to a halt. A key responsibility for leaders is to try and relieve the stress on their team so that they can be effective in identifying solutions and mobilising to implement an agreed plan. Crises are also characterised by ambiguity and uncertainty as often only limited information is available and the nature of the crisis continues to change leaving leaders constantly attempting to catch up.

We consider the many difficulties of leading during the COVID crisis and how leaders and teams can improve their performance during crises. We discuss the key elements of leading during crises and how to prepare for the next crisis, which will no doubt arrive from an unexpected direction. We consider how to create and seize opportunities during crises. Competitors are often struggling with exactly the same challenges which create a short-term focus in managing through the current difficulties. Those who can look beyond the crisis and position the organisation for the new future are those that in the long run will thrive.

Making Key Decisions in a Volatile, Uncertain World

Decision making is underrepresented in the leadership literature despite being the most likely reason that leaders may find their tenure terminated. Getting the 'big calls' right on strategy, people, and crises is often the difference between whether a leader is remembered as a success or failure.

Take UK Prime Minister Tony Blair who held office for 10 years from 1997 to 2007, his achievements are largely overshadowed by his decision for the UK to join the United States in the Iraq war. Similarly, David Cameron, who held the same office again for 6 years from 2010 to 2016, will be remembered for his decision to opt for a referendum on Europe and then losing the vote.

We will look at models of how leaders can improve their decision making and what key elements lead to poor decision making. How can we develop capability in making decisions for developing leaders of the future? Effective decision making normally requires experience which raises the question as to how new leaders can gain experience before they too are confronted with major decisions.

Clearly teamwork has a role to play, and we examine when the process of decision making should involve the team and when that might be unhelpful. We also consider how to select the right people, and where to direct questions when faced with significant decisions. Finally, we all have biases, how can we question our own biases?

Ethics and Values: Negotiating a Complex Minefield

Never has the concern for ethical practices been more important both within a business and when assessing those with whom you may be enacting business. Ethical standards are no longer 'nice to have' but absolutely critical for survival and are becoming a central requirement of leadership. However, most leaders will admit that it is the ethical elements of leadership decision making that provide the greatest challenge. Dubious ethics have a habit of returning to haunt you in the future. On the other hand, pious decision making with little regard to value creation runs the risk of failure to meet organisational objectives. Leaders tread a very fine line between value creation and poor ethical decisions. We investigate this 'line' through the medium of a number of case studies. What decision would you make in each case? What are the likely short-, medium-, and long-term consequences? Information and evidence may be inadequate but there may still be victims. What are your values?

Ethical considerations are a complex minefield for any leader and maintaining good values is often under pressure from circumstances which require a degree of pragmatism if organisational objectives are to be negotiated and achieved. We will explore some of the ethical areas that leaders face and relevant theory which helps to make for a better ethical culture in organisations.

The second section, 'Philosophical Underpinnings and New Directions', includes the following chapters from Associate Professor at Warwick Business School, Doctor Dimitrios Spyridonidis:

Leading Change in Turbulent Times

It does not take a genius to realise that as environmental change accelerates organisations have to adapt more rapidly. Indeed, one can argue that those that can readily adapt and change will ultimately be the victors. Those that are slow to realise that change is necessary, or do not wish to change, or simply are not capable of change will struggle to survive. The graveyard is full of such organisations. However, most organisations still struggle with major change initiatives. John Kotter, a Harvard Business School professor viewed by many as a major influence on change management thinking, contends that 70% of major change initiatives materially fail. Prime candidates include culture change programmes, organisational change, and major information system projects. Most change initiatives are judged against projections of outputs as well as time and cost. Few achieve what was originally expected, and indeed the basis for why funding was approved in the first place. Indeed, Kotter contends that the main reason is a failure to lead the project. This chapter considers a number of perspectives to improving outcomes which are based in leadership rather than process.

The chapter is accompanied by a case study which explores the importance of leadership and the roles of responsibility, accountability, and the power of internal politics when implementing major projects.

Creating the Capacity for Strategic Leadership

Any book on leadership needs to consider the relationship between the vision and purpose of a business and its strategy, ethics, and culture. Many successful organisations create an alignment between these factors which transmit through the staff to customers who are, at least in part, buying into the vision and culture of the business as well as the product/service. Disney is an example where the vision and culture integrate along the lines of family values. This transmits through the staff or 'actors' to customers. Starbucks similarly attempts to live high ethical values and a positive culture which staff are trained to transmit to customers. Clearly that culture needs to have a variety of positive characteristics if it wants to successfully negotiate increasingly volatile and complex conditions. Strategic leadership not only involves creating and developing the vision, strategy, and ethics but also a culture which can cope with constant and rapid change and display resilience during difficult times. Such leadership capabilities will necessarily require high levels of team involvement, creating a clear sense of urgency amongst teams. In effect strategic leadership is leadership on a grand scale which starts by determining the core values, direction and purpose of an organisation, and the leadership infrastructure to support achievement of these key features (Fig. 1.2).

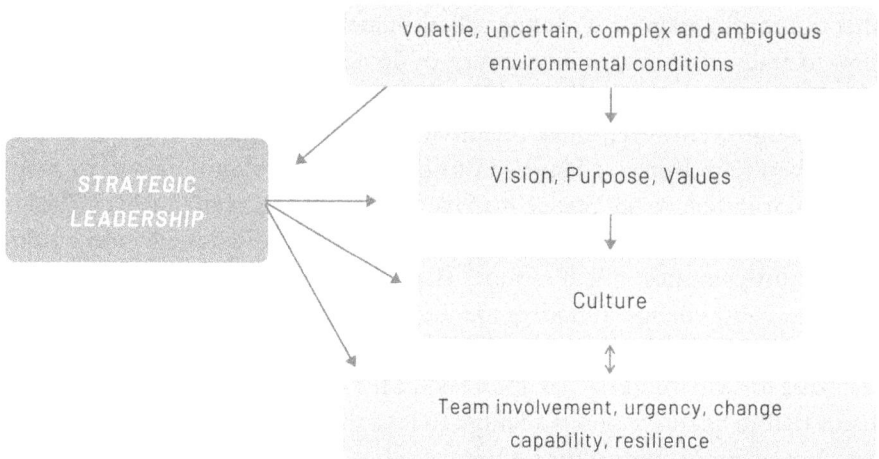

Fig. 1.2   Key elements of strategic leadership

Responsible Leadership and Sustainability

This chapter considers the emergence of a brand of leader who is concerned about the risks to the environment and upholding ethical and moral standpoints. Most leaders have concerns regarding reputational damage through customer and society criticism. Concerns emanating from environmental damage or poor treatment of workers are likely to affect sales levels and damage shareholder earnings. Indeed 'greenwashing' has become a common approach to managing stakeholders with high publicity given to relatively minor initiatives. Some institutional shareholders are moving investments towards Environmental, Social, and Governance (ESG) companies which has resulted in much repackaging of credentials to comply with the new demands. However, 'Responsible' leadership goes beyond this to upholding modern day values and 'authentic' principles. This sees leaders and stakeholders connected by a shared sense of meaning. We study Paul Polman, CEO of Unilever from 2009 to 2019, who successfully achieved excellent financial returns whilst at the same time driving the environmental and sustainability agenda in the business.

The third section, 'Communications, Education and Coaching—Tools for Leading During Crises', offers unique perspectives from three contributing authors, Tim Wray, Alan Matcham and Bob Thomson, and comprises the following chapters.

The Purpose and Power of Leadership Communication

In periods of uncertainty, communication fulfils the critical role of reducing anxiety and creating direction. Communication disseminates the confidence that someone is in charge, that there is a plan to escape the current circumstances, and that the new future will be attractive and a reason for optimism. It provides the motivation for personal involvement and team mobilisation. Whilst leaders attempt to transmit confidence (and that rather depends on their previous track record), a more powerful form of communication flows through informal networks. Communication has to be two ways and people need to believe that they have leaders who are listening and moving rapidly with an understanding of current circumstances.

How can leaders improve their communication skills? How can they create a strategic narrative which is fully understood and that people are willing to believe? We consider communication from the perspective of 'Authentic Leadership' and the views of Bill George and Peter Sims as to how to be authentic and communicate in a manner which transmits your beliefs. An

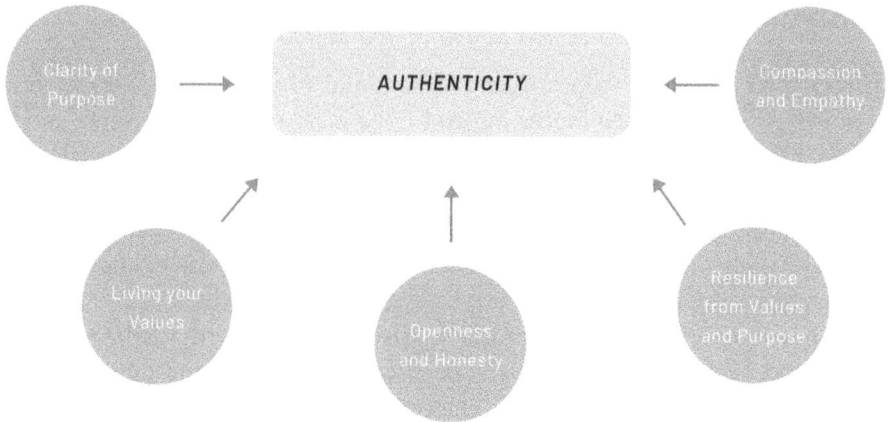

Fig. 1.3 Demonstrating authenticity when communicating

integral part of authentic communication is the power of stories which not only bridge the gap between theory and practice but illustrate the ideas in a manner which captures people's imaginations (Fig. 1.3).

Paradoxes in Executive Development

This chapter is written from the perspective of a long-term professional engaged in leading executive development programmes. The main paradox is that the relationship between traditional approaches to executive education and actual achieved organisational change is somewhat remote. Instead, such development programmes should be about challenging the status quo, asking fundamental questions, creating effective innovation and generating ideas. This perspective of leadership is difficult to achieve when leaders have full diaries which do not leave time for opportunities that might offer more scope for modern leadership approaches. Through a series of apparent paradoxes, traditional hierarchical leadership approaches are contrasted with flexible arrangements, cutting across functional and geographic boundaries to produce collaborative outputs and ideas. A view is constructed that in volatile, uncertain conditions, strategic and responsive leadership requires the ideas and motivation which less hierarchical structures can provide.

Coaching for Leadership

Unprecedented leadership has a clear focus on the relationship between the leader and the team members. We have discussed at some length how team and individual development both improves the performance of the team and alignment between the individual team members and the team and organisational objectives. The coaching approach has proved itself successful at enhancing team and individual performance and development. The coaching industry has expanded enormously in recent years and most major businesses now draw on coaching services, often throughout the organisation from board level down. This chapter explores how leaders can coach themselves and their teams to establish a coaching culture.

Our 'Conclusions' chapter considers the main themes and content of the book in the context of the future.

Unprecedented Leadership for Unprecedented Times

This book is motivated by the increasing difficulties which leaders face when negotiating rapid and major change as crises and major challenges arise. Its content provides practical dilemmas to illustrate the difficulties leaders negotiate, and theory forms the basis for the analyses with a pragmatic filter. The essence of leadership is found in the relationship between leaders, their teams, and organisational objectives. We explore many different perspectives and accept that there is no one right way. Leaders have to feel comfortable with their own values and approaches, but remain aware that team performance may necessitate evolution of their style. We provide plenty of practical options.

Part II

Crisis from the Ground Up

Recommended Reading for 'Crisis from the Ground Up'

Grint, K. (2010). *Leadership. A very short introduction*. Oxford University Press.

Jackson, B., & Barry K (2008). *A very short, fairly interesting, and reasonably cheap book about studying leadership*. SAGE Publications Ltd.

Kotter, J. P. (1990). *What leaders really do*. Harvard Business Press.

Kotter, J. P. (2008). *A sense of urgency*. Boston Harvard Business Press.

Lencioni, P. M. (1998). *The five temptations of a CEO*. Jossey-Bass.

Lencioni, P. M. (2002). *Overcoming the five dysfunctions of a team*. Jossey-Bass.

Pfeffer, J. (2010). *Power: Why some people have it—And others don't*. HarperCollins

Radcliffe, S. (2009). *Leadership plain and simple*. FT Publishing.

Ward, A. (2003). *The leadership lifecycle*. Palgrave Macmillan.

2

Crises Global and Local: When Leadership Becomes Critical

During 2020 the world saw a global pandemic that killed in excess of one million people, a death toll likely to increase once final figures are available. A crisis of this magnitude, that demanded complete lockdowns has set economies and relative affluence back by decades. Debt levels have soared whilst future tax increases and cuts in public services appear inevitable. Over this period, few governments have garnered public confidence and popularity. Instead, they have been criticised for their reluctance to make decisions, communicate the truth and mobilise effective tracing systems, and making unpopular decisions in allocating health care. The handling of this crisis in the UK provides the opportunity to review important components of crisis management and wise decision making.

During the COVID-19 pandemic governments faced a series of major challenges which placed them in the difficult position of having to select one of numerous non-ideal options. Some of the more difficult decisions are listed in the discussion box below.

Political, Economic, Social, and Technological Dilemmas for Government Decision Making During the COVID-19 Pandemic

- Lockdowns: Health of the Nation vs Economy
- Rationing of Health Services: Who Loses Out? COVID-19 Priority Patients vs Cancer Treatment? Young vs Old?
- Funding COVID-19: Economy Now vs Future National Debt and Taxation

- Public Services: Ability to Cope vs Opposition to Private Contracts
- Industries: Which to Support and Sacrifice Through Government Support
- Costs of COVID-19 Treatment: Funding Cost Effective Potential Treatments
- Speed vs Quality of Decision Making in Circumstances of Limited Information. Do Governments Wait for Better Information Whilst COVID-19 Spreads?
- Communication and Transparency: What Information Does a Government hold Which is Inaccessible to Others?
- Directive vs Consultative Decision Making: Does the Government Tell or Consult First?

This list is far from exhaustive but encapsulates the critical facets of a crisis unfolding: ambiguity, prolonged pressure, rapidly changing circumstances, and real fear—a blend that rarely supports good decision making. New leaders, faced with a major crisis for the first time often 'freeze', delay and fail to make timely decisions when time is of the essence.

It is essential to note that it is not the government or any one body alone that has been thrust into recent crisis management mode—all businesses have, in some way, had to confront testing situations, diminished budgets and limited choices that all require rapid decision making. Leading businesses in hospitality and tourism, culture, sport, manufacturing and construction have all faced collapsing demand and difficult decisions. Despite this, rents, taxes, administrative services, and property costs all continue to be due. As debt piles up, decisions have to be made as to who to dismiss and who to keep, whether to close the business temporarily or permanently, how to manage suppliers and the real possibility that insolvency looms.

While the COVID-19 pandemic has crystallised the critical role of effective crisis leadership, it is valuable to note that crises on a much smaller scale can and do occur in the business environment on a regular basis. At their core they share similar characteristics to large-scale crises, and it is now argued that, as the speed of change accelerates and systems become more interconnected, crises and their sphere of impact are ever-increasing (Heifetz et al., 2009a).

This chapter draws on the work of Ronald Heifetz, whose concept of 'Adaptive Leadership' is developed more fully and from different perspectives elsewhere in this book. Essentially, Heifetz believes that, in times of crisis, the top down, single-figure model of leadership does not work effectively. His approach is to enable individuals to manage the challenge and adapt to the evolving environment as a team; the role of the leader is to develop the capacity of the team to do so. We also draw on the 'Centre for Army Leadership' (2020) which may well be one of the most experienced and practical training colleges for leading in crises. In many ways they are the real experts.

Whatever biographies of famous leaders may say, everyone has to learn to lead, and crises are a fast-track but challenging opportunity to do so. If previous learning has been fruitful, then when crises do arise later in one's life, the leader can move with greater agility, address the key issues, and mobilise their team whilst already thinking towards possible consequences.

This chapter addresses the following questions:

- What are the key elements of a crisis?
- How can you manage your fear when under prolonged pressure?
- What are the essential steps in the leadership of a crisis response?
- How can leaders prepare?
- How can you seize opportunities in crises?

UK Plaster Crisis

In addition to theoretical critiques, this book is intended to provide practical advice. This section recounts a real-world crisis that I experienced whilst in the role of Managing Director of a large building products business. With the benefit of hindsight, I can see a myriad of decisions I would now make differently in order to manage the response far better than I did. In honesty I was consumed by pressure and slow to mobilise the team who, I now know, were essential to finding solutions, or at least actions to mitigate the crisis more rapidly.

Amongst its product range, this business manufactured and distributed a plaster-based product used in 95% of new UK housing. The product required unique raw materials mined in the vicinity of the plant and a special manufacturing process. For these reasons competitors had found the product difficult to replicate. Previous management had pursued the strategy of concentrating production and investment in one site which had the capacity to supply virtually all of the UK's requirement. Immense capital investment had automated the process to the extent that around a million tonnes of mineral was mined in extensive underground mines, processed, calcined, mixed, bagged, stocked in an automatic warehouse and loaded by a total mining and manufacturing workforce of around 130 employees. The automated processes produced a cost base that was so low that no one else would be able to compete.

Shortly after I became Managing Director of the business, an explosion occurred in the plant. The plant was out for four days and, when reopened, could only work at around two thirds of its previous output. Although long-term expectations had been for declining sales, at the point of the explosion, demand had still been rising and the plant running at maximum capacity. As the product had a short shelf life there had been limits to maintaining stock, and so the auto-

(continued)

(continued)

mated warehouse was only able to cover five days of sales. By the end of the four days, the market was already falling short, and the restricted output level was likely to continue for quite some time. The supply chain of distributors also kept little stock, largely due to the high service levels they received from the manufacturer; typically, an order before 3.00pm would be delivered when premises opened next morning.

As stocks in the supply chain were rapidly depleting, the market went short, and as there were no real substitute materials, building activity was curtailed. On the back of one event new house-building was curtailed and repair and maintenance across the country stalled. There was press coverage across all national newspapers, the phone lines were besieged by, if not media, then customers demanding priority for the meagre available supplies. As TV cameras arrived at the gates of the Head Office, tempers ran high.

This was not a crisis that was going to be solved rapidly, and I suddenly found myself to be everyones' villain, and in most peoples' eyes, the one responsible. The main board of the business were equally irate as they too became besieged by questions and complaints. The stress and fear over this prolonged period felt extreme and there was a surprising degree of complexity and ambiguity in terms of how we could resolve or at least mitigate problems in the short term. We knew that eventually the plant would be fixed, but that required specific parts to be made and further work necessary to reconstruct the damaged part of the plant. All this would take months.

Ultimately, the answer lay with the senior team; they did not have the same pressure and also had the expertise which could help. High levels of communication were needed to keep all stakeholders informed of the progress and plans, principally so they knew we were doing our utmost to fix the problem. Certain products made at the plant that did not need specialised processes we could arrange to have made at sister plants in Europe. Our Irish sister company could make a similar product but had only limited capacity that was soon shipped out.

We produced an allocation plan to customers which was transparent and fair to ensure they did not believe favour was being given to our biggest customers. Due to demand far exceeding supply, distributors started selling the product at exorbitant prices to their customers so as to profiteer from the situation; we made it consistently clear that our prices were entirely unchanged.

Eventually the allocation system, together with our other mitigating actions, brought supply and demand closer to equilibrium, but the process had been gruelling. In retrospect, I did not move rapidly enough to set up the team and provide enough communication. In major crises, it is often the case that the person at the top becomes very isolated. Usually, main board functional directors would be in frequent contact but at the time of crisis most evaporated away, unwilling to be tarnished by any involvement, but were then quick to materialise at any sign of success.

In this case, our eventual success was a result of teamwork: a collaboratively produced plan, communication, and ultimately our shared values. There were many internal challenges that would test the robustness of our plans, the validity of our alternatives, and maintaining a sustained tempo in dealing with the many issues and stakeholders. It was a tough learning experience, but we all learnt how to deal with a crisis; the next time we would move much faster and in a more organised fashion.

It is difficult to train for, or even fully describe the personal experience of managing unexpected crises such as this one. There is no artificial means of replicating the prolonged pressure and anxiety of a mind relentlessly turning over and discarding possible solutions to an ever-escalating problem. Only by way of case studies and probing questions can we encourage you to reflect on your own business practise, regardless of what stage of your leadership career you are at.

Anatomy of a Crisis

So as to distinguish the term 'crises' from more minor terminology such as 'misfortune' or 'difficulty' it is important to restate what we mean by the term in a practical leadership context.

A crisis will generally exhibit the following:

* Fear
* Prolonged pressure
* Ambiguity
* A rapidly changing environment

There are three key areas of crisis leadership that we will now look at more closely (Fig. 2.1):

* Leading the self

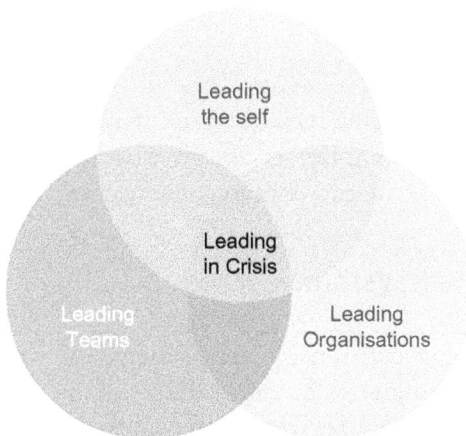

Fig. 2.1   Leading in crisis

- Leading teams
- Leading organisation

Leading the Self

Although many great things may have emerged from periods of pressure, that of the leader is different, simply because its associated emotions are far from conducive to the requisite balanced decision making. A team may be in a similar state of anxiety, but it is the leader who, ultimately, will carry personal responsibility for a crisis outcome. The consequence is stress: tension, poor concentration, a lack of clarity ('brain fog') and ability to make effective decisions, or even ascertain what decisions need making.

Greater previous exposure to crises does, we have established, help in recognising and deploying mitigating actions, however leadership teaching frequently underplays the importance of taking care of the self. Being physically and emotionally robust will be crucial to your success; you can achieve none of your leadership aims if you sacrifice yourself to the cause (Heifetz et al., 2009b). Although we are change agents, tasked with championing, motivating, and providing direction, we as leaders are also an impacted party with our own fears and uncertainties. To be an effective leader of change, you must be aware of your own needs as well as those of the people you lead.

It may sound simplistic, but no one can understate the most basic advice: take a lunch break, switch off your phone, and do not do emails late at night.

Leading Teams

There is little doubt that true leaders come to the fore in crises, and this is when leading self and leading teams become critical. The British Army have invested significantly in defining specifically what a leader needs to do when confronted by a crisis as this may be a frequent occurrence for their personnel.

Lead a Connected System

Leadership thinking in a crisis needs to be systemic. Do not forget the role of the increasingly interconnected economy during periods of crisis. Global supply chains have become so intertwined and complex that nobody can predict, for example, how significant the impact of COVID-19 might be. Leaders need to change their mind-sets from the individual or the organisational level to the broader interdependencies within their organisation, rather than just focus on their own line of business. There are many challenges around business continuity and the choices made during a crisis which will help build resilience and agility through extended periods of uncertainty. Those decisions have to include all stakeholders in order to maintain the viability of the system, or systems of which the organisation is part.

For example, as a result of the COVID-19 pandemic, leaders have had to make decisions that significantly impact their bottom line, potentially shutting down their business, which impacts their staff and their subsequently their families. There's been sporting seasons cancelled, theme parks closed, conferences postponed—the list goes on and on. Indeed initially much of the economy was shut down. Those were all decisions that leaders made with other peoples' best interests in mind. In crises, decision making may be influenced by the personal cost to ourselves. Leadership is losing the right to think about yourself. If you're going to lead well it has to be with others' best interests in mind.

Lead with Facts, Not Fear

During the COVID crisis we were engulfed by misleading information ('fake news') about the disease. Official health advice competed with conspiracy theories on social media, ineffective cures and false claims about how the virus was transmitted. In many ways, fake news may have delayed effective response to the virus itself. Indeed, even scientists held very different precautionary views in relation to government policy.

Leaders require the right kind of wisdom to help their businesses deal with a crisis situation. Don't lead with fear, but with facts. One of the best ways you can lead others during a crisis is to lead yourself well, so try to become aware of what's actually happening and surround yourself with others who are like-minded and have a similar appetite for facts and wisdom.

Establish Clear Objectives and Purpose for the Team

What are we trying to achieve in a crisis and how does that fit with the organisation's overall objectives? Critically this is where the team comes into its own. A team under less pressure, allowed to work together with their knowledge and experience, are more likely to design and deliver an effective response. It is also where leadership matters most. Crises are major events which may take weeks or months to resolve. Responding to the COVID-19 pandemic clearly met the criterion of a crisis. It also became apparent that the various authorities had little idea of what they were dealing with during the earlier period of the pandemic.

Various questions had to be analysed—such as where and how it is transmitted, which environments encourage the spread and what mitigates?—for example 'do face masks work?' Research frequently produced inconclusive findings which proved unhelpful; governments were driven by public opinion and the media was constantly changing positions. It is clear that the long-term fate of many governing parties would ultimately be determined by their response to COVID-19 as concluded by public opinion.

Recently formed and inexperienced governments often had a significant proportion of ministers with limited previous experience of power, and were unused to the pressures of real responsibility. Learning curves were steep all round.

Produce a Collaboratively Developed Plan

When in a crisis, it may become apparent that your team has relevant experience and expertise which needs to be fully exploited. They will be more committed if they have input to the plan and understand critically what the team is trying to achieve. It will not only increase their alignment with objectives in the various tasks but also increase their ability to work together cohesively as a team.

Leadership can be lonely, but leaders need people with whom they can discuss concerns and potential options. A leadership group who is not afraid to voice their opinion and share new facts will help you in your decision making processes. Leaders need to be self-aware and acknowledge that during a crisis they are under significant stress and being asked to make difficult decisions that are anything but clear. Having support and challenge from reliable voices will help you to lead with wisdom.

Decision Making and Calculated Risk Management

Ultimately the leader does have to make the decisions after team consultation. However, a team discussion does help determine the options and explore the pros and cons of each. This does also facilitate final decision making. There is usually a tension between available time and extent of team consultation.

Sometimes there simply is no time to consult and a directive decision has to be made. However, these situations are rare, and consultation is usually preferable where time allows. Involving the team in the decision not only aligns them with each other in attempting to achieve clear objectives but also creates deeper understanding of why the chosen approach was selected. It also helps to develop the team improving their contribution and ability to mobilise rapidly and effectively.

Develop a Challenge Culture

Many leaders do not like challenge. They view it as undermining and plays to their insecurities. Often subordinates are recruited who are not willing to question plans or decisions. Leaders may feel more comfortable with less forthright debate. However, the team may well have better ideas than the leader, some may have expertise in an area, and others may see flaws in a plan which needs addressing. Ultimately a better plan will emerge after challenge, followed by some further evolution. Leaders do need to have trust in their team and set aside their own insecurities in arriving at better decisions. However, once a decision has been made by the leader, the team does need to accept that is the end of challenge until implementation. Most decisions still need some adjustment during implementation. Few military plans withstand first engagement with the enemy and so it is with crises. Perhaps reactions are not as predicted or more important information becomes available which means the plan needs adjustment. Leaders need to keep open minds and alternative options in mind. However, no one wants a leader who is constantly changing their minds. Adjustment to plans is necessary but pointless chopping and changing is not. Think long and hard before making major changes.

Teamwork and Sustained Tempo

Activity is important in maintaining morale and mutual support ultimately comes from the way the team works together. Inactivity usually results in an ineffective response. The fundamental basis of leadership is that teams working together will achieve far more than individuals alone and through carefully set objectives they can achieve far more than any might have believed. Maintaining momentum is important as once it is lost it may be difficult to recapture motivation and progress. Motivation, activity, and progress go hand in hand and are self-reinforcing.

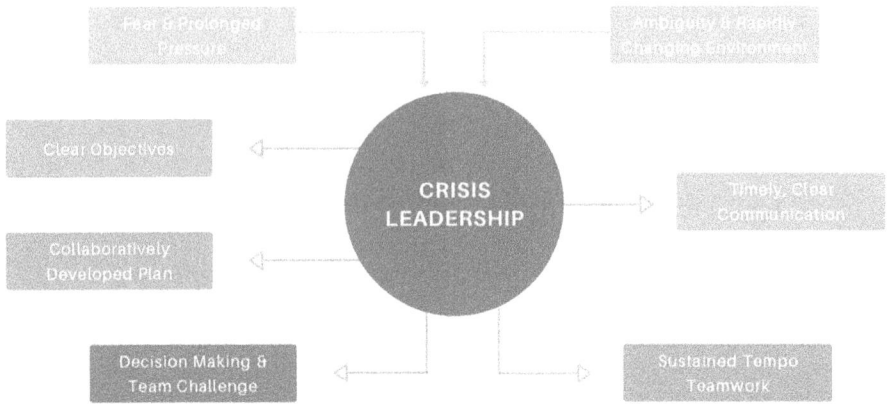

Fig. 2.2 Elements of crisis leadership

Timely and Clear Communication Is Key

As we have seen in our examples there are usually many stakeholders with a keen interest in the outcome, besides the team themselves. Communication needs to be simple with clear messages. Usually, the message has to be repeated several times as otherwise it could well be missed under the pressure that comes with crisis. If stakeholders understand the issues and the rationale for the necessary decisions, they will be much more supportive than if they are kept in the dark. During periods of crisis, leaders not only need to speak up, but they also need to act. Mistakes will be made, and wrong decisions will happen so leaders need to accept that they are fallible and that getting most of the important calls right comes with experience (Fig. 2.2).

Leading Organisations

Tell the Truth

When a crisis first emerges, there is a temptation to minimise the extent and impact of the developing event. We have seen this with many governments which have been slow to initially recognise the magnitude of the likely impact of COVID-19. There was denial in that they didn't want it to happen and so they pretended it was not occurring. The consequence was a weak initial response. This was followed by consistently denying the scale of what was happening. Concern then switched to the way the media would portray events such as the appalling video from Italy showing overcrowded hospitals and patients on trolleys in corridors. Then governments attempted to find others to blame such as China where the disease originated. This denial resulted in continuing to underestimate the impact of the event and failing to take adequate measures to control the disease.

This was followed by exaggerated promises which are never going to be fulfilled as a distraction for stakeholders in the hope that the crisis abates. Failure to deliver was followed by more unrealistic promises which were usually not met either, nor indeed had any real hope. There was 'being positive' and there was failing to recognise the gravity of the situation. Churchill in his famous wartime speeches to rally the UK people never underestimated the strength and threat of the opposing forces. He was careful to describe the threat as accurately as he could. Yet he still managed to motivate the nation who believed in him.

Telling the truth is important during crises as failing to do so results in lost credibility with stakeholders and the organisation. They start to wonder whether they have the right leader if there is a failure to recognise the scale of the crisis. The Trump versus Biden US Presidential election has been viewed by some as a vote on the effectiveness of the COVID-19 response. There may well be plenty of other countries that might similarly conclude that they no longer have the right leader.

The organisation also has to have confidence in their leader and candour is a two-way matter. The team expects the truth and in return they will be honest with the leader.

'Keep it simple' is also good advice as complexity confuses. Try and avoid detail unless it is truly necessary. Be brief, accurate, honest, and authentic.

Maintain Values

Whilst we have not explicitly included values in this chapter, crises are a real test when difficult decisions, often with no attractive prognoses, have to be made: sometimes it is simply about selecting the 'least bad' option. Subsequently the leader will become answerable for the consequences. The question underlying all leadership decisions should be 'is this morally right?'

During the UK COVID-19 crisis, it rapidly became clear that the National Health Service would most likely be unable to cope with the deluge of extremely sick people. Whilst measures were being taken to expand capacity, decisions still had to be made regarding the rationing of what had become scarce resources. Evidence is starting to arrive which supports the anecdotal reports at the time that, as a matter of policy, people over 80 became viewed as a lost cause and failed to receive intensive care. Many were transferred to nursing homes which lacked the facilities to provide high levels of medical care. Whilst this is in dispute and responsibility is being passed around in the ensuing blame game, it has become increasingly clear that in the heat of the moment such blanket decisions were made. It may well be that inadequate resources justified the decision however unpopular. However, governments are unlikely to own up to such decisions.

Make Decisions

Whilst the ultimate preserve of the leader, decision making may be the hardest part as leaders need to step back and be calm so as they can understand the context and perspective in which the decision is to be made. When under pressure being calm is almost impossible. However, you also know that instant impulsive decisions are usually wrong. People may say 'sleep on it', although that luxury may not always be available in a crisis. If it is available, take it as it invariably adds context and improves the quality of the decision. Calculating the time available to make a decision is often the first task of decision making. In business often more time exists than might initially seem to be the case. Don't procrastinate and also do not rush important decisions. A rushed decision is often wrong, and procrastination can end in no decision. Whilst a short wait often means that more important information becomes available which may well change the decision.

Some suggest waiting until 70% of relevant information becomes available. However, that is difficult to know. The outstanding information may be critical. In crises, earlier decisions are preferable to delayed decisions with better information. Stakeholders want to see action and organisational members need mobilisation. The ability to change your mind must remain an option if it turns out to be the wrong decision. Pride for many decision makers prevents this option which sometimes is necessary.

Be Visible

During a crisis there is often a rising sense of panic and sometimes a lack of advice can create chaos and confusion. During these times it's more important to both speak up and be seen. Even with staff working remotely, a leader needs to be visible, appear in control, and be a re-assuring presence during such uncertain times. Offering support that will make a difference for everyone, providing hope, and telling people it's going to be okay all become essential.

Short-term objectives to get through the crisis need to be communicated repeatedly. Leadership teams have to be regularly visible, often reaching out to and engaging with employees. People need support and help and may be reluctant to admit that need.

We are certainly learning that agility is key when events are moving so rapidly, as is keeping a calm head. Calm minds will prevail during periods of crisis, and this applies not only at the top leadership level but also throughout the organisation.

Learn and Recover

Hopefully your organisation will emerge intact after the crisis, but there will be lessons to be learned for the next one and even for how you operate in normal times.

How do we ensure we've got the right skills in the right place at the right time during this period? Some organisations have already implemented an agile workforce management capability with underlying analytics that can quickly adapt to long-, medium-, and short-term changes in demand. Although there are criticisms of this approach (see Cross et al., 2021.

Others are also adept at flexing between full-time and part-time contingencies and working with third parties. However, I would say that very few organisations are likely to be ready for this level of disruption for a prolonged period of time.

Specifically, to the COVID-19 situation, the outbreak may be the start of a revolution in remote working. Although we've seen a significant transition to remote working for some time, the COVID-19 pandemic has compelled more people to work from home. Having the ability and flexibility to shift workers to home wherever possible might be a lesson for leaders going forward. Maintaining a balance between the two options is gathering support for the 'best of both worlds' (Fayard et al. (2021).

More broadly speaking, in China the coronavirus pandemic has fast-tracked the 'testing' of robots and drones in public, as officials seek out the most expedient and safe way to grapple with the outbreak and limit contamination and spread of the virus. Leaders need to see new ways of operating that can disrupt the existing status quo.

Opportunities and Silver-Linings in Crises

However regretful, most crises provide opportunities to create a better future. Amidst the fear and pressure, leaders need to be searching out opportunities to reposition their business in a variety of ways. Employees and stakeholders will be anticipating any chance to exploit the opportunity and make significant changes which may have been needed for some time. Crises could well provide the rationale and circumstances to make those changes.

The COVID crisis will result in future governments formulating more agility in the management of pandemics. Already they are developing the ability to research, develop, manufacture, and distribute vaccines at scale and with speed. Hospitals and medical facilities are at work, discussing how, where, and when they provide greater flexibility in both the short- and long-term response to pandemic outbreaks.

Increasingly we are seeing organisations taking opportunities to cut costs and refinance so that when they emerge, they are better positioned to exploit demand. The so-called walking dead or zombie businesses are, historically, those encumbered with high levels of debt to the point that they are left unable to invest and grow. Leaders should focus on opportunities when managing crises to create a better future.

Conclusions

Ultimately crises are the true test of a leader's ability to lead themselves and lead their teams in order to ensure the organisation's continued ability to perform.

It is this time when team members who the leader may have held concerns about may well fail, and regret not having addressed the team composition earlier. It is also when leaders within the team come to the fore—it may be their dynamism, motivation, and ideas which will help drive both the team and organisational performance.

Learning Points

- Crises expose leaders to fear and continuing pressure whilst negotiating the challenges posed by ambiguous circumstances and a rapidly changing environment.

- Activity and involvement of the team is the key element in responding to crises. They are under less pressure, their ideas and ability to mobilise rapidly to an agreed plan are the key ingredient of an effective response. Truthful communication with stakeholders outlining the issues and how they are being addressed are important.
- Leaders must provide clear objectives and vision, a collaboratively produced plan with the team, and sustained activity and tempo whilst remaining positive.
- Quality of the team is more important than ever as weaknesses become exposed which should previously have been addressed. Teams used to working together with good people are more likely to succeed.
- There are always opportunities in crises. Identifying a positive future path and using the crisis to manage the transition to that future is frequently an available option.

Reflection

- Have you ever either been involved in a crisis or had to lead in a crisis?
- If you were involved in either, what would you do differently now if faced with similar circumstances?
- What lessons from this book would you apply?

References

Centre for Army Leadership. (2020). *Leading through crisis: A practitioner's guide.* www.army.mod.uk/leadership

Cross, R., Gardner, H. K., & Crocker, A. (2021, March–April). For an agile transformation, choose the right people. *Harvard Business Review.* https://hbr.org/2021/03/for-an-agile-transformation-choose-the-right-people

Fayard, A. L., Weeks, J., & Khan, M. (2021, March–April). Designing the hybrid office. *Harvard Business Review.* https://hbr.org/2021/03/designing-the-hybrid-office

Heifetz, R., Grashow, A., & Linsky, M. (2009a, July–August). Leadership in a (permanent) crisis. *Harvard Business Review.* https://hbr.org/2009/07/leadership-in-a-permanent-crisis

Heifetz, R., Grashow, A., & Linsky, M. (2009b). *The practice of adaptive leadership.* Harvard Business Press.

3

Making Decisions in a Volatile, Uncertain World

Technological development has brought many changes to our lives, largely due to new pace, complexity, and global reach; the impact of critical decisions has never spread so far and fast, which means getting important decisions right is critical. Leadership guidance rarely has much that is both relevant and relatable to say about this core area, primarily because each decision is entirely unique in its context. Yet we often stand or fall by the decisions we make—especially the big calls—and so it is important to discuss the process in the context of crisis management.

One thing is certain—in a crisis state, a leader will find themselves inundated with data intended to inform a response; good leadership is about establishing what is relevant and when to make the decision. This chapter considers challenging questions such as whether to wait for more data to arrive, or act in the hope that the data already available to you will lead to the right decision. Sometimes this is something of a gamble.

Early on in the COVID-19 crisis, many governments were 'following the science', awaiting solid data before making key decisions, a wait that meant the difference between life and death for many thousands of people. Governments fought and indeed still fight criticism from many quarters for their perceived slow responses; as leadership bodies they learnt the hard way that in some situations we have little option but to go with what we have.

We reiterate throughout this book that leadership success is built on the foundations of a high-performing team. In this chapter we will consider how decision making can be used effectively to develop, motivate, and align that team towards the best possible decisions.

© The Author(s), under exclusive license to Springer Nature Switzerland AG 2022   **41**
J. Colley, D. Spyridonidis, *Unprecedented Leadership*, Palgrave Executive Essentials,
https://doi.org/10.1007/978-3-030-93486-6_3

We consider Victor Vroom's particular interest in team development through decision making. We also explore research contributions from Sir Andrew Likierman at the London Business School, whose concern lies with the quality and diversity of available information.

Through specific case studies we examine how and why capable leaders make questionable decisions, and develop a discussion of how we might detach ourselves from personal biases in order to gain more objectivity and ultimately make better decisions.

This chapter will seek to address the following questions:

- How can you improve your decision making?
- What can you do to avoid common and costly mistakes?
- When and why should you involve the team in making the decision?
- How do you pick the right people?
- Should you recruit externally or promote from within?
- How can you learn which key elements to probe and question?
- How can you learn to question your own biases?

The Legacy of Our Decisions

Leaders ultimately stand or fall by the success or otherwise of their decisions, indeed, they are a leader's main legacy. Whilst many would argue that the ability to make decisions is only one aspect of a leader's necessary capabilities, it is the predominant factor which determines the extent of a leader's tenure.

Getting the big decisions wrong usually ends badly for the leader, even if at the crucial moment there may have been widespread support for the choice. If they prove successful in outcome however, then it is onwards and upwards.

A memorable example of this would be the UK Prime Minister Margaret Thatcher, who in 1982 made the decision to send a fleet to the Falklands Islands following occupation by Argentinian forces. As the UK was in the midst of a severe recession this decision received widespread opposition at home. If that mission had failed, Margaret Thatcher's tenure would very likely have been cut short, but it did succeed and, despite enduring and in places, extreme unpopularity, she was re-elected in a landslide victory the following year.

Case Study: Mike Coupe at Sainsbury's

Often whether a decision works out or not dominates almost all other necessary leadership characteristics. An interesting example can be seen in the case of Mike Coupe, CEO of UK grocery chain Sainsbury's. Coupe exhibited most of the positive aspects one would expect from a leader: he is hugely knowledgeable about the grocery industry, charismatic, supremely confident, and a natural communicator, widely respected across the industry.

However, Coupe made two major bad decisions during his tenure. The first in 2016 was to acquire Argos, the online and catalogue seller of an extensive range of household items. You may well be familiar with the company's unique format which involves customers browsing the catalogue, filling in a form, and the item being produced almost instantly from an attached warehousing facility. This format had considerable popularity with a consumer group arguably very different to that of Sainsbury's. The latter predominantly attracts customers who are willing to pay more for Sainsbury's long upheld standards, including the experience of their spacious, pleasant stores.

A problem facing much of the European grocery industry at the time was that maintaining large ranges were costly to service and not valued by many customers. Trade was being lost to competitors with small ranges at much lower prices. The main grocers were actively having to reduce their range in order to cut costs. One consequence was that Sainsbury's had spacious stores and subsequently, scope for shops within shops. Argos was therefore seen as one economic solution to this, considering Sainsbury's already stocked some household and homeware ranges.

Initially the acquisition appeared successful, although there was a lack of hard evidence owing to the fact that figures were rapidly merged into those of Sainsbury's. Some years later it became apparent that over 500 of the Argos standalone stores were to be closed with attendant closure costs, and fewer shops within shops were to be created. The differing nature of the customer base is one reason this may have failed.

In 2019, Mike Coupe opted to merge with a direct competitor, Asda, owned by the US group Walmart, which would have led to a combined dominant market position of more than 30% of all UK grocery sales. No doubt, if the motivations behind the venture—reduced costs and economies of scale—had been a success, it would have led to an unassailable position. However, after many months of deliberation, during which Sainsbury's were steadily losing market share, the UK Competition and Markets Authority turned down the proposal, leaving Sainsbury's with a bill of £50 million in advisory fees. Following the failed bid, Mike Coupe announced his resignation from the board.

Sadly, these examples are the rule rather than the exception for overly confident decision making. So, what drives CEOs and boards to make such poor decisions after a track-record of success?

Case Study: Megamergers and CEO Hubris

Experience has shown that when a business decides on high-risk megadeals, the senior management usually pays the price. A brief review of the major deals in 2015/16 shows that very few senior management teams remained in place. This was typically the consequence of bad strategy, paying too much, or failed integration bids. The resultant loss of market share and failure to realise predicted benefits were soon followed by the loss of key personnel. One contributor to this pattern is that the management were too distracted by what is essentially an internal reorganisation and failed to recognise the warning signs of deteriorating performance.

In the agribusiness arena, German-owned Bayer bought US-based Monsanto for $6 bn, only to find that it had acquired enormous claims liabilities from people producing and using its weed killer 'Roundup'.

An £11 bn UK-based 'merger of equals' between investment fund managers Standard Life and Aberdeen Asset Management resulted in a major loss of customers and slow realisation of cost benefits. The chairman and both company CEOs left.

The global leading brewer Belgian-based AB InBev acquired the world's second largest brewer headquartered in South Africa, SABMiller, for $106 bn to create a global market share of almost 30%. Unfortunately, they paid far too much, only to find the various competition authorities did not like the deal and all relevant acquisition assets in North America, Europe, and China had to be disposed of at a fraction of the price originally paid. Most of the AB InBev top team left and the merged business continues to limp on with enormous levels of debt.

Why Do Capable Leaders Make Bad Decisions?

Some leaders struggle with decision making. Others spend much of their careers making good decisions, but on reaching the top job, manage larger decisions badly (Fig. 3.1).

The Founding Components of Decision Making

'Judgment can be defined as the ability to combine personal qualities with relevant knowledge and experience to form opinions and make decisions' (Likierman, 2020a). The component which is most likely to let us down is personality. Sir Andrew Likierman goes on to say that 'Judgment is not a synonym for being cautious. It implies action and making decisions. You will never have all the information before acting. The judgment call involves recognising when you have to act but also recognising the limits of your knowledge'.

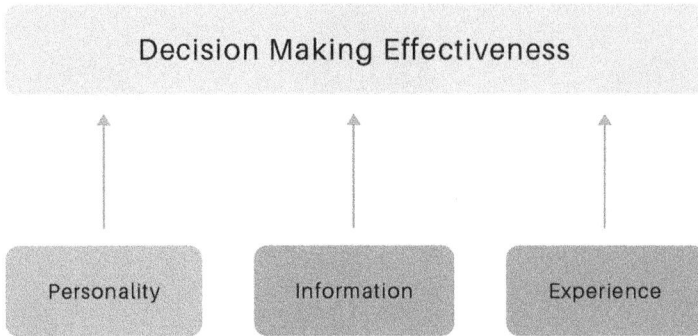

Fig. 3.1 Key elements of effective decision making

Any crisis decision is a product of available time and information. More time will bring more information, but it may mean that circumstances have developed to the point at which action is too late. In the case of government decisions relating to COVID-19 lockdowns any delay that results from waiting for more information means more deaths.

In many decisions, waiting a little longer, if time permits, allows for potentially important information to arrive. It can also be a rationale for failing to make a decision, which in a crisis situation is unforgiveable (Fig. 3.2).

The Five Roads to a Bad Decision

Hubris

'Excessive pride or self-confidence; arrogance.' (*Oxford English Dictionary*)

This generally afflicts leaders with a successful track record. Their subsequent confidence often means they start to believe their own publicity. Perceiving themselves as infallible and disregarding the contributions of advisors is a hubris that often prematurely ends the careers of previously successful leaders.

Sir Terry Leahy at Tesco serves as a possible example. During his 14-year tenure as CEO, he built a huge empire of supermarkets across a number of countries including more than 30% of all UK grocery sales and in 2011 return Profit Before Tax of £3.5 bn on sales of £67 bn. Sir Terry believed that he could also conquer the highly competitive US grocery market, despite optimal locations having been pre-empted, having no supply chain, and without a known brand. Also large well-known and efficient competitors were already

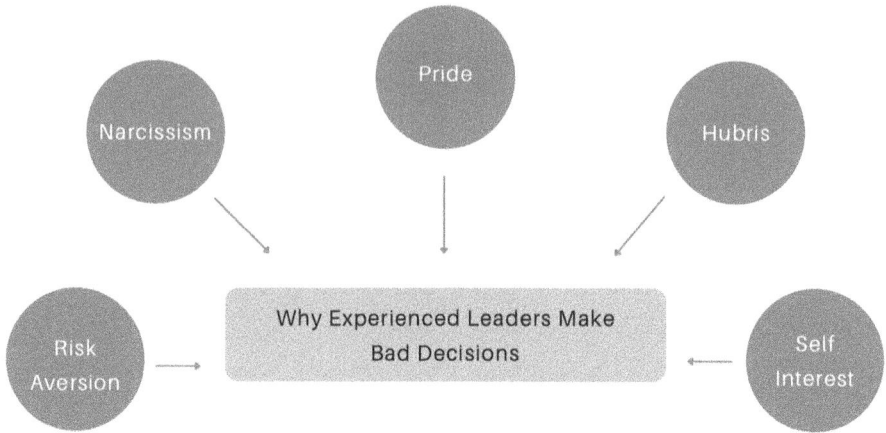

Fig. 3.2 Decision making distortion through personality influences

there. Late entrants without a significant source of competitive advantage or compelling customer value proposition have little prospect and so it was for Sir Terry Leahy. He subsequently retired from Tesco in 2011, and the US excursion was sold off at a vast loss.

Narcissism

'Inordinate fascination with oneself; excessive self-love; vanity.' (OED)

Individuals with this particular egotistical character trait often overestimate their abilities and acquire an excessive need for admiration or affirmation. This may be accompanied by a limited ability to empathise with others or experience emotions. In terms of decision making, this results in decisions being made to impress rather than in the best interests of the organisation or stakeholders.

When the UK government decided to grant India independence from British rule in 1947, Lord Mountbatten was asked to oversee the withdrawal. A partition of predominantly Hindu India from Muslim Pakistan was agreed; however, Mountbatten allowed only four months for this to be implemented. This resulted in chaos and violence erupted as people of respective religions were relocated across the countries and over one million people are believed to have died. Some believe deciding on such a short transition period was more to gain admiration for efficiency from people in Britain than in the best interests of India.

Whilst this example is extreme, recent years have seen a number of narcissistic leaders come to the fore with decisions made for effect as opposed to the greater good. They allow their own career progression and accolades to take precedence rather than the good of the organisation.

Pride

'A high or inordinate opinion of one's own dignity, importance, merit or superiority.' (OED)

In many ways this is an inability to admit there may be better ways of running a business than those previously employed. It exhibits as a reluctance to change as there may be an implicit admission that there are better approaches than one's previous decisions and methods. A common occurrence in manufacturing is the decision to introduce new working methods such as lean, 6 sigma, world-class manufacturing. Typically, they involve the collection of detailed data at the shop floor level and analysis, followed by a review and correction of the sources of waste, such as raw materials, machine time, and improved quality and productivity. The strongest opposition to introduction is normally exhibited by plant management who see this approach as questioning their previous methods. Resistance is often to the point that the plant management have to be replaced.

Risk Aversion

'A strong disinclination to take risks.' (OED)

This is evident in a leader that calls continually for supplementary or marginal information, in the hope that the data will make the decision itself. It seldom does. There is a thin line between having enough information and simply procrastinating on making a decision.

There is evidence to suggest that CEOs in particular become more risk averse as their careers develop. First-time CEOs are often willing to take greater risks and instigate far more change than second-time CEOs, who may be more aware of potential risks and less willing to take them (Hildebrand et al., 2021).

This avoidance of personal responsibility also often manifests in the formation of committees to make decisions and take collective responsibility. Whilst committees may ensure appropriate consultation, they can result in very different and divisive decisions from those made by an individual alone. They can also leave committee members vulnerable to manipulation by individuals.

Favouring Self and Friends

'The practice of giving special treatment to a person or group.' (OED)

We have already discussed the need for some leaders to make decisions in their own best interests rather than those of the stakeholders they represent. Many also surround themselves with cronies who may be no more than 'yes' people when challenge is needed. Friends are also not necessarily the best team you can find. When crises occur or the organisation comes under real pressure, then leaders need the best team they can find. Weak team members will always let you down at the most critical of times.

Meanwhile, friends and cronies are viewed by the rest of the team as not having been selected on their own merit and can create both a lack of motivation on behalf of others, and a lack of respect, none of which is good for the team.

When to Involve the Team in Decision Making and Why?

Many leaders adopt the same approach to decision making regardless of the nature of the decision in question. With some exceptions they fall broadly into two camps: those that consult extensively before almost any decision, whilst others more routinely decide for themselves and then communicate their decision to those who need to know. Indeed, in some organisations, this latter approach may be expected by the team and consultation may be viewed as weakness or vacillation.

It is important to be aware however that different cultures and business environments have diverse approaches. For instance, prior consultation is almost mandatory in knowledge-based organisations, whose workers are unlikely to offer the same motivation and cooperation if they feel they have been excluded from decisions.

Conversely, in manufacturing environments there is often the assumption that decisions will simply be relayed and executed. In effect, an autocratic, decisive approach such as this is expected by many: the hierarchical business structure expects commands, whilst the flat, knowledge-worker structure expects consultation. This can also apply in different countries and cultures. For example, Swedish culture is highly consultative and direct commands are unlikely to be successful, whilst in Greece and some other Mediterranean countries, decisions with limited consultation may be the norm.

Victor Vroom (Vroom, 2003; Vroom & Sternberg, 2002; Vroom & Yetton, 1973) proposes approaches to decision making based on key factors which determine when and how to consult the team. As he explains, there are various approaches from consulting individuals or as a group, to facilitating a discussion or indeed delegating the decision entirely. We take the view that leaders vary their decision making approach depending on variables, such as how much time is available to make the decision, what expertise the team has to contribute, and how likely they are to implement the decision effectively without consultation. Figure 3.3 provides a brief summary of some of the factors which may help a leader to decide how a decision might best be made.

What Factors Mitigate Against Team Involvement?

- **Self-interest**
  Decisions which involve terms and conditions, remuneration, relative status, and especially terminations are best served with limited group discussion. Consultation in these circumstances is easily interpreted as a negotiation, and much time and energy can be expended trying to reach a solution deemed satisfactory by all. Senior management can be particularly status-conscious and so cars, offices, and other conspicuous signs of status are debates best avoided. Indeed, many would argue that they are best removed altogether, whilst others may deem this to be unrealistic.

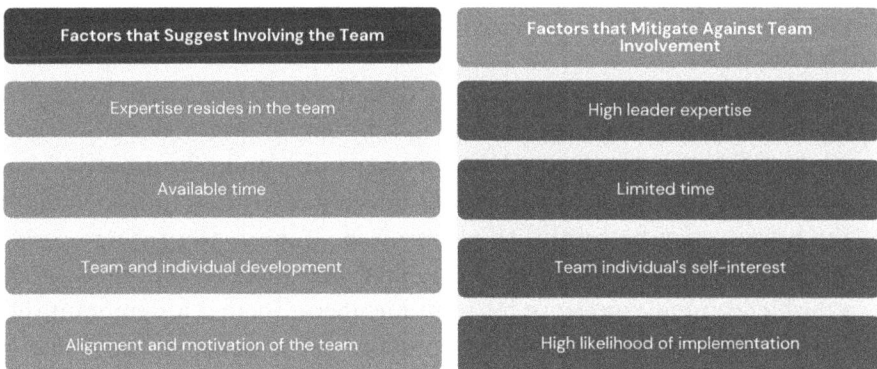

Which factors suggest team involvement is the best choice for a given situation

Factors that Suggest Involving the Team	Factors that Mitigate Against Team Involvement
Expertise resides in the team	High leader expertise
Available time	Limited time
Team and individual development	Team individual's self-interest
Alignment and motivation of the team	High likelihood of implementation

Fig. 3.3 When to involve the team

- **Time**

  If, as in crisis situations, there is limited time, then it may simply not be possible to consult as extensively as one would like. However, even in fast-moving crises, it's important to consider where the expertise and experience may reside within the team—they often have the capability to solve major problems beyond your knowledge-base. On other occasions, the decision may be relatively minor, and time and resources would be wasted by protracted discussion.

What Factors Suggest Consultation with the Team Is Advisable?

- **Expertise**

  In senior positions, detailed expertise in certain areas often resides at a lower level. For example, a Finance Director might have separate managers for tax, treasury, legal, management and financial accounting, information systems and estates, to name a few. In reality, the real knowledge in those areas resides at that level, and so consultation on issues concerning them has to take place either with the relevant manager or the team. The FD's job is to ensure that their team is working in the best interests of the organisation and supporting its strategy. Similarly, at the board level, the CEO may have functional directors for marketing, sales, operations, finance, and so on; each will have a much greater knowledge of their own area than the CEO or MD, making consultation both advisable and efficient. On occasions though, the CEO or MD may take the view that they have enough expertise or experience not to consult.

- **Development**

  Ultimately, developing a cohesive, motivated team is best served by involving individuals in decision making, and to some extent, making decisions successfully has a strong experiential element. To a point the more decision making one does the better, and so introducing developing individuals into the process may be helpful to all involved. Consistently sitting outside leads to double-guessing based on limited information, and rarely offers valuable learning experience for team members. There is a significant difference between having the responsibility for a decision and being a bystander. The views from each side are quite different.

  The objective of any leader is to develop their team to optimum effectiveness and ultimately provide both succession and better-quality resources for the organisation as a whole. Team members do not always share the same enthusiasm for more difficult work, which decision making ultimately is. For some it may seem safer to do the easier jobs and avoid the inevitable responsibility associated with decisions.

- **Delegation**
  Leaders will only find the time, energy, and clarity to lead if they are not hindered by doing the work of the team. Delegation is absolutely key. Delegation and open leadership develop the team whilst still allowing the leader to create the agenda. It also ensures the work of the team closely supports and develops the strategy of the organisation. The job is to motivate, lead, and to make the important decisions to the best of your ability.

- **Alignment and Motivation of the Team**
  People are more motivated if they are consulted at the time of making a decision. Being part of the process helps people understand the reason for certain decisions, and gives them the opportunity to suggest improvements. Clearly, in some time-bound circumstances, such as crisis management, teams should understand a lack of consultation and still support implementing decisions. However, when time is available, team members are more likely to align with both the organisation and team's objectives if they have been part of its development.

Many at the CEO level will tell you that the hardest part of the job is persuading board members to work cooperatively. Each will have their own ideas on how the business should be run; if they have had the motivation and ambition to reach the top table then they may not necessarily work well with other major egos in achieving the organisations' ends. Whilst they may appear friendly, courteous, and open to cooperation, they may also have elements of the 'Five Routes to a Bad Decision' addressed earlier in this chapter. The leader must constantly focus on facilitating teamwork.

How Open-Minded Are We?

My personal approach to decision making is usually to consult with two or three of the most senior directors separately, before proposing a decision to the Executive Committee for discussion. As Managing Director, I found the key was to avoid making a decision with which I did not feel entirely comfortable, unless, of course, it is a matter entirely within the jurisdiction of one director, in which case they must take responsibility for the outcome.

The decisions you feel uncomfortable with but allow to proceed are those you regret most. In effect, retain a veto on important matters. Having said that, my mind was typically in varying stages of commitment to a decision. For some, I might have effectively decided what I wanted to happen before hand; whilst for others I had a completely open mind. Whatever your thoughts are, little is to be lost from discussion. New solutions, ideas, and concerns all add to the balance.

When it came to picking the top team however, it was my prerogative alone. Human resources may offer an opinion, but I took the view that success or failure resided in the team. If they did not perform, then it would be me, not human resources that paid the price, so who was selected had to be my decision. On occasions there would be pressure from the CEO to take someone from head office, which I would advise anyone to be cautious of—it is rare they are as good as their publicity suggests and may not fully 'fit' in a new environment and business culture.

Ultimately, when it came to big decisions on which my own future rested, I had to be happy with the decision.

Whose Got Your Back? How to Pick the Right People

In their 2007 paper 'Making Judgment Calls', Noel Tichy and Warren Bennis situate the key decisions senior leaders may face into three categories—people, crises, and strategy (Tichy & Bennis, 2007). As leading in crises and strategy are dealt with elsewhere in this book, here we will focus predominantly on people.

Key Decisions—Strategy, Crises, and People

Recruiting the right team is critical. When crises arise, weak members will be the first to let you down. Indeed, weak members can reduce the motivation of others and be a constant source of distraction and difficulty. Pulling together the right team is anything but straight forward and in many organisations—particularly those with the added challenge of cultural and structural barriers—present major problems. Where extensive attempts at remediation and development of an underperforming individual have failed, then removal, transfer, or promotion elsewhere may be advisable. A leader must have influence when it comes to selecting their team.

Case Study: Right for the Role?

A long-term colleague was recruited to the CEO position of a smaller listed company. His main strengths included an immense network of contacts, a sociable personality, and excellent communication skills. He was also highly popular as an empathetic and supportive team leader.

The business was previously owned by private equity and an entrepreneur who had sold their shares by floating the business on the stock market. The previous CEO had lacked the communication skills vital in the major transition from private equity to listed company leadership, where the sentiments of stakeholders are paramount. It rapidly became apparent to the new CEO that the Finance Director could not manage the demands of his role.

The new CEO was unwilling to make changes, adamant that he could develop the team to manage the new challenges ahead. After a period of poor performance, the FD explained without warning to the CEO that they had seriously breached their banking covenants. This was the first the CEO and board had heard of what was an extremely serious mistake. Immediately a stock market announcement had to be made, the shares collapsed, and the bank assumed various rights, opening an immediate investigation into the financial situation of the business. Only then was the FD invited to leave the business two years too late. The failure to replace the FD had been a catastrophic failure of judgment.

Appointing a Team: Internal or External?

A key dilemma facing leaders when making appointments is whether to recruit from outside the organisation or from within. The general and logical rule is that if the team or organisation is running well, then an internal appointment may be most appropriate. If performance is disappointing, however, and change is necessary, then the successful candidate may well be better found externally. In these circumstances the key consideration is to identify and invite new thinking, new blood, and a change in strategy. You must be prepared to expect that external appointments may well bring wholesale change. Typically, new leaders bring a new strategy and make a number of changes to the top team. Sometimes the entire team may be replaced, which also means the loss of a long-standing body of knowledge and experience. In the UK and US, the average tenure for CEOs of listed businesses is less than 5 years and that figure is ever-declining. Constituencies making such appointments need to be clear on the degree of change they want to see before making the decision. As the opening of this chapter stated, technology has brought with it pace, reach, and volatility; organisations today have to survive major change more frequently.

Turnarounds are typically performed by leaders external to the organisation. Without the psychological 'baggage' of continuation they may provide the necessary objectivity to see what needs doing, unimpeded by previous strategy, past initiatives, or team loyalties. This also may mean they will select their own best team to make the necessary transformation.

Case Study: Tesco's Post Sir Terry Leahy

Tesco, the UK's most dominant supermarket chain, was led by Sir Terry Leahy from 1997 until 2011. During his tenure, Sir Leahy massively expanded activities and diversified into a wide variety of other markets including software, cafés and restaurants, mobile telecoms, banking, toys, and furniture. International expansion into Turkey, Japan, Thailand, Poland, USA, and six other countries was also pursued. Sales turnover reached £67 bn in 2011 with Profit Before Tax (PBT) of £3.5 bn.

Looking for continuity as opposed to overhaul, Leahy's successor was an insider, Philip Clark. However, Tesco's market share began to fall under pressure from cost champion German supermarket chains Aldi and Lidl. The overseas investments began to underperform, diversifications were questioned, and, following various unrealised profit forecasts, there arose the view that Tesco had over expanded and needed significantly scaling back.

Therefore in 2014, Dave Lewis was recruited from Unilever to replace Philip Clark who was viewed widely as having been dealt a bad hand and only partly responsible for Tesco's misfortunes. By the time Lewis voluntarily stepped down in 2020, it was generally accepted that he had addressed the key issues: many previous diversifications were disposed as were a number of the overseas operations. The US Fresh'n Easy venture closed at a cost believed to be £1.2 bn. Cuts in the UK included 43 stores closing and a further 49 proposed new stores cancelled. Food counters and bakeries were closed, and suppliers pressured into better terms. Product ranges were reduced and prices cut. Market share has stabilised at around 27% (from 30.6% in 2011) and profits reached £1.6 bn in 2019 in much more competitive markets. In this case, it required an external leader to turn the company's fortunes round and make the brutal but necessary cuts.

In Peter Capelli's, 2019 Harvard Business Review article, 'Your Approach to Hiring is All Wrong', he bemoans the deteriorating diligence in hiring as businesses more and more look for their talent outside and overlook the talent within. However, hiring mistakes can be extremely costly, particularly in more senior jobs. Capelli makes the point that very few businesses routinely monitor the success or otherwise of their newly hired recruits.

Khurana and Nohria (2002) explored this further, studying CEO recruitments made from outside the organisation compared to providing succession from within. They examined data from 200 organisations over a 15-year period identifying four different scenarios (Fig. 3.4):

Internal vs. External

Previous Firm Performance	New CEO Performance	
	Internal CEO	External CEO
Good	Remains Good	Deteriorates
Poor	Remains Poor	Improves

Fig. 3.4 Business performance before and after CEO change

1. Insider promoted in a high-performing firm.
2. Insider promoted in a badly performing firm.
3. Outsider hired in a firm doing well.
4. Outsider hired in a firm doing badly.

In both 1 and 2, the firms continued much as before and in effect, progression from within was accompanied by limited change—ideal if the business is doing well, but less so if doing badly. In 3, performance deteriorated significantly, suggesting that internal succession would have been much better for the business. Whilst in 4, the firms improved significantly, indicating that if major change is necessary, then an outside candidate is the better option. The conclusion arrived at was to only recruit from outside when a turnaround is needed; otherwise, internal succession is better for the business (Fig. 3.5).

From an extensive literature review Fernandez-Araoz, Nagel, and Green's paper 'The High Cost of Poor Succession Planning' (2021) concludes that getting CEO appointments wrong comes down to five factors:

- Lack of succession attention.
- Poor leadership development.
- Suboptimal board composition.
- Lazy hiring practices.
- Conflicted research firms.

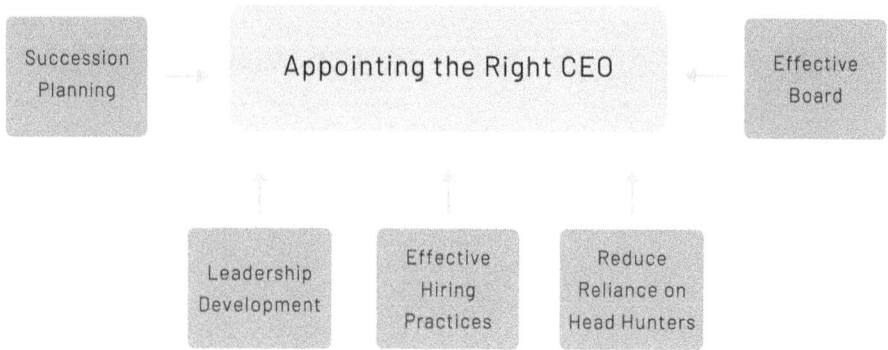

Fig. 3.5 How to appoint the right CEO

The first three of these are about preparing for the future. Sometimes identifying and developing potential successors can make CEOs feel insecure and unwilling to act. In these circumstances, the Non-Executive Directors (NEDS) should be insisting that a proper process and training are put in place.

The final two factors can sometimes only be solved by outsourcing, for example, using headhunters to provide more independence into a selection process. However, headhunters frequently charge large fees that might be unnecessary had a CEO been preparing their own successors. Incentives for headhunters are aligned towards appointing outside candidates, earning them a far greater fee than looking inside an organisation.

The Potential Risks of 'New Blood'

Let us consider the extent of risks associated with bringing in 'new thinking' and 'new blood' from outside.

- **Limited Knowledge**
  Although they may look good on paper and perform well at interview, you still have little knowledge of their strengths and weaknesses—information that they will hardly disclose and that may cloud judgement when looking internally. This is a significant advantage external candidates have over internal options where both strengths and weaknesses are known in some depth.

- **Repeat Performance?**
  Historic success can be difficult to replicate when the environment, business circumstances, culture, and timing are quite different. Success may be as much a case of luck as it is of skill. Different circumstances bring differing outcomes.
- **The Learning Time-lag**
  Getting to know a business—its market, culture, and competition—takes time, a learning process that may delay the effectiveness any new leader may have to offer.
  Subsequently, they may feel under pressure to act, and force rapid decisions based on limited understanding.

It is clear that there are significant risk factors to both external and internal appointments. Some may be discouraged from considering the latter simply by overlooking an individual's ability to grow into bigger jobs and, given the chance, contribute new thinking. Knowing the business and its workers well may mean they are able to initiate changes rapidly, and with an understanding of what they are inheriting, the possibility of destroying competitive advantages is far less likely.

In regard to outside hires, perhaps a third subsequently have to be despatched after much cost and damage to the business, even if only through treading water during their tenure. Another third may well be acceptable to the degree that it is not worth changing them, but we might question whether we would recruit them again. The final third typically achieve expectations and perform as we had hoped. Overall, we should perhaps give more consideration to how our existing management can be further developed.

Case Study: BPB plc—Global Leader in Plasterboard

In the decade between 1995 and 2005, BPB plc became the world leader in plasterboard, with a global market share of around 20% and operations in more than 50 countries. The business was acquired in a hostile takeover by the French multinational St Gobain for a headline £3.9 bn although the total cost with buying out share options and funding pension schemes was around £4.6 bn.

At its simplest, the plasterboard business is a capital-intensive manufacturing process which relies on finding and developing local gypsum reserves. These are naturally occurring, although also arise from desulfurising emissions at coal-fired power stations.

In the decade of rapid expansion from 1995 up to acquisition, the main growing pain was the lack of leadership talent required to run new operations in Russia, South America, Southeast Asia, China, and India.

Problems began in the early 1990s when the retiring chairman and CEO selected an external CEO to run the business. Like the above scenario, they lacked conviction that there were internal candidates adequately skilled for the

(continued)

(continued)

demands of such posts. The recruit was highly charismatic, articulate, and well-connected yet then proved disinclined to develop any real depth of knowledge in the existing business. He focussed instead on diversification, exploring, and acquiring other major, but often unrelated building material producers such as roofing tiles and cement manufacturers. This was a risky path to take and the CEO was sacked after just one year in office.

The next two CEOs were internally sourced and far more successful. They stuck with what they knew and, by focussing on plasterboard and plaster systems—the organisations' original purpose—developed a rapidly growing global lead in the product.

A number of senior management positions were filled from outside the business in an attempt to bring 'fresh eyes', but far less were successful than expected. There were few competitors within the respective countries to recruit people from who might have industry knowledge, and although those appointed were highly presentable, spoke a variety of languages and talked of doing a great job, they showed a marked reluctance to develop any depth of understanding in the industry. Most left; although a small number of notable successes did bring much needed new ideas.

Improving Your Decision Making

As a long-standing researcher in the field of decision making, Sir Andrew Likierman of the London Business School has plenty of advice for developing leaders (Likierman, & Stern, 2020). Much of his advice is appropriate at the board level and is useful in providing a 'gateway' to ensuring that decisions are thoroughly considered and consistent with the organisation's objectives. Individual biases and personal interests discussed earlier in this chapter may apply just as much to leaders of divisions, sections, and subsidiary businesses who submit their plans for approval; whether you sit on a board or not, the basic concepts still apply to how you approach decision making.

Much of Sir Andrew's advice concerns the quality, reliability, and extent of information presented, plus the adequacy of available options and whether the ability and resources to implement them are available. He suggests that the leader making decisions should approach all supplied information with a high degree of scepticism and, where he is not satisfied, be willing to request more. He also advises the need for diversity of thought within the decision making body and discusses strategies as to how to deal with implicit biases which can influence opinion. Consider the following factors that contribute to the most suitable decisions at a given time (Fig. 3.6).

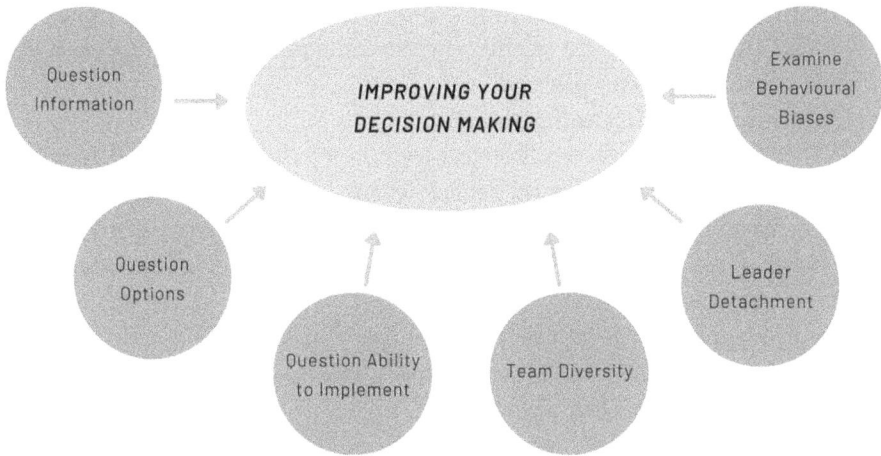

Fig. 3.6 Improving your organisation's decision making

Asking the Right Questions

- **Question the Information**
  Data and information arrive frequently from team members, but what of this is relevant and what irrelevant? Some data will already have been interpreted by others: does it have an inbuilt 'spin' or 'positioning'? Other reports may later be ascertained to be 'fake' news, accidental or otherwise. Sorting the 'wheat' from the 'chaff' is a critical leadership skill.
  Similarly, you must ascertain what is *not* there: are there inconsistencies that raise suspicion? Unless it really is a time-sensitive critical decision, then ask for more information, especially if there are holes and inconsistencies in what has been presented.
- **Question the Available Options**
  Limited options are often presented which may initially look to narrow and simplify the decision, but are these the only options? If time allows, ask to discuss or brainstorm more options, evaluate possible outcomes, and consider what would happen if the team chose to do nothing.
  Example: A business subsidiary wants to build a new manufacturing plant at a cost of £70M as the forecast demand looks set to increase beyond existing local capacity. Is the forecast accurate though? Can the business import from a nearby group company? This option is often unpalatable for local management but attractive to the organisation. What are their motives?

Local management may well want to be in control of their own plants in order to retain the profits of their own manufactured sales rather than lose them through transfer pricing.

- **Question the Ability to Implement**

  Who will reliably execute the decision? Does the organisation have the resources and capabilities to deliver within the planned time and cost? Enthusiasm and optimism may sometimes engulf management into approving schemes, have they fully appraised whether resource requirements are really available?

  Example: A business with demand collapsed by COVID-19 was attempting to rapidly reorganise itself from five plants to three whilst also closing the head office. Too few managerial individuals were available leading to inevitable consequences: poor service, major cost overruns, and protracted delays.

  Ultimately the cost base was significantly reduced, but a number of important customers were lost. Whilst circumstances may have made the move time-critical, the planning and availability of resources should have been given more attention and, if necessary, more external resources introduced to help.

- **Question the Diversity of your Team**

  Many organisations have a template for recruitment and progression based on their rubric of an 'ideal' company employee. However, this inadvertently but easily precludes diversity of thought and background within a team.

  Examples:

  - In a major French multinational company, all of the board's executive directors were male, French, and had been to one of two schools. Needless to say, they had a similar approach to making decisions and strategic thinking, which did not necessarily guarantee the best interests of the business, particularly in a more volatile environment.
  - In private equity, virtually all the partners have strong financial backgrounds and are recruited from quite limited areas, such as investment banking. However, they do recognise the limitations of this and consciously introduce management diversity into running their investments.
  - Multinationals should have diverse boards. They contribute a broader perspective to worldwide business practices. However, few boards do, or appoint 'token' employees to create an impression of diversity yet remain aligned to home country thinking. Similarly, gender diversity enriches

debates and encourages more innovative solutions that bring better solutions.

- Team members should be selected for their ability to recognise and communicate what you need to know, rather than what you want to hear. A frequent complaint issued by CEOs is that bad news travels slowly up an organisation; trusted people tell you what you need to know, however unpalatable.

- **Question Objectivity**
  We all have biases and carry allegiances to people and past decisions. Perhaps we have previously supported or introduced failing initiatives and subsequently struggle to admit defeat or curtail investment. Are there colleagues we have built good relationships with but who cannot manage an increased role and should be replaced? There are things which cloud our judgement when making decisions and reconsidering strategies. Detachment means stepping back, taking time to think, and adopting as objective a view as possible. This may be difficult for those that have built a team and business over some time. Turnaround leaders almost invariably come from outside the business for exactly these reasons—they have no allegiances to people or the business and will do what is necessary to change its fortunes.

- **Examine Behavioural Biases**
  Similarly, decision making bodies and individuals tend to suffer biases. The most common may include:

  - Confirmation bias: looking for information to support a decision you have already made whilst discarding suggestions that don't fully support it.
  - Anchoring or latching onto an early idea and then ignoring what comes after.
  - Desperation for consensus in meetings that lead to a lack of progressive solutions.
  - Appetite for risk varies between leaders. Some struggle with the risk associated with decision making and engineer deference. Others may be impulsive and act before fully appraising available information. Sometimes they simply want to look decisive or get the decision out of the way.

These are all biases a leader must acknowledge and negotiate within a group decision making process.

Learning Points

- A major threat to effective decision making is allowing certain character traits to develop; identify hubris, narcissism, pride, impulsivity, or risk aversion: Intelligent people make poor decisions when not vigilant to personal flaws.
- Unless lack of time precludes, then team consultation for major decisions is valuable. It taps expertise, motivates, aligns, and critically helps develop a team. Leadership is principally about developing your team to outperform.
- Actively seek diversity of thought and background. Recruit the best team you can find. Although they may be more difficult to manage, people who offer challenge in its proper place usually result in more innovative decision making. 'Yes' people tell you what you want to hear rather than what you need to know.
- External recruitment is high risk. The internal development of talent not only reduces risk but permits the evolution of strategy and trains potential successors. When major change is required, then recruitment from outside sometimes supplies necessary objectivity. However, do not be too quick to assume internal candidates lack productive and innovative ideas as to how the business can be better run.
- Be sceptical of information, options, and ability to implement decisions. Question deficiencies and inconsistencies. Ask for more options and an implementation plan if you are concerned.
- Leaders and teams may suffer from behavioural biases such as anchoring, confirmation bias, and achieving consensus. Awareness of these potential inclinations contributes greater objectivity to the process.

The ability to negotiate fast-moving, complex business environments are some of the greatest challenges faced by today's leaders; often solutions lie with the capability, experience, and ability of the team. The decision making process can improve and develop the team, their ability to work together towards a common purpose, and their subsequent capacity to support and challenge the leader. In the current business climate, it is our teams which will decide whether we win or lose. Pick them wisely and, where possible, fully involve them in your thinking and decision making.

Reflection

- To what extent and in what circumstances would you involve the team in making decisions?
- Can you think of ways of drawing the team into the process?
- Consider carefully: will this improve motivation, alignment, and team commitment?

Bibliography

Capelli, P. (2019, May-June). Your Approach to Hiring Is All Wrong. HBR May-June.

Fernandez-Araoz, C., Nagel, G., & Green, C. (2021). 'The High Cost of Succession Planning.' HBR May-June.

Hildebrand, C. A., Anterasian, C., & Brugg, J. (2021, Jan-Feb). 'Predicting CEO Success: When Potential Outperforms Experience.' *Harvard Business Review*. URL??

Khurana, R., & Nohria, N. (2002). 'The Performance Consequences of CEO Turnover.' Working Paper.

Likierman Sir, A. (2020a). The Elements of Good Judgment. HBR Jan-Feb.

Likierman Sir, A., & Stern, S. (2020). How to exercise your judgment during a pandemic. Think at London Business School.

Tichy, N., & Bennis, W. (2007). Making Judgment Calls. HBR Oct.

Vroom, V. H. (2003). Educating managers for decision making and leadership. *Management Decisions, 41*(10), 968–978.

Vroom, V. H., & Sternberg, R. J. (2002). Theoretical letters: The person versus the situation in leadership. *The Leadership Quarterly, 13*, 301–323.

Vroom, V. H., & Yetton, P. W. (1973). *Leadership and decision making*. Pittsburgh Press.

4

Ethics and Values: Negotiating a Complex Minefield

This chapter is entirely case study based, intending to develop your understanding of ethics and values that are fundamental to organisations. Through analysis of practical examples and applied theory, it will invite questions as to how you as a leader might respond to crisis situations in an ethically considered way.

Why do ethics and values matter?

- How can you lead effectively amidst the ethical challenge of globalisation?
- How can you create an ethical culture in a highly driven environment?
- What is the nature of ethics and leadership with the hidden culture of 'white-collar crime'?
- How can you manage product recalls when the stakes are high?
- Do ethics have a role amidst boardroom battles?
- How can you spot an unethical culture?

During times of crisis and turmoil, leaders are often required to make decisions that include a strong ethical component. Such decisions, if handled thoughtfully, can serve to bring stability, humanity, and hopefully profitability to an organisation. If handled badly however, they can cause not only personal regret, but significant damage to the organisation. Some decisions in times of crisis may simply prove wrong however they are viewed, others may have adverse moral and ethical implications that lie with the decision makers themselves. All leaders must be aware that pressure, fear, and uncertainty can act to distort the decision making process.

© The Author(s), under exclusive license to Springer Nature Switzerland AG 2022
J. Colley, D. Spyridonidis, *Unprecedented Leadership*, Palgrave Executive Essentials,
https://doi.org/10.1007/978-3-030-93486-6_4

A topical example can be drawn from the early stages of the UK's response to the COVID-19 outbreak. Hospitals assumed that younger COVID-19 sufferers might respond best to intensive treatment using ventilators and breathing assistance. With cases multiplying every day, medics and government elected to free up beds by transferring elderly COVID-19 patients back to care homes. Sadly, the bulk of care home sufferers did not have access to similar treatments, resulting in a disproportionate rate of loss compared with all other demographics.

In a situation where little was still known about the virus, a section of the population was disadvantaged for the greater good in an imposed form of utilitarianism (Driver, 2014). Rightly or wrongly, there were further decisions to be made in the next year regarding restricted visits to elderly care home residents. Undoubtedly the confusion and isolation of these accelerated dementia-related symptoms made for a cruel reminder of how vulnerable we are to the decisions of our leaders.

Despite restrictions intended to limit the means of transmission, death rates in care homes—the most vulnerable and closely quartered sectors of society—were enormous. Moreover, this protracted situation was only declared discriminatory by UK courts a year later. A more rapid implementation of visitor testing, or later still, vaccine passports could have reduced the emotional pain of this situation.

People are by default supreme followers, so it is imperative that our leaders pay serious attention to their ethical conduct. Scholars argue that ethical leadership has always been paramount, yet both research and practice suggest that individuals and organisations find it difficult to exercise. We live in an ever more technologically interconnected world and this wider reach alone makes ethical leadership more critical than ever.

Leadership Ethics: Ongoing Debate

Leadership ethics can be traced back to some of the earliest classical philosophers, including Plato, Socrates, and Aristotle (Ciulla et al., 2018). Many of their core writings were founded on justice, fairness, and democracy, teaching that ethical leadership is an essential tool for building solid and prosperous communities. Being a leader involves power and influence, but also responsibility for individuals, groups, and society as a whole. The capabilities or virtues ascribed to leadership are evidence of a certain set of values, referred to here as ethical or moral.

More recent critiques of ethical leadership in business have focussed on the organisation and interpersonal dynamics between leader and follower. In these theories, humility is also a defining moral virtue that creates trust, commitment, and conscientiousness within an organisation. To be an ethical leader is to empower others to create high trust cultures of organisational excellence (Caldwell et al., 2017).

A perspective that has gained increasing approval in recent years is that of **Transformational Leadership** that, by way of rigorous research, has established a strong connection between successful leadership and high moral reasoning. These findings led to the development of the Multifactor Leadership Questionnaire or MLQ (Turner et al., 2002)—a psychological leadership assessment tool (Northouse, 2016, p. 189) valuable in assessing personal leadership style.

Equally relevant to Transformational Leadership are its followers and their aspiration to higher moral standards and levels of functioning. The original concept of Transformational Leadership derives from James McGregor Burns' theory of 1978 and has since been developed into a new paradigm for leadership theory. Its basis is not so much on leader–follower transactions, but on the motivation and morality the leaders provide to those surrounding them. Ultimately this means Transformational Leadership is most applicable to an organisation's long-term goal (Northouse, 2016, pp. 161–62).

Collins' (2016) concept of level 5 leaders applied to those that combine professional excellence with humility; these are the leaders most capable of taking their company 'from good to great'. The values ascribed to level 5 leaders fit into the concept of Transformational Leadership (Caldwell et al., 2017), but also share similarities with the theory of **Servant Leadership** in which humble leaders adopt the role of servant in order to understand their own strengths and weaknesses.

All theories have their limitations, however. Although they create paradigms for leader conduct, they often fail to differentiate whom its benefits are aimed towards, whilst the Transactional Leader acts alone and the Transformational Leader for the sake of their organisation, the Servant Leader is intended to be entirely altruistic and not necessarily profitable; in short, none make for a balanced pragmatic approach within an organisation.

We know that no matter the values espoused, there comes a point at which policies meet pragmatism and leaders face the difficult negotiation of upholding ethical standards whilst under pressure to generate economic value. Compromises are bound to ensure, and, in this case study, we investigate the difficulties which surround such decisions. Timely responsiveness nearly always calls for distributed leadership, trust, and development (Bolden, 2011) to avoid sub-optimal decision making. The relationship between organisations, teams, and leaders has never been more important than when dealing with decisions with a significant ethical component.

The Case Studies to Follow

The format of this book is to present you with narrative case studies of commonly encountered situations. These are followed by questions that ask you to reflect on your own leadership practise in regard to ethical conduct. We consider the work of Epley and Kumar (2019) in relation to developing an ethical culture and what actions a leader needs to take to reach that end. How often are a business's actions at major variance with the espoused statement of ethics emanating from boards? How can a business drive those values into their culture such that they become the norm? Does the board 'walk the talk' and 'practice what they preach'? These will be among the questions addressed.

- In **'The Russian Way'** we consider how a leader might encounter local opposition to the construction of new plants overseas. We refer to the pitfalls of such investments and how knowledge of antecedent corruption may prevent potentially damaging business decisions.
- **'A Poison Pen Letter'** addresses the role of the whistle blower, what issues commonly arise by whistle blowers and the difficult decisions that must be made regarding source credibility and what accusations may expose about an organisations ethical culture.
- People working in organisations are likely to be familiar with **'white-collar crime'** such as bullying, sexual harassment, bribery, and dubious accounting to name a few. This is often a 'submerged' culture—its activities may rarely travel up an organisation but can be only too apparent to those working amongst it. We discuss solutions to this in the context of Healy & Serafeim's, 2019 work, with guidance as to how leaders identify white-collar crime. Reference is made to the 1995 case regarding the BBC journalist Martin Bashir's interview with Princess Diana using forged documents and what measures should be taken to protect potentially vulnerable individuals and sensitive information.
- **'Uber'** enables us to look in detail at how values have suffered in environments where technological development has gone hand in hand with associated business growth. Uber exhibited signs of subjugating standards in pursuit of growth targets which led, as of 2021, to a business worth in

excess of $100 bn, despite previously being accused of disregarding rules and laws. Prior to this unprecedented growth, the organisation was accused of unethical conduct. We will study Uber's dominant market position, alongside major efforts to improve values and ethical culture in recent years.

- A shorter case study reviews the potential damage to reputation and internal organisation dynamics as a result of faulty products and the need for their recall. This is a chance to reflect on how a leader responds even when they know the fault to be correctable and localised.
- Finally, we consider the politics of the board room and how discord amongst higher management easily percolates down, impacting an organisation's overall success and ethical culture.

In considering these cultures, leaders must remember how the consequences of poor ethical behaviour are now more broadly accessible. The easy deployment of social media means chances of suppressing knowledge of unethical decisions are significantly reduced. As a result, the importance of clear ethical statements and consistent actions has never been more important.

Reflection

- Have you ever had to deal with issues in which ethics and values were a significant component?
- How did you take measures to address the issue?

Case Study: The Russian Way—Little Is What It Seems

Construction was going well on a new Russian brick production plant sited a few hundred miles to the west of Moscow. The £100 M scheme was progressing after an arduous delay in obtaining the permits needed to buy land and build the plant. This was the first foray into Russia for the multinational business and progress had definitely been slow. Globally the product was penetrating markets rapidly and the business had now built plants in more than 30 different countries around the world. Russia had been selected for the next plant as the economy was accelerating rapidly and Western businesses appeared to be welcome. Despite a reputation for corruption following the Yeltsin era, significant progress was being made with regard to cleaning up the approach to business and the backing of the Regional Governor had been the necessary accelerant. The scheme would create several hundred well-paid jobs in an area of relatively high unemployment; it would inject much needed cash into the regional economy. However, the multinational's International Director was aware that this may be met with some challenge.

(continued)

(continued)

Foundations were in place and the plant was rising from the barren wasteland on which it was being built when the local Regional Governor was promoted to a higher position in central Moscow and a new one appointed.

Some months later disturbances began when local boar huntsman claimed that their traditional hunting grounds were disappearing as a consequence of the scheme. This was a cultural issue previously unknown to Western management, and that now rapidly started to gain more traction and news coverage. Attempts were made to contact the huntsman community to discuss their concerns but with little success; they simply did not wish to engage.

As the campaign gathered support, the local governing body made a decision to retract all permits and prevent the scheme progressing. This was something of a disaster for the International Director after such a sizeable investment had been made and that now looked to be in severe jeopardy. A meeting was hastily convened with the new local Governor.

The International Director laid out the situation to the Governor and explained that he could not understand why these objections had arisen at such a late stage and permits so categorically withdrawn. The Governor sympathised with his predicament but said there was little he could do in the face of such strongly opposed public opinion.

As the International Director was about to leave following this fruitless discussion, the Governor suggested, 'had you thought of a local public relations campaign to persuade hearts and minds that this scheme is in everyone's best interests?' The Director responded that this had already been tried with various local PR businesses and had even garnered some positive TV, radio, and newspaper coverage, but that little had been achieved. The Governor thought for a minute before producing a card: 'Try this firm. I have heard they are very good at resolving this type of issue'.

Reflection

- What should the International Director do?
- What would you do in the circumstances?

Discussion

Transparency International (Transparency.org/cpi) is an independent organisation which attempts to expose the scale of worldwide corruption in the public sector. They define corruption as 'the abuse of entrusted power for private gain'. In their words, corruption 'erodes trust, weakens democracy, hampers economic development, and further exacerbates inequality, poverty, social division, and the environmental crises'.

A corruption league table of 180 countries is published annually (Corruption Perceptions Index) together with an explanation of the extensive methodology and the key issues which businesses may face in each country. The top ten 'clean' countries usually include the four Nordic countries together with New Zealand, Australia, and Canada. However, once a country falls out of the top 50 it can be assumed that corruption is largely endemic; India, China, Russia, together with many Eastern European and Balkan countries are included in this category. A business setting up or running operations will have to manage corruption in some form, directly or through agents such as lawyers, public relations firms, or venture partners.

Although largely shrouded in darkness at the main board level, corruption is the major issue in need of management for Western-based corporations entering international markets. Boards are often well aware of potential cultural challenges, but seldom the sheer scale of them.

Public sector corruption is illegal in most countries (Fleming et al., 2020); however, the degree of enforcement varies enormously. In corrupt countries, the exposure of corruption usually involves score settling or deposing of a rival. It is a highly selective means of maintaining political control or power, whilst a significant number of politicians may actually be involved in unchallenged corruption.

In some Western countries, independent authorities will investigate whistle blower testimonies; in fact, a significant number of corporations—Walmart, Airbus, Goldman Sachs, Siemens, BAE Systems, Alcatel-Lucent, and Rolls Royce, to name a few—have suffered major fines for industrial scale bribery in international markets.

However, this underestimates the scale of the problem and exposes only some major corruption cases. Corruption is often endemic as illustrated in the example.

Western corporations are placed in a difficult position since, if they wish to internationalise beyond a limited list of countries, then they have little choice but to manage corruption one way or another. This is usually through intermediaries to blur the audit trail and attempt to create distance. There still remain major ethical issues to consider. Corporations often claim to be 'clean' through their public relations but what other choice do they really have?

There are also discussions about the arrogance of Western nations inflicting their moral values upon other countries. A counter argument is that the local laws usually make corruption illegal. Ultimately, it is the people who suffer. They see their taxes being stolen, which encourages behaviour towards evading tax. Ultimately public services cannot then be adequately funded and the quality of life for all deteriorates.

Leadership does embrace making difficult decisions and applying judgment (Shotter & Tsoukas, 2014). If Western corporations choose not to enter many transition economy countries due to the extent of corruption, this will hinder country development and reduce the opportunity to fight corruption. Many countries are so corrupt that they suffer this fate. However, there are others which may ultimately be redeemable, which makes the leader's task still harder. They face the difficult question of how to flourish in a country without experiencing the ill-effects of corruption.

Reflection

* Is your business active in countries which have low transparency ratings?
* Do you know how values are managed in those territories?

Why Do Ethics and Values Matter?

A 'Poison Pen' Letter

Tucked in amongst the post was a handwritten letter on personal writing paper, post marked from Perth. To Adam, recently appointed as CEO of a large service business, it looked like a poison pen letter, always interesting but not necessarily accurate. The letter had been handwritten in capitals as an attempt to disguise the identity of the writer and with its various spelling errors certainly looked authentic.

The letter detailed the behaviour of the local Area Manager's Personal Assistant, apparently a force to be reckoned with in the regional business. The writer claimed that people who crossed her, particularly in administration, usually ended up losing their jobs. Several instances were specified in some detail. There was a suggestion that on occasions she did bully people and as a consequence appeared to wield an authority which went well beyond the powers of an Area Manager's Personal Assistant.

The further allegation was that she was conducting an affair with the companies' Operations Director who sat on the board. The Operations Director in question was married and had previously been Area Manager in South West Australia. During the last year, he had been promoted to his current role and his deputy promoted to manage the area. The area was sizeable and employed around 500 employees. The letter alleged that the Personal Assistant's power was a consequence of her ongoing relationship with the Operations Director.

The business had previously experienced a difficult period in regard to operations directors. Around three years previously, the then Operations Director had retired, and he had been replaced with an external recruit. Despite major efforts to embrace the culture and introduce modern management methods, overall performance had deteriorated substantially, and the external hire was eventually released. The new internal appointment was previously the South West Area Manager who understood the culture and was now starting to restore better levels of performance throughout the business. He still lived in the Perth area with his family, despite the company's head office being in the east.

(continued)

(continued)

Adam called in the HR Director and showed him the letter. The HR Director, Mike, had been with the business many years in a variety of roles before being promoted to his current position. 'Is this true?' asked Adam. 'It may well be' replied Mike. Adam sensed that Mike knew far more about this than he cared to admit. 'I will make some discrete enquiries and get back to you', responded Mike. 'By the way' asked Adam, 'Do we have a policy on relationships between staff, particularly where there is a line of management?' As the Kent Area Manager reported to the Operations Director and the Personal Assistant reported to the Area Manager, it meant there was a direct line of power influence. 'I'm afraid not', responded Mike. 'I think we are going to need one, Mike', retorted Adam.

Adam reflected that there seemed to be a force field around him which prevented bad news from being received. Good news seemed to arrive rapidly, whilst matters he should have known failed to make it into his office. Clearly, if the letter was true, then the South West Area Manager was in a difficult position as his boss was having an affair with his assistant, which was probably undermining his position. But would that really explain why the assistant was able to wield such power?

A week later Mike returned and explained that the letter was largely correct or so it seemed. He had made enquiries through a number of employees he knew well at the area and they largely substantiated the allegations. However, he felt that it was unlikely that anyone would offer formal evidence, on the grounds that should there be an absence of managerial action then there could be reprisals.

Adam's thoughts were that clearly this situation could not be allowed to persist and action was needed. What should Adam do in view of the circumstances?

Discussion

The illustrative case identifies several key problem areas when dealing with decisions which have a significant values element. For senior managers, this may amount to a substantial proportion of their decision making. Clearly the instigator of the letter is concerned that their identity may become known and that there could be reprisals, hence anonymity. This may also signify a lack of confidence in management to effectively resolve the situation. 'Whistle blowers' are rarely treated well (see below). Secondly there is a concern to 'right a wrong'. Of course, this might be a score settling exercise too.

Breaking down this example further, the business does not have a policy so whatever it does might be subject to some form of legal challenge. Perhaps it goes without saying that running a business does involve some risk and there is always a temptation to do nothing, which effectively maintains the status quo. However, is that really feasible in this case? We also know that the current situation places the Area Manager in a difficult situation as his assistant appears to be having an affair with his direct boss, which undermines him. We also know that the assistant appears to be unfairly using the relationship to develop power, which she may be abusing. There will also be resentment and jealousy amongst staff that the personal assistant may be receiving other advantages from her relationship.

There is also the question of the real evidence. The letter is anonymous although the HR Director, who has an excellent network which he has tapped, is suggesting that the letter appears to be accurate in its claims. However, it is unlikely anyone would want to formalise his or her evidence or stand by it. If there were to be no effective action then, they would have exposed themselves to retribution from conceivably both the assistant and Operations Director. A summary of some of the difficulties to be considered in such cases (see Fig. 4.1):

- Issues are often ambiguous, complex and lacking in information.
- Even with a policy in place, there still remain difficulties in collecting adequate evidence to act. People may offer information but only 'off the record'. Formal processes often ensure fairness and legitimacy but fail to resolve the continuing issues. Those supplying information have the concern that grudges may persist post the investigation.

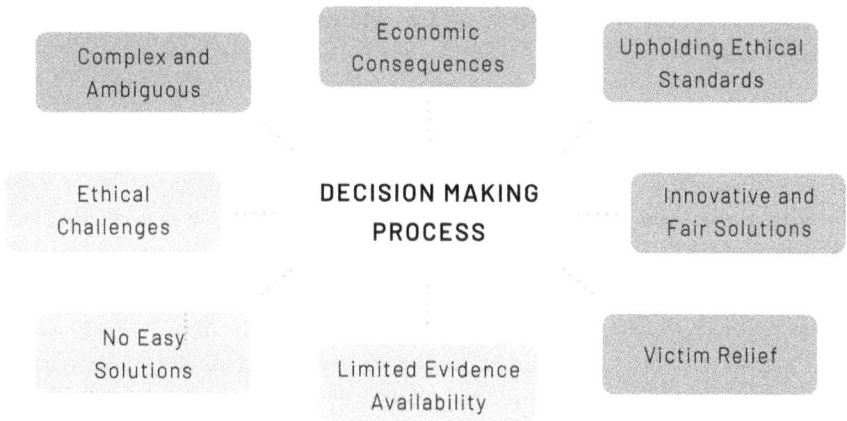

Fig. 4.1 Key characteristics associated with ethical decision making

- There is often no right answer or easy solution and whatever decision is made could well have some adverse consequences. This may result in, either victims who do not feel justice has been done, or the accused perceiving they have suffered injustice; claims and litigation may ensue.
- There are frequently issues about balancing economic value to the business versus upholding decent ethics standards. The cost of good values can be economically substantial.
- Of primary consideration are the victims, current, and, unless the situation is resolved, future. This means that doing nothing is not a realistic option.
- Resolution of difficult issues such as this requires decisive action and imagination. It is important that values are seen to be upheld and the solution viewed as fair. Ideally it should be difficult to legally challenge, although any decisive action often carries that risk.

Even if there were a policy in place, the business would not wish to lose the Operations Director, particularly given he had turned around the poorly performing operations activities. As the costs and risk in trying to find another, equally effective Operations Director are significant, what should Adam do? (Fig. 4.1).

There are greater issues here, outlined by Epley and Kumar in their 2019 article for the Harvard Business Review, 'How to Design an Ethical Organization' (2020). Firstly, many organisations have clear statements of high morals on paper. However, it is actions and incentives that link these statements and policies to an ethical culture. If those actions of senior management are not consistent and fail to uphold the principles, then, for all expressed purposes, those principles are not being implemented.

Similarly, incentives mean consequences. If there are no consequences for behaviour which fails to meet the organisation's standards, then it will continue and proliferate. These situations are often seen by managers as too difficult or time consuming to address. They are also likely to be unpleasant and messy. Managers have to take a view as to whether their superiors will really support them in any sort of action, and they often do not. The likely consequence is that it is easier to do nothing or simply speak to the parties concerned but take no further action, allowing the situation to persist. Responses to these kinds of situations define the culture and ethics of an organisation.

Whistle Blowers

'Whistle blower' is a term typically used to describe an employee who exposes information about activities which may be illegal, fraudulent, unsafe, abuse of public money, or bullying (Fotaki, 2020).

Whistle blowers can be categorised by public and private organisations, and internal and external. Externally is usually to media, or law enforcement. Internally may be to senior management. Public institution allegations often concern public money misspending or abuse of position.

What we do know is that whistle blowers are almost universally badly treated by their organisations. External leakage of information usually involves termination of contract. Organisations are concerned about their image and carefully manage the flow of information to media or external bodies. Termination sends a message to others regarding whistle-blowing activities.

Many countries have laws to protect whistle blowers, however their effectiveness is questionable. Those who are not fired may suffer internal action to make their lives less comfortable such as a major increase in workload. Organisations are often required to have internal complaints systems to provide anonymity, however employees may have limited confidence in such systems.

In 1995 the BBC journalist Martin Bashir procured an interview with Princess Diana using forged documents. Princess Diana was viewed by many as a 'vulnerable' person. The subsequent interview resulted in Princess Diana losing royal support which ultimately ended in divorce and the loss of her royal title. A subsequent investigation by long-term BBC director Lord Hall determined that Bashir did not have a case to answer and that no wrong doing had occurred. Various whistle blowers were fired as a consequence of leaking material to the media. A recent investigation by Lord Dyson determined that the allegations were correct and that the interview was procured using fraudulent means. A question put to the BBC by a journalist was why had no one been sacked by the BBC as a consequence of the affair other than whistle blowers?

Reflection

- Have you had to deal with difficult staff issues?
- To what extent did you find policies helpful in resolving the issues?

White-Collar Crime

One can argue that all companies suffer from some white-collar crime. It can take a number of forms, including the following.

- Conflicts of Interest
- Sexual harassment and bullying
- Bribes or inappropriate gifts
- Accounting irregularities
- Antitrust violations
- Theft

The extent and depth largely come down to the nature of the culture which, more often than not, takes its lead from the actions of top management. Such white-collar crime can bring about significant trust and reputational damage as well as cost billions of pounds. In the case of the major UK clearing banks, they have paid several tens of billions in compensation to customers who have been mis-sold inappropriate products. An example of such a product is loss of employment insurance which has been structured so that there are few circumstances in which it will pay out. The bank's current share prices are less than half the level before the various scandals were identified. The main drivers were sales bonuses for selling the products and an unwillingness to challenge the morality of the products. In effect, the four banks saw each other making money from these products and felt they could benefit from entering these dubious markets.

Healy and Serafeim (2019) have identified that the main driver of such crimes is weak leadership and a culture of making the numbers at all costs with a blind eye turned to dubious practices. Their solution is that leaders need to broadcast to all their employees that crime does not pay. They must punish perpetrators equally, and hire managers known for their integrity. Some industries, such as waste disposal, have a reputation for dubious practices or anti-trust activities (common to many industries). In these circumstances recruiting from outside the industry may be necessary. They must also create decision making processes which reduce the opportunity for illegal or unethical acts, and champion transparency. Involving the entire team in decision making helps reduce the propensity for unethical decisions, particularly when the leadership is clear on what is not acceptable.

> **Reflection**
> - How often does bullying and harassment occur in an organisation without being reported or acted upon?
> - How does your own organisation perform in relation to 'white-collar crime'?

What are Business Ethics?

Business ethics are moral principles that guide the way a business behaves. These include norms, values, unethical and ethical practices which guide the business. It is distinguishing between what is morally right and wrong when selecting courses of action that are often complex. This frequently involves the interaction of profit maximising behaviour with non-economic concerns and the impact on other stakeholders.

> Ethics is concerned with the study of morality [...] and the elucidation of rules and principles that result in morally acceptable courses of action. Ethical theories are the codifications of these principles. (Crane et al., 2019)

Businesses often have ethics codes and social responsibility charters to provide guidance to employees. These are intended to regulate behaviour in areas of concern which go beyond what is covered in government regulation and the law, but which may be viewed as unacceptable to the business and its stakeholders.

Many of the questions we face are equivocal in that there may not be a definitive 'right' answer. Choosing between different courses of action may involve a complex consideration of many different ethical aspects and widely varying points of view.

Some of the most prominent ethical issues encountered include:

- Employment and comparable worth (Amazon and low pay, zero hours contracts)
- Discrimination (age, race, gender, disability)
- Workplace safety
- Marketing ethics (inappropriate product/service claims—mis-selling, distortion of perceptions)
- 'Greenwashing'
- 'Pyramid selling'
- Consumer fraud
- Corruption
- Misuse of business resources (executive pay and allegations against Carlos Ghosn of Renault)
- Child labour, slavery, exploitation
- Environmental destruction (BP)
- Tax avoidance
- Sustainability and climate change

Shareholder, Stakeholder, and Stewardship Theories

The following theories are useful in analysing motives and rationale behind events.

Shareholder theory is the view that the only duty of a corporation is to maximise profits accruing to shareholders. Other stakeholders are satisfied only to the extent of safeguarding shareholder returns. So poor reputation could restrict sales and reduce shareholder returns. Similarly relations and management of customers, employees, suppliers, government, and environmental concerns are with the objective of preventing damage to shareholder returns. In terms of legal activities it could be argued that the business only complies with the law to the point that conceivable consequences of breaching regulation are worse than the profits made from such breaches.

Stakeholder theory considers the business from the perspective of creating value for all stakeholders, not just shareholders. In effect there are multiple constituencies who have a legitimate interest in the corporation. This includes the environment which does not have a voice. The theory assumes two principles:

- That of corporate rights which demand the corporation does not violate the rights of others.
- That of corporate effect that the corporation is responsible for the effects of their actions on others.

Hence businesses have a responsibility to create employment and pay fair wages. They have strong environmental credentials which go beyond reputational damage. Sourcing would be ethical despite increased costs even though this may not be a potential source of competitive advantage through reputational improvement (such as in the case of B2B).

Stewardship theory is the view that ownership does not really own a business but looks after the business on behalf of all constituencies. There is a higher vision or purpose beyond shareholder satisfaction. The theory assumes that managers left on their own will act as responsible stewards of assets on behalf of the owners. In a choice between self-serving and pro-organisational behaviour people will choose the latter. They are trustworthy collectivists who have a belief in a higher vision.

However the CEOs operate the business on behalf of the owners or intended beneficiaries (e.g. charities). This tends to contrast with agency theory which considers that the owners and managers of the business pursue their own interests and objectives, which necessarily diverge. In effect this model assumes a high level of trust unlike the agency model which believes that objectives diverge where there is the passage of limited information on the business performance.

Case Study: Uber and Kalanick—Always Hustling!

Garrett Camp and Travis Kalanick had one thing in common—they disdained and were frustrated by the US city approach to taxis. The 'medallion system' adopted by many cities was designed to ensure drivers were reasonably remunerated through metered rates and that they had been subject to certain checks and were registered. However, the system created taxi shortages and the meter system ensured that passengers had no idea what the journey would cost until it was complete. It also made trips expensive. So not only were taxis in short supply at rush hour but passengers had to put up with expensive fares of indeterminate amount, plus demands for cash payment and a sizeable tip. Drivers safe in the knowledge that they had a job for life and decent remuneration could be discourteous. In one form or another, similar systems were in operation in many cities around the world. The passengers were receiving a poor deal and the system was loaded in favour of the drivers.

Camp and Kalanick devised the genius idea of a ride hailing app which might, on occasions, ignore regulations but provide a far better deal for travellers. They would provide a quote through the Uber app and give an estimate of when the taxi would arrive. There would be no tip to pay, and all transactions would be by pre-registered credit card. A mutual assessment system would be in operation so that passengers could assess the courtesy level of the driver and vice versa. Hence future drivers and passengers could identify lower ratings in advance before entering into the transaction. In addition, Uber, the app provider, would simply link drivers to passengers and take commission on the deal. They would set the rates and collect payment from the passengers and pay the drivers after deducting their commission. Uber believed that they were merely providing a platform that connected travellers to drivers, and were therefore not responsible for the various parties involved in the transaction.

They were also aware that, in this market, being first was critical, as was creating network effects as a barrier to followers. So the more passengers Uber could attract the more drivers would want to sign up wanting to earn more. The more responsive the service became through having more drivers, the more travellers would wish to use it. Each would drive what are two-sided network effects. Once created, this provided a major barrier to potential followers wishing to copy the approach. Rates were a fraction of those offered by metered taxis.

Camp and Kalanick knew they would have to pump prime the model by offering incentives to drivers and passengers to build scale rapidly. They also anticipated challenges from the authorities as they may have disregarded regulation and operated on the edge of legality. Indeed, regulation said little about ride hailing platforms and so they operated in a legal grey area. They would meet authority challenge by growing the service rapidly so that, if eventually banned, large numbers of drivers would lose their jobs, and customers would lose cheap

(continued)

(continued)

and convenient travel. Customers and drivers are voters in local government elections. Uber would invest heavily in public relations and lobbying local government and authorities. The objective was to make it as difficult as possible for politically sensitive local politicians to oppose them.

Funding the Venture

Travis Kalanick had made money from a previous venture ('Red Swoosh)', but had been fired by venture capital investors as they sought to accelerate development of the enterprise. As Travis famously said, 'It is in the Venture Capitalists (VC) nature to kill a founding CEO. It just is'. Following the success of Facebook, Google, and Amazon, Kalanick was not going to offer VC that opportunity again. VCs were desperate to invest in technology start-ups. So Kalanick introduced two classes of share: founder shares with most of the votes and VC shares which had little in the way of voting rights. Cheap money, booming device ownership around the world, and the ability to develop software infrastructure rapidly using Amazon Web Services generated significant opportunities. So in 2009, Uber Technologies came into being and headquartered in San Francisco. In total it raised over $25 bn to fund the global development of Uber taxis plus a variety of other ventures, including takeaway food delivery, freight services, bikes, and autonomous vehicle development.

By 2019 Uber claimed 78 M users, a 67% market share in the USA and revenue (commissions) of $14.1 bn. Its operating income was a loss of $8.6 bn. Indeed, with COVID-19, results for 2020 looked likely to produce losses at a similar level. However, despite Uber having a consistent history of major cash losses each year, the stock market valuation at the end of 2020 still stood at $94 bn.

Ethics and Values in a Driven Culture

Kalanick was famously driven and believed in 'always hustling', in short, pushing at the regulatory limits wherever beneficial. His view was that achieving targets for revenue and user growth were prime means by which investors valued the business. He appeared less concerned with how his teams achieved the targets or the nature of the high-spirited culture. The pace of Uber's growth was staggering as driven and highly remunerated teams were set up in major cities throughout Europe, India, Southeast Asia, and China. The goal of these teams was to generate growth. Money was little object as venture capital money was so easy to come by. As each growth target was achieved, Kalanick would organise a party for staff. The famous 'X to the X' party after achieving sales of $1 bn was believed to cost some $25M. Kalanick rapidly acquired business guru status, producing and presenting his own philosophy of business, as had many Silicon Valley founders. Tellingly, his philosophy did not mention values or ethics. He surrounded himself with similar thinking people who believed that regulation merely presented a business opportunity. However, challenges started to mount up, including:

- Increased traffic congestion as the business boomed. When Uber entered the London market in 2012, total taxi drivers increased from 65,000 to 120,000 in 2017, and Uber rapidly developed a claimed 3.5 M customers and 45,000 drivers. Previously most customers might have used public transport, bikes, or walked.
- Safety concerns developed as allegations of sexual molestation amongst drivers mounted. Indeed, in a one-year period in London there were 26 complaints of Uber drivers' sexual offences against passengers. There were also criticisms that Uber had not reported these allegations and failed to cooperate with investigations.
- Once the initial driver incentives were withdrawn by Uber, drivers became concerned that they should have employee benefits rather than be treated as contractors on a trip basis. Legal challenges were issued in many territories.
- Google commenced major litigation that Uber had stolen their 'Waymo' autonomous vehicle technology by recruiting a senior staff member.
- An Uber autonomous vehicle struck and killed a pedestrian whilst being tested, and the supervising engineer was accused of watching videos at the time.
- 'Greyball' software was alleged to be used which denied traffic inspectors and government official's rides by presenting an alternative, limited picture of Uber taxi availability.
- Employees claimed that a toxic culture existed in which sexual harassment was commonplace. Following an internal investigation, 20 employees were fired in 2017.
- There were two occasions of major data breaches being disclosed. The second in 2017 disclosed personal data of 600,000 drivers and 57 M customers.

Despite this saga, Kalanick was proving difficult to move from his position. The board was largely powerless as non-founder shareholders had little voting power. Whilst venture capital investors (VC) were represented on the board, some of the Non-Executive Directors were colleagues of Kalanick. What was increasingly apparent was that an initial public offering on the stock market would not be possible unless values improved, and Kalanick was gone. In effect cashing out would not be available for investors including Kalanick and

Camp unless there was major change. After negotiating his exit, Kalanick resigned and left the board with several billion dollars and Dara Khosrhowshahi became CEO. He had many issues to resolve with proliferating litigation claims and regulatory authorities to deal with. Uber also needed to make money at some stage.

Discussion

Mike Isaac in his 2019 book *Super Pumped: The Battle for Uber* described the story as 'a tale of hubris and excess set against a technological revolution … a young leader surrounded by "yes men" and acolytes given nearly unlimited financial resources and operating without serious ethical or legal oversight'.

Despite the level of losses Uber was still valued at around $94 bn at the end of 2020. Despite the dubious values and suggestions of a toxic culture the founders and venture capital investors have been well rewarded.

Upper Echelons Theory proposes that a business's values are largely a consequence of the behaviour of the top management team. In turn, that behaviour is a product of their previous experiences. Certainly, in the case of Uber we can conclude that behaviour of management took its lead from the top team. Uber has not been in existence long so there has no previous culture that could have served to moderate behaviour. Instead, the swashbuckling attitude to rules, regulation, and other staff left much to be desired. Indeed, the major celebration parties had been deliberately marketed as an opportunity for excess behaviour.

There has been a cost to Uber, both at the time and subsequently, due to costly litigation and a loss of trust. Transport for London has now twice banned Uber from having a license to operate. On both occasions, Uber have successfully appealed the decision but are now granted short-term licences and have to comply with ever more demanding regulation. Regulation relating to labour practices is tightening and Uber is seen as an early target for legal action due to their historic responses, which are unlikely to attract judicial sympathy.

In the USA, Lyft was able to develop a more significant position as a consequence of Uber's adverse publicity. Outside the USA, Uber has major competition in every market and there is some doubt whether they will ever make money outside the USA.

Travis Kalanick was handsomely paid off, but his reputation is damaged, and it is likely he would still rather be running Uber. He certainly did not leave without a fight. However, the financial markets have rapidly forgotten the many dubious actions and remain willing to invest significantly in a business they believe will eventually be highly profitable.

Uber had a board with NEDs which ultimately failed to create good ethical standards. They may well have had policies and statements but these need to be connected to behaviour through specific actions and incentives. In reality, the investors were faced with being unable to list unless they resolved the ethics problem. Governance arrangements may be satisfactory on paper, but without clear links to incentives and actions, they are ineffective. In this case, founder shares presented a major barrier to any sort of action in terms of building an ethical workplace and ethical culture.

Reflections

- In view of the outcome to what extent does ethics and governance really matter?
- Whilst a governance structure existed, why was it ineffective?
- Is a driven high-spirited culture, pushing at the boundaries of regulation, bound to fall foul of accepted standards of ethics?
- What does this case say about governance, ethics, and leadership?

Building an Ethical Culture

Culture emanates from the top team although cultures can be very resistant to manipulation particularly in businesses with long histories. Changing attitudes require high levels of communication and publicising the good things that employees do. The business should present clear rationales for decisions, in particular where some stakeholder groups are disadvantaged or have to bear the brunt of necessary measures for example redundancies or closures. These need to go beyond just saving money.

This means creating an environment that enables people to do the right thing and reminds them that wrongdoing is not allowed. As a leader, your job is to make it known that doing things the right way is necessary.

A problem leaders face is ensuring that they are not holding their followers back in exhibiting ethical behaviour. Ideally, leaders want their employees to come forward and feel comfortable voicing any concerns regarding perceived unethical behaviour. As leaders, we have to make an effort to nurture a work culture in which they feel comfortable in doing so. Unsurprisingly, it is upper management and leadership that most frequently breach ethics (Downe et al., 2016), and the probability of a leader disregarding ethics increases with seniority. As a leader, your most important job is to make sure that you establish your own personal moral code and make sure that *your* practices and policies follow that moral code. Then you need to build your team around people that can be relied on to follow that moral code and provide support in creating an ethical workplace.

An important element in creating an ethical climate is to frequently raise the issue of ethics. The more leaders emphasise positive behaviours, the more willingly people will follow. Leaders need time to determine their workplace values and create the ethical code that they want people to follow.

Be Careful of Ethical Hazard Zones

Sometimes good people can be caught up in unethical behaviour known as ethical hazard zones (Messick & Bazerman, 2001). Watch out for its most common features (Fig. 4.2):

- **Contradictory Targets**
  Ethical standards can start to deteriorate when people have to meet performance goals at all costs.
- **Evasion**
  When unethical behaviour is overlooked, it can incentivise others to act in a similar way.
- **Declining Standards**
  Once someone has committed an unethical action and avoided the consequences, more become conceivable and so standards decline.

Fig. 4.2 Creating an ethical culture

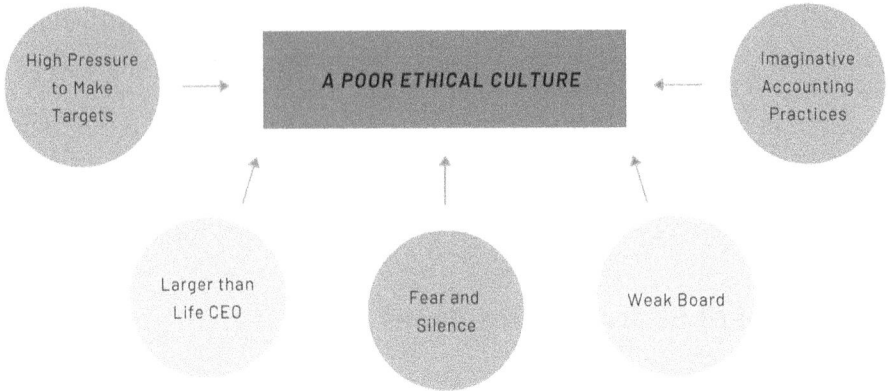

Fig. 4.3 Signs of a poor ethical culture (adapted from Marianne Jennings 'Seven Signs of Ethical Collapse')

How to Spot an Unethical Culture

By way of summary, it is worth summarising some of the views of Marianne Jennings in her 2006 book *Seven Signs of Ethical Collapse*. She identifies several symptoms of an unethical culture, including significant pressure to make the numbers, a larger-than-life CEO, fear, and silence internally, and a weak board, usually selected by the CEO. Other symptoms include using charitable activities as a cover for an unethical culture, imaginative accounting approaches, and conflicts of interest at senior leadership levels. If an organisation exhibits several of these symptoms, then it may well be sick. Ultimately, organisations are likely to pay the price for poor ethics one way or another (Fig. 4.3).

Product Recalls

A problem experienced by manufacturers and increasingly service providers is the issue of faulty products and services which have to be remedied. In the service field, there has been the mis-selling of various financial products and insurances which are of poor value, or entirely inappropriate to the client's needs. UK authorities have subsequently offered retrospective protection and compensation to consumers of complex financial products which few understand, including those that sell them. This has cost the banks some tens of billion pounds in compensation.

Case Study: The Blame Game

Imagine that you manage a building materials business in the Netherlands, and you are informed internally that a manufacturing process has been defective for nine months and that substandard materials are now in 5000 properties across the country. Worse still, it may not be possible to trace all the buildings as the materials pass through distributors. If there were to be a fire it is possible that those materials may not perform to tested standards. The costs of removing and replacing would far exceed your levels of insurance, to the extent that the business would almost certainly become insolvent. However, if fires were to occur, then there should be other fire prevention precautions in buildings specified in building regulation. The chances of the products in question being identified and subsequently tested are unlikely except in the case of a major fire.

We assume that in all circumstances the plant problem is immediately fixed and the plant stood down until the issue was resolved. Secondly, we also assume that a reliable testing regime is introduced across all products to prevent any future recurrence.

Reflections

- How would you respond to the discovery of faulty manufacturing, regardless of how minor?
- How might you manage social media and act in a socially responsible and ethically transparent way?

Recently recalls have become more frequent. Manufacturers attempt to do this quietly to prevent bad publicity. However, this may now be expedited by government departments who mandate the manufacturer to identify all owners and require action. Car manufacturers can be slow moving due to the expense of a recall and the perceived reputational damage.

However, reputations can be enhanced if there is a rapid and decisive response. This can be used to send a clear message about values and a supplier who is responsible and cares. This is more likely in the retail industry in which supermarket chains demand suppliers stock cleanse all product on the shelves and in stock at their own expense, and fund a returns scheme for all product sold. In these circumstances, the costs are largely identifiable and there is a 'policeman' in the supermarkets ensuring rapid action.

Board Games: Do Ethics Really Matter?

The two brothers sat behind the desk on the Zoom call saying little. When they spoke, it was usually to issue orders or some form of ultimatum. They were clearly used to being obeyed and instructing whilst discussion seemed rather alien to their approach. Their family business, Dresden, had been successful and was now listed on a local stock market. The father had been the driving force in building the business and had now retired taking a back seat to his two sons. In recent years, Dresden had developed beyond Germany into the Netherlands and Belgium, with various minority interests in Denmark.

Between these two brothers, the one with the beard spoke to outline the terms that they were willing to offer for investing in the Austrian business Proteus. 'We will offer a bullet loan of $5.0Mn repayable in 2 years, plus 60 days trade credit on raw material supplies from our plants. The equity will be $3.0 Mn and management will have control at 51%. You will need to find the pro rata portion from your own funds'.

As chairman of the business, he certainly did not sound like the brothers were negotiating, more akin to a statement. I asked if we could have a few days to discuss amongst ourselves as we had to find over $1.5 Mn between the three of us. He responded, 'You have 2 days'. It was by far the best offer we had received but working with these two looked to be a real challenge as there was no real scope for a relationship and the COVID-inspired Zoom calls did not help in resolving this!

COVID had resulted in Proteus falling into difficulties as sales had collapsed and the business was already heavily indebted. It needed a major reorganisation to reduce the number of plants and cut overheads which would cost several million pounds in reorganisation costs. We needed a partner to provide the funding and Dresden's offer would provide $12 Mn in total, which would allow for a much lower cost base and help see us out the COVID epidemic. Private Equity had been approached but their offers were significantly inferior to this, which at least granted us, the management, control. Clearly, we had little choice but to accept.

Discussion

This is a difficult situation, the temptation being to fix the problem and then say nothing. However a key issue has to be the risk to life of the product fault. If that is increased then there is little choice but to come clean and admit the problem. In such circumstances the government may pick up funding if it is evident that the business is not capable of carrying the burden.

The chances of the problem becoming known may be unlikely as even if there were a fire, then it would require a number of different fire safety precautions to fail. However, despite the unlikely prospect, a full risk assessment should be undertaken to identify where the real and significant risk exists. To what extent does the product failure increase the overall fire risk? Is it significant? For example, hospitals, schools, and care homes followed by multi-storey buildings should be risk assessed. This review should be

Challenges Emerge

Around three weeks after the deal was signed and the major reorganisation commenced, we received a call from a board director at Dresden. They wished to merge Proteus into a similarly sized independent Austrian competitor, MF, to which they had been talking. This seemed a strange and certainly unexpected request. 'So, what do we get?' I enquired. 'We will give you shares in the new larger business but sadly we will not need you to manage the business'. 'Well, that sounds attractive'. I thought. It seemed an easy decision to decline the generous offer. Their rationales for the merger were greater economies of scope and scale, and increased market power. However, they seemed to have forgotten that they had ceded control to us. We suspected that this was really about another raw materials supply contract at elevated prices from Dresden's upstream operation. The proposed deal made little sense as major reorganisations are hard enough to do well anyway, but whilst merging into another business, there was little prospect of success. In reality, management's shareholding was unlikely to yield much value and losing their jobs was scarcely attractive. The refusal was not received well, and the resultant Zoom calls were at best stilted, verging on disagreeable. The concept of discussion seemed as far away as ever. Explaining our position cut little ice as that was of no interest to them. They had changed their minds and that was that.

A month or so passed and Dresden then made an offer to the management team to buy all their shares at twice the original price paid. The proposed alternative was that management paid the same for Dresden's shares and paid back the bullet loan. After consultation with financial advisors and some modelling of options, the management team accepted the offer to buy out Dresden and repay the loan. They believed they could fund it out of business profits over the next year. The brothers promptly withdrew the offer. They clearly had thought that management would not be able to raise the money and so would be unable to accept their proposal to sell out.

A couple of months later Dresden started to reduce the trade credit. Proteus looked as though they were dependent upon this trade credit for cash during the difficult winter months when demand was low anyway. The third COVID lockdown along had further reduced demand so that Proteus was dependent on the trade credit. As always, cash forecasts were shared with Dresden who claimed that the business was not viable and would need another $2.0 Mn to survive. They proposed that there should be an equity issue shared pro rata to shareholdings, so management would need to find another $1.020 K out of their own pockets to stay in control. Otherwise, Dresden would buy up any surplus shares and take control. This would no doubt be followed by an unwelcome merger with MF and the management team losing their jobs.

To me, we did not need more cash as the business was improving rapidly in results as we removed cost. Our forecasts showed rapidly increasing cash and profit once we had navigated March and April when certain major payments were due. My guess was that the brothers had realised that the business value was set to increase rapidly and if they wanted to take control, they would have to do it before valuations rocketed. So their approach was to cut credit and force a share issue believing that the management team could not afford to stay in the game. In effect, their aim was to increase the stakes for all and trade on their bet that Dresden had deeper pockets than the team.

undertaken in conjunction with the insurers and the relevant government agencies.

I politely declined their generous offer on the grounds that the business did not need it. Their response was to have their 'independent' accountants conduct a review of the accounts. It would not be too hard to guess what their opinion would be. Even with independent accountants 'he who pays the piper calls the tune'.

Reflection

- How ethical is this in your view? Is it anything more than boardroom power politics?
- Clearly choosing a partner carefully is important. Do you think this battle for power is unusual in joint ventures?

Discussion

In boardroom battles, there are no rules other than complying with the law and the governance processes on which the business is established. Economic value seems to trump any other values and ethics. Indeed, the articles and shareholder contract provide the legal framework within which the battles for power operate.

In joint venture type relationships such as this, it is usual for the objectives of the partners to develop and diverge over time. This frequently leads to disputes between the partners who are effectively married under the contracts. Exiting is very difficult, as it is almost impossible to sell a significant share of a business with a disaffected partner attached. As a consequence, the exit of either partner is normally at an under value as they can only sell out to the other partner. In such a limited market for the shares, they will be cheap. Around 80% of joint ventures are sold to one partner. Around 50 to 70% end up in failure and value destruction as a result of diverging objectives.

In this case, one partner somewhat unusually changed their objectives almost immediately, once the deal was done. As they had not considered the position of the management team when changing their minds, they were somewhat surprised by a refusal. After that, rather than offering a sensible figure to buy management out they indulged in various devious activities to buy the business on the cheap.

In board games, few are interested in what is fair and reasonable but rather how they can extract value; others are viewed as needing to look after themselves during the battle for power.

Lessons

- **Be very careful whom you trust in business**. When it comes to money, trust can become a scarce commodity. Do not believe that friendly reasonable sounding people are not interested in extracting maximum value from whoever controls it.
- **The objectives of partners often change over time**. This may create tensions and ultimately lead to divorce. One side of the JV shareholders, if not both, usually has ambitions regarding overall control that may not have been previously discussed with the other partner.
- **Joint ventures frequently develop into battles for control either in the boardroom or by controlling the management team**. Other means involve the functions, technology, or raw materials supplied by each side to the business.
- **Consider with whom you make strategic alliances**. There has been enormous growth in joint ventures over the last 20 years as firms realise that co-operation can yield significant benefits. However, exits have to be carefully planned before marriage occurs to avoid major disputes when objectives change.

Reflections

This chapter has identified several key issues and questions:

- Why ethics and values matter and the potential consequences of poor ethical standards.
- When globalising the decision to enter many countries is accompanied by ethical risk of varying degrees. How will you manage this risk without creating unacceptable risks for your people?
- Perceived unethical behaviour of the top team has a significant influence on the organisation's culture and the way challenges are managed.
- Boards are rarely aware of the true state of ethics within their organisation unless they conduct regular confidential surveys of their staff (Soltes, 2019). To be effective surveys need a top team response.
- An organisation's ethics and values are placed under real stress when stakes are high. However, maintaining and upholding values usually has a lower real cost than anticipated and significant long-term benefits in terms of perceived ethical reputation, both internally and externally.
- In boardroom battles, ethics are rarely a consideration in the quest for control. Be careful when selecting partners.
- Unethical cultures often exhibit certain symptoms. Be aware of those symptoms and be willing to ask the important questions.

References

Bolden, R. (2011). Distributed leadership in organizations: A review of theory and research. *International Journal of Management Reviews, 13*(3), 251–269.

Caldwell, C., Ichiho, R., & Anderson, V. (2017). Understanding level 5 leaders: The ethical perspectives of leadership humility. *Journal of Management Development.* https://doi.org/10.1108/jmd-09-2016-0184

Ciulla, J. B., Knights, D., Mabey, C., & Tomkins, L. (2018). Guest editors' introduction: Philosophical approaches to leadership ethics II: Perspectives on the self and responsibility to others. *Business Ethics Quarterly, 28*(3), 245–250.

Collins, J. (2016). *Good to great: Why some companies make the leap and others don't.* Instaread.

Crane, A., Matten, D., Glozer, S., & Spence, L. (2019). *Business ethics: Managing corporate citizenship and sustainability in the age of globalization.* Oxford University Press.

Downe, J., Cowell, R., & Morgan, K. (2016). What determines ethical behavior in public organizations: Is it rules or leadership? *Public Administration Review, 76*(6), 898–909.

Driver, J. (2014). The history of utilitarianism. In E.N. Zalta (Ed.), *The Stanford encyclopedia of philosophy.* https://plato.stanford.edu/archives/win2014/entries/utilitarianism-history/

Epley, N., & Kumar, A. (2019). How to design an ethical organization. *Harvard Business Review, 97*(3), 144–150.

Fleming, P., Zyglidopoulos, S., Boura, M., & Lioukas, S. (2020). How corruption is tolerated in the Greek public sector: Toward a second-order theory of normalization. *Business & Society, 61*(1), 191–224. 0007650320954860.

Fotaki, M. (2020). Whistleblowers counteracting institutional corruption in public administration. In *Handbook on corruption, ethics and integrity in public administration.* Edward Elgar Publishing.

Healy, P., & Serafeim, G. (2019). How to scandal-proof your company a rigorous compliance system is not enough. *Harvard Business Review, 97*(4), 42–50.

Isaac, M. (2019). *Super pumped: The battle for Uber.* WW Norton & Company.

Jennings, M. M. (2006). *Seven signs of an unethical culture.* St Martin's Press.

Messick, D. M., & Bazerman, M. H. (2001). *Ethical leadership and the psychology of decision making.* Emerald Group Publishing Limited.

Northouse, P. G. (2016). *Leadership: Theory and practice.* Sage Publications.

Shotter, J., & Tsoukas, H. (2014). In search of phronesis: Leadership and the art of judgment. *Academy of Management Learning & Education, 13*(2), 224–243.

Soltes, E. (2019). Where is your company most prone to lapses in integrity? A simple survey to identify the danger zones. *Harvard Business Review, 97*(4), 51–55.

Turner, N., Barling, J., Epitropaki, O., Butcher, V., & Milner, C. (2002). Transformational leadership and moral reasoning. *Journal of Applied Psychology, 87*(2), 304.

Part III

Philosophical Underpinnings and New Directions

Recommended Reading for 'Philosophical Underpinnings and New Directions'

Ayes, J. (2018). *The theory and practice of change management*. Palgrave.

Barton, M. A., Christianson, M., Myers, C. G., & Sutcliffe, K. (2020). Resilience in action: Leading for resilience in response to COVID-19. *BMJ Leader, 4*(3), pp. 117–119.

Bennett, N., & Lemoine, G. J. (2014). What a difference a word makes: Understanding threats to performance in a VUCA world. *Business Horizons, 57*(3), 311-317.

Bolden, R., Witzel, M., & Linacre, N. (Eds.). (2016). *Leadership paradoxes: Rethinking leadership for an uncertain world*. Routledge.

Caluwé, L., & Vermaak, H. (2004). *Change paradigms: An overview*.

Joiner, B. (2008). Leadership agility: Five levels of mastery. *Strategic Direction*.

Kotter, J. P. (2012). *Leading change*. Harvard Business Press.

Maak, T., & Pless, N. M. (2006). Responsible leadership in a stakeholder society–a relational perspective. *Journal of Business Ethics, 66*(1), pp. 99–115.

Painter, M., Hibbert, S., & Cooper, T. (2019). The development of responsible and sustainable business practice: Value, mind-sets, business-models.

Sinek, S. (2009). *Start with why: How great leaders inspire everyone to take action*. Penguin.

5

Leading Change in Turbulent Times

No one could have anticipated the nature or magnitude of crises in recent years; you will find that each of these chapters explicitly or implicitly reiterates that leading change in turbulent times is fast becoming a part of everyday life as a leader. The recent past has demonstrated that change can be unforgiving towards all types of organisations, whether they are corporate or non-profit. The ability of firms to change and adapt to this constant flux is crucial to their relevance and, as COVID-19 has demonstrated so brutally, even survival.

Leading organisational change has long been an area of considerable challenge. Innumerable studies have provided insights on change processes, management, leadership, and organisational change, and only more recently progressed to focus specifically on what makes for successful change (Croft et al., 2021; Bolden et al., 2021; Northouse, 2021). The hierarchical nature of organisations alone is acknowledgement that there is little chance of success without leadership playing an active, positive role in mobilising change.

Hollander's theoretical comments are simple but true: 'leadership is a process, not a person' (Hollander, 1992); change cannot happen in isolation, and it is the responsibility of the leadership to ensure the conditions are right. Whilst it may be activated unexpectedly by complex external events and threats, a planned organisational change is one that is managed through clear phases of intervention.

The aim of this chapter is to look at the process of change during periods of crisis. It discusses tools and frameworks for change implementation, reflects on pertinent case studies, and prompts readers to reflect on their own experience.

J. Colley, D. Spyridonidis, *Unprecedented Leadership*, Palgrave Executive Essentials, https://doi.org/10.1007/978-3-030-93486-6_5

There are three key areas to examine here: leading the self, leading teams, and leading the organisation that will be considered in turn.

Leading Self

Nothing so conclusively proves a man's ability to lead others as his day-to-day personal conduct in leading himself.

This is the wisdom followed by Thomas Watson, legendary CEO of IBM, who oversaw the rise of its global empire from 1914 until his death in 1956. Watson understood that in order to be effective, a leader must develop their self-awareness; only having recognised your personal strengths and weaknesses can you surround yourself with people that compensate or contribute skills in those weaker areas. Leaders, we must remember, are human, incomplete, and imperfect; they can only be consolidated by a high-functioning team.

The most significant skill required of a leader therefore is the ability to lead the self. In turbulent times leaders may need to change how they think and how they practice; it may seem obvious, but only when they have helped themselves can they help their team. This means taking care of both mental and physical health, demonstrating the work-life balance that can be seen as exemplary to others.

Develop Self-awareness—taking time out for reflection on your leadership manner is essential in evolving the often dismissed 'soft skills' needed for emotional engagement—a sense of humanity is more valuable than any technical knowledge when it comes to managing highly stressful situations, such as the myriad of concerns spidering out from the pandemic.

Be Honest About Anxieties—if they are ever to create a culture committed to taking care of each other and feeling supported, leaders need to be honest about their anxieties. It is an extremely difficult, but underestimated skill that differentiates effective leaders from the rest. As well as observing and reflecting on their personal impact, leaders may find it necessary to consult others as to how they might improve.

Question Your Assumptions—what do you assume about the future? What might you be able to test? What do you assume about your job, your organisation, and your industry? More importantly, if somebody in your team thinks differently, are your assumptions about that person, and most importantly, are their assumptions correct? What do we assume about our customer and competitors', especially when considering non-traditional competitors? This is the starting point and an opportunity to challenge your assumptions, to start thinking differently.

This last point lies at the heart of leading change: recognising your assumptions and challenging your beliefs. The global pandemic has created great uncertainty, but it has also brought a new appetite for change.

In the context of this book, you will frequently encounter the acronym VUCA (Volatility, Uncertainty, Complexity, and Ambiguity). These are the defining facets of a crisis and the four things that will require leaders to repeatedly challenge. Leaders in fact need to be able to do two things at once: carry on with business as usual and delivering results, whilst also maintaining business as unusual—the VUCA that may work for or against you. These simultaneous conditions require a leader to stop and give careful consideration to what a post-pandemic future might look like for their company, what place they might have and how far their value systems will survive in it.

Business as Usual, Business as *Un*usual

In times of heightened uncertainty about the future, change in the usual way won't work. To plan for 'business as unusual' suggests that the problem-solving techniques usually used by leaders are not fit for purpose in this context.

Crisis requires leaders to change the way they think about their teams. The days are long gone of telling people what to do; clever leaders employ people to tell them what to do. A strategic leader needs to cultivate an environment where people are willing and able to contribute ideas and challenge the leadership.

Leading change means thinking about the future and creating an environment that focuses people's minds on development and growth. It is about developing the organisational capacity for ongoing change, for constantly questioning and reinventing. It is also about creating an organisation that is able to learn in a productive fashion and be prepared where necessary to challenge the assumptions of the leadership referred to earlier.

All of this needs to take place whilst coping with the short-term pressure of delivering results and meeting targets. Unilever did this by developing a very clear purpose around sustainability and how it might act to lessen its environmental impact. It was a mission that was bigger than both the leader and the organisation, eclipsing short-term corporate goals that satisfy shareholders.

This is the binary approach leaders must now embrace: as businesses struggle to survive and cope with the pandemic, they must also look to the future and reimagine a new operating model. Amidst this crisis, they have to maintain hope and envision potential new opportunities for their organisation.

It must again be articulated—Leaders need to lead themselves, challenge their assumptions and beliefs before encouraging questions from their team. Build a cultural ecosystem that has a place in the aftermath of a crisis situation.

Adaptation from Uncertainty

As public life slowly begins to stir, and aspects of our 'old' normality returning, the future of work and our organisations will still feel unclear, and may do for some time to come. Even the most skilled and experienced executives will face challenges unlike any they have encountered. Such seismic changes may well be an opportunity for business leaders to transform work and the workplace for the better.

Throughout the pandemic, we've consistently been told that we will never return to normal. The reality is not quite as clear-cut. COVID has changed the traditional workplace, but different employers will prioritise different ways of working. Some organisations in the financial sector have said they want to return to the traditional office culture, but a number of companies, technology companies in particular, may well allow employees to work remotely indefinitely.

Rather than looking for solutions externally, I argue that strong leadership starts by looking at ourselves. We must learn to lead ourselves before we lead others. That means understanding your own wellbeing, your mental health, and your physical health. If you can't understand how to create a healthy work life balance for yourselves, how are you going to show others?

We know that productive, sustainable organisations must have leaders who are emotionally intelligent, resilient, and empathetic. COVID-19 has created one of the biggest emotional rollercoasters of our lives. It's more important than ever for executives to understand the human aspect of leadership. Empathy and compassion are important traits in leadership, but you must instate these traits in yourself first.

The workplace has not always been conducive to allowing executives to grow and progress. Organisations recognise the value of learning and development at every level, but budget constraints, long working hours, and the simple daily pressures of working life can often mean that workplaces cannot offer the necessary space for executives to evaluate and reflect or sharpen their skills. This is one of the greatest difficulties encountered by leaders, that in a fast paced, pressurised environment, they are unable to stop, think, reflect, and potentially redefine their organisation's future.

It might seem overwhelming, but with help, it is possible to make self-reflection as much a part of your daily routine as a cup of coffee. Take time to stop, think, and take care of yourself. Self-awareness is often seen as a soft skill, but such a classification underestimates its role in both personal and organisational core values, and incorporating it into your critical thinking should be part of a leader's standard practise.

Leading Others and Organisations: Why Is Change Important in Times of Crisis?

Organisational transformation during crisis requires significant shifts in routines and operations (Wischnevsky & Damanpour, 2006).

The twenty-first century has already posed major challenges for leadership teams with its stream of global crises, from the developing impact of Brexit in the UK and Europe, the elections of new global leaders around the world, ongoing conflicts in the Middle East and Northeast Asia to the unprecedented COVID 19 pandemic (Gowing & Langdon, 2016). Regardless of whether these are viewed as sources of challenge, opportunity or both, these unknown threats have accentuated antecedent uncertainties already felt by many. These events emerge rapidly from political, economic, or societal shifts, that even the most skilled leadership teams could not have anticipated. They are indicative of the new world in which we live; one of change and complexity, driven by digital technology, globalisation, and demographic change. Such developments are creating levels of disruption which fundamentally change the way organisations function and create new levels of risk for leadership teams.

Businesses face the need to transform now more than ever before. Failure to do so can easily mean a slow decline, receding market share, declining profits, and at its worst rapid extinction (Kotter, 2008). As shifts in the market context occur, consumer attitudes also shift rapidly, turning a historically high margin industry on its head almost without warning. New entrants of substitute products or technology to the market can dramatically change the industry landscape, not to mention the impact of economic shifts. These more frequently changing external factors have the power to render existing ways of doing things no longer fit for purpose. For business leaders, this creates an increasingly volatile environment in which their organisations must exist (Reeves & Pueschel, 2015).

Against this backdrop, organisations which are unable to achieve change are vulnerable, yet those able will have developed a powerful competitive advantage. History is littered with examples of failed transformations and missed opportunities. Against such an uncertain backdrop, change in the market environment is the only constant; organisations must learn to transform in order to survive.

Warning: Change Efforts Often Fail

Blockbuster in the UK is an example of an organisation that was unable to successfully transform itself from a bricks-and-mortar video rental business in the face of online and mail order video models, inevitably they did not survive. Kodak fared little better—once the pioneering and dominant name in cameras in the 1970s they went on to develop the first digital camera range in the 1990s. Despite this its attachment and reliance on traditional film rendered them obsolete and the business was forced to file for bankruptcy in 2012. Blackberry and Nokia, global leaders in their respective markets for mobile phones, both themselves were under threat by the arrival of the Apple iPhone in 2007. Nokia went on to sell their mobile phone business to Microsoft in 2013, whilst Blackberry announced they would stop making phones entirely in 2018.

The common theme among these examples is that these organisations were disrupted by technological shifts in the world around them and consumer behaviour. Such changes are occurring faster than ever before (Keller et al., 2010), which explains why the average life expectancy of an organisation is surprisingly short; in 2015 the average life expectancy of a fortune 500 company was 40–50 years (Handscomb & Thaker, 2018).

Yet, organisations which embark on transformations rarely achieve their desired outcome. McKinsey and Company found 70% of transformation efforts fail (Ewenstein, Smith, & Sologar, 2015), and a leading cause is that leaders fail to overcome employee resistance to change (Kotter & Rathgeber, 2006).

Why Does Transformation Often Fail?

Organisational change has a rational and an emotional dimension. All too easily, leaders may neglect the emotional needs of employees.

Transformation efforts usually necessitate a paradigm shift and for which leaders must meaningfully engage their employees. It is not uncommon for transformation efforts to fail and one of the key reasons is that leaders ignore the emotional dimension of change over the course of the project (Bartunek et al., 2006; Handscomb & Thaker, 2018). Emotions in fact provide the fuel for transformational success; without loyalty, honesty, motivation, and pride in their work (Kahn, 1990), transformation projects less likely lead to positive outcomes (Lasrado & Kassem, 2020).

To achieve a successful transformation project, employees must feel intellectually stimulated by it (Bass & Steidlmeier, 1999). Wherever possible transformational leaders must take time to help employees establish a link between their work and the change strategy. This process is intended to empower employees and understand how best to carry out their work, to understand their valued contribution to a 'bigger picture'.

However, radical change takes time to achieve (Kotter, 2008). It frequently requires employees to give up old habits, practices, routines, and norms, and accept new ways of working (Lewin, 1947). This takes demands to sustained effort, but will be far easier if a leader is emotionally intelligent. During periods of significant change, it is not uncommon for employees to become disengaged or frustrated (Kotter, 2008). Over time, overloaded employees may experience burn out and fatigue, leading to resistance, friction, and toxic behaviours. Leaders must be prepared to adjust their leadership behaviour, model and champion new practices, and engage employees with good communication and mentoring.

Leaders of successful change projects must therefore be sensitive to the demands placed on their employees as the project unfolds, take steps to eliminate unnecessary work, and provide extra resources when early signs of fatigue begin to appear. Successful transformational leaders must therefore be able to detect and treat negative emotions that, left unchecked, cause in-fighting between teams, wilfully withholding support and in extreme cases, sabotage a company's goals (Bartunek, 2004). This provides one explanation for why transformation projects rarely achieve the performance outcomes expected.

Treat Negative Emotion with Individualised Consideration

In the midst of a transformation project when leaders are struggling to prioritise pressing issues, finding the time to show individualised consideration for staff members can prove difficult. However, its acknowledgement of employee welfare and strain can calm negative emotions before they have a chance to become problematic (Avolio et al., 1991). To improve the chances of success, leaders must make as much effort as possible to remain attentive to the individual needs of employees when they begin to buckle under the strain of the project.

Creating a safe climate where the employee can talk freely and safely is critical to allowing him or her the opportunity to share their sources of frustration and irritation safely (Bruch & Vogel, 2011). Moreover, it provides a direct feedback channel between the ground level work and strategic decision making at leadership level. On the one hand, if negative emotions can be detected early enough, individualised attention can minimise instances of employee disengagement.

Summary

Leaders believe that decisions within organisations should be made logically and rationally. But how is this possible when we know that people do not always share similar views of that logic and rationale? Many clear-headed leaders excel at building a rational case for change but are less adept at appealing to people's emotional core, which is ultimately where real drive and momentum for transformation lie. It is critical that leaders understand and communicate the emotional case for change if they are to avoid divisive behaviours.

Why and How Are We Going to Change?

Change management communications need to be individualised or tailored to each segment of a team and delivered in a two-way fashion that allows people to make sense of the change. Change is a people process, and people being creatures of habit are typically resistant to adopting new mind-sets, practices, and behaviours.

The transition curve (Kübler-Ross, 1973) reminds us that change is a gradual process; different individuals pass through the curve at different speeds and employees have to be supported through the process by their managers. The transition curve reminds us that change is not a linear journey nor necessarily a progressive one; people need an anchor and motivation that must be established by leaders.

It may be necessary to deploy interventions related to communication, education and training, coaching and counselling. Symbolic gestures can also be helpful in helping people let go of the past and understand of what is expected of them in the future. It is common for people to convince themselves that the change isn't actually going to happen, or if it does, that it won't affect them. People carry on as they always have, may deny having received communication about the changes, make excuses or avoid participation in forward planning. As an example of this at a national level, these are all elements seen in the response to Brexit.

Communication is key. Reiterating what the actual change is, the effects it may have, and providing as much reassurance as possible will all help to support individuals. Don't assume that because you know what you want to communicate, others will automatically agree and comply.

Human-Centred Change

A colleague of mine, Andrew Vaid, Managing Director at Firestone, always reminds not to ignore the Human-Centred Change. He advises that, during crises as difficult as COVID, leaders need to prioritise putting people being at the centre of the change. Doing so can be the essence of success, connecting them in a meaningful way with their employees and giving them greater enthusiasm to design and implement that change. Vaid's framework (Vaid, 2022) summarises key areas to be taken into account including "Answering the Why's, Communicate Constantly, Expect Casualties, The power of Networks, What do you believe in and Understand what motivates people".

McKinsey carried out an extensive study that verifies what most leaders already know—transformational changes will often struggle to deliver positive outcomes on many levels. Due to the complexity and individualised circumstances, there is no straightforward answer. Organisations must therefore initiate change sparingly, to minimise fatigue and subsequent disengagement of employees. Moreover, badly planned and implemented change simply won't deliver the required outcome. We encourage leaders preparing to undergo major change to consider *all* options carefully before. If entirely necessary, implementation should be done with employee sensitivity, and its progress continually reviewed. In short, do it well, or don't do it at all.

There is a worrying culture emerging, particularly in Western societies, that embraces change without considering its longevity. It has been said that the only thing that is true today is change, and to some extent this is correct, particularly in crisis times when it may occur with unexpected speed. Before launching a new product, or offer, ask yourself what it is all about, whether it is necessary and how confident you are of its success.

Answering the 'Whys'?

Simon Sinek suggests that inspirational leadership begins with the question, 'Why?' In the context of change leadership, this is the crucial prelude to even *attempting* change, and the one thing a leader must be ready and able to explain to their employees. Often what leaders do or say is, 'We need change because the share price will go up', or 'We'll open a new office'; most people don't care about that. Leaders have got to find a way to frame 'why' so as to connect on a human level, in short, what is the mission of the change?

There may be a hundred different reasons as to why people go to work. Ask yourself what motivates your employees to come to work? What motivates them in life in more general terms? Obviously financial elements matter. People want to be part of a successful organisation and gain rewards from it. To really make change matter a leader must explain it in these human terms— growth, enthusiasm, and satisfaction, as many employees will switch off when they hear corporate blurb. Simon Sinek offers some excellent suggestions about this in his TED talk and we would advise you listen to them.

What Do You Really Believe?

"Oh, it's always our people who make the difference. People are our greatest asset, you know, we wouldn't be anywhere without our people, right?"—Have you ever heard or known of something similar?

If, as a leader, you genuinely believe this to be true, and that each member of the team makes a difference, then you have to put them at the heart of change. There can be no excuses. You can't say that they are the most important asset the organisation has, only to allow new technology or the brand itself to become the central focus.

Here is the hard part: leaders know that some of their people don't and probably won't make the difference. If a division, an office, or a factory in some part of the world cannot contribute to the organisation's vision, the leader must consider how they are going to manage a situation in which some people understand they may not matter.

This is one of the most difficult situations you will encounter as a leader, particularly if you consider yourself to be an emotionally sensitive leader. Understand that not everyone is of equal value in this change. Don't pretend they are; be transparent, tell the truth with as much sensitivity as possible without offering simplistic platitudes.

Expect Casualties

Many change initiatives end up with people being uncomfortable and potentially leaving. Losing people in the middle of a change project is inevitable. The critical concern is that these people could very well be your best people, since those in the best position to leave are typically the ones who are most wanted by the market. It is important therefore that you know who your best people are. So many companies, whether they be small organisations, big charities, or large enterprises, have not entirely understood exactly how their best people are.

Determine who your 'keepers', are. Ask yourself who are my best people? How do I make sure that my best people know they're my best people? And how do I stay close to them throughout their career? Again, this is a real challenge, because you must also motivate those who may not be of the same value, but are still needed. Think through various scenarios and consider all angles. Remember, casualties are inevitable when you are going through change.

The Power of Networks

Human beings are social creatures and gravitate towards living in societies and tribes. We are all connected through human networks, and we need to recognise that reality. In every organisation—whether small, medium, or large—there are networks in action that don't necessarily follow the hierarchical line from the CEO down. If you're going to lead a change, you need to grasp what networks are at play within the organisation. This is especially challenging if an organisation has offices all over the world, spanning diverse cultures and including different partners, suppliers, and customers.

What you need to ascertain is who the key influencers are. Again, this takes careful consideration, sit down and think about where the power lies in your organisation or within your broader ecosystem. In addition, you've got to have some understanding of who the main players are. What is their disposition towards the change that you're representing? Are they absolutely behind it? If so, that is great, and they can help you promote it. But consider also if there are neutral individuals, or even those with the potential to sabotage an initiative because, whatever their reason, they don't want it to succeed. You've got to find a way of connecting with those people. Obviously the best dialogue would shift employees from a negative to a positive position; more realistic however is to find a means of connection that at least shifts them from a negative to neutral position.

Having a plan for this kind of dialogue is essential. Consider what might happen within these networks, as they will be playing an important part in propagating their objections should they have them. You may find these networks to be highly resilient, and become more so in the face of merger and acquisitions. A good leader will connect with these employees the right way. Maintain a constant dialogue, and don't make the mistake of looking to more senior people, as in many organisations the real influencers may lie elsewhere.

Communicate Continuously

The worst type of change is that emailed out by senior management. Perhaps they will hold a virtual town hall, a blog or blog newsletter, and consider that to be requisite communication. Most people will not read it attentively, nor necessarily even understand its rationale. If a leader hasn't made an authentic human connection, then it's not communication.

It is far harder than people presume to sustain a constant dialogue that is delivered in a simple and authentic way. Given that over 80% of communication is nonverbal, one of the greatest obstacles of recent times is being unable to meet in person. As we all know, COVID-19 made this an impossibility for many organisations, but the written word can't be the only substitute for face-to-face communication.

It is important that you solicit and acknowledge feedback from the people you're communicating with: What's their response? Have they understood what you're trying to say? Unless followed up in this manner, people will forget, or presume you won't do anything meaningful with their feedback. Use it as a means of opening up that critical dialogue. Though you might start your communication with one position, as you get feedback and engage with people, you could well move towards adjusting it. This is not an invite to make unrealistic promises in your responses, but simply **acknowledge what people are saying to you and deduce whether it is something you could or should do something about**.

Understand What Motivates Humans

Many leaders fail to think about the core motivations of people when leading change. If they can satisfy some of them, then a leader is more likely to connect meaningfully and help their staff feel better and more prepared to support change. These might include things such as creating a sense of belonging, feeling valued and secure, especially during such crises as the COVID-19 pandemic. Even when this crisis has passed, leaders should still be thinking about their people in this way—How is this change affecting our employee wellbeing and sense of belonging? **Human values must remain of paramount importance**.

Corporate Change: Harder Than It Looks?

With each passing year, the pace of change demanded of organisations increases. Those that cannot cope with continuously changing environments and markets will ultimately join the ranks of history. Those that can anticipate market trends and technology-facilitated change are those that win out in the long run. Retailers who started early with online offerings are those that have survived COVID-19 and are thriving, such as Zara, Next, and Tesco, whilst the late movers such as Top Shop and the other Arcadia businesses have become insolvent with little more than the brand remaining. Technological change reshapes supply chains and distributors and retailers must adapt or surrender. Many of these changes have accelerated during the COVID-19 lockdowns and we can be sure that the future will be a very different place.

Sustainability has come to feature much more highly on almost everyone's agenda. This can be seen not only in customer attitudes towards preserving the environment and the treatment of workers, but also in product selection, such as the creation of new opportunities for meat-free products. Investors are now choosing funds with good Environmental, Social, and Governance (ESG) credentials, and taking action to improve their performance in areas other than shareholder returns.

Within organisations, there are often strong forces opposing change, which all too frequently slows down efforts to transform the business and reduce effectiveness. Forces such as organisational inertia, internal politics and power struggles, inflexible organisational structures, initiative overload for management, and a lack of leadership to drive change.

A strong rationale for organisations to evolve rapidly may exist but effective change capability is often far more limited (Fig. 5.1).

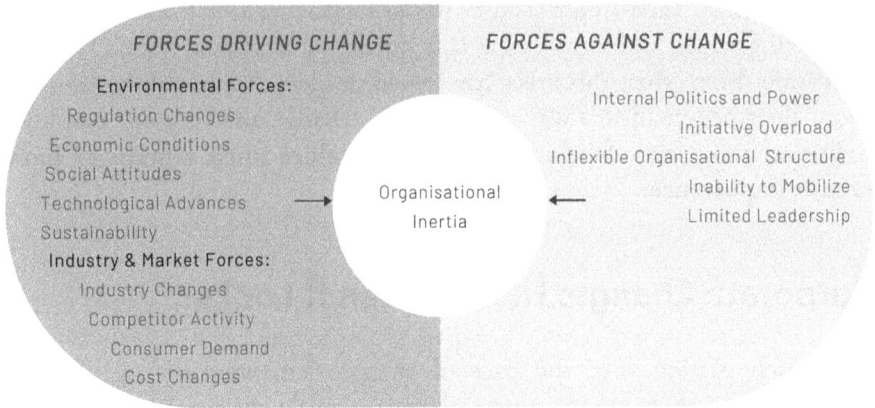

Fig. 5.1 Forces for and against major change

Case Study: The Price of Globalisation?

As a rapidly globalising and largely decentralised business, TVS now organises a senior management conference in a different country each year. This particular year it was hosted in Chicago with the top 150 employees invited. These were predominantly leaders of subsidiary businesses and were therefore accustomed to a significant degree of autonomy. In addition to the functional directors, the world management had been divided into three regions, each with a Regional Director (RD) the Executive Committee (EC) which ran the corporation consisted of the Functional Directors and the three Regional Directors who together held much of the power.

Traditionally at the annual gathering, the CEO would give a 'state of the nation' speech outlining current performance and key objectives for the coming years. He stated that:

> It is time the business embraced globalisation and introduced standardised information systems across our entire operations. This will reduce costs and allow us to more rapidly integrate acquisitions, whilst producing timelier and better-quality information.

There was a silence from the assembled throng who were doubtlessly thinking 'he has been talking to strategy consultants'.

The CEO continued, 'James Read, our new Group Finance Director will lead the project'. To the audience this did not augur well. James had been with the business for only two months and was a polished, highly intelligent financial communicator, ideal for stakeholders and an experienced FD. He was not however the ideal candidate to lead a complex global project in the likely face of strong opposition. It was also clear that the CEO, well aware of the associated risks, was not going to lead the project and would be maintaining his distance from it. New system implementations rarely went well and he did not want to spend every board meeting for the next three years explaining to the Chairman and Non-Executive Directors its latest difficulties each month.

At present, the business had three very different legacy systems: Americas, Western, and Eastern Europe. They worked well enough with but could not communicate with each other, and all data to the head office had to be fed back through various interfaces. The Executive Committee had been divided in discussion of the new £20M investment (although almost everyone believed that it would cost many multiples of the quoted figure). The functional directors were strongly opposed to the proposal, as they were party to better information, whilst the regional directors were equally reticent, aware that they would have to provide the resources for the implementation. They also perceived that they would lose power in the near future as the functional directors increased their influence. This was not helped by geography, given that the functional directors were located at the head office with the CEO, whilst they were in their respective regions. Their access to the CEO was more difficult and they usually ended up on the wrong end of head office politics.

Two months later the Group Finance Director announced that he was appointing a 'Director of Information Services' responsible for implementing the new project, despite not sitting on any boards.

First of all, a new system was to be selected. It soon materialised that this was to be the system used in the Americas where the CEO had risen to fame and so was the only system he knew a considerable amount about. The Europeans viewed this system as unsophisticated and ill-equipped to deal with more complex operations and marketplaces existent in Europe. There were further concerns about future ownership and development of the proposed systems.

A central team was assembled to develop and implement these new systems. The pilot implementation was to take place in the UK and France, each of which had a different system, culture, and market approach. The idea was to avoid rejection by the other country, something they thought might occur if they focussed initially on just one country. France and the UK were old rivals and, moreover, the two largest and most profitable countries.

There was jargon-heavy talk of 'cash burn' in testing and development and 'workarounds' necessary to take into account the complexities and eccentricities of the current systems.

The three Regional Directors did not interfere and stayed out of the implementation, appearing neither to support, nor help lead it. Senior Functional Directors were also notably absent; they were more politically astute and did not wish to be accountable for a likely disaster. In reality, the entire project was driven by the IS Director, with benign backing and support from the Group Finance Director.

After around two years, the day arrived for the 'go live' in France. A variety of objections and additional requirements were produced by the French management. Money was starting to run low and confidence in the new systems was fast ebbing away. What was becoming clear was that this would be an enormous job, that it would take several years to implement, and that its functionality would be limited in the face of enormous costs. Concerns were rising and the pilot implementations were once again delayed.

At this point a completely unexpected hostile takeover bid arrived from a much larger business. After a long struggle and several increases, the bidder triumphed. They fired the majority of the board almost immediately, offering jobs only to the Regional Directors who held much of the power and influence over the management. Two of the three accepted. Their next immediate announcement was that they would be implementing their own systems throughout the entire business. Strangely, the new implementation was an unexpectedly seamless and largely successful venture.

Reflections
- What were the main causes of the project failure, and how could this have been remedied in future?
- What recommendations would you make regarding leadership?
- Major projects are likely to face some internal opposition either of a passive nature or more obstructive nature? How might these be overcome?

Commentary and Analysis

Most major change initiatives fail to meet expectations, either by overspending, by taking too long, or by providing limited functionality. Indeed, many fail on all three dimensions. Information system projects are especially high up the league table of failures. Let us examine why that might be by analysing the case study.

First of all, there is the fundamental problem of leadership. Was the project ever really 'led'? The CEO and GFD did not wish to lead it and the RDs had not been sufficiently convinced of its benefits to drive the project forward. Instead, an external candidate was recruited but was given insufficient power to be effective.

The vision was unclear and few were convinced by it. Little was explained regarding its benefits and there was suspicion that this would facilitate a major senior management reorganisation. Proposed cost saving benefits seemed unlikely as more modern systems tended to have far higher ongoing costs than legacy systems. Whether this should be treated as essential infrastructure or not, it seems inadequate efforts were made to sell the benefits to the senior management.

Although a timetable existed and some progress was made, the timetable continued to slip. Review meetings simply accepted ongoing slippage as being usual for IS projects.

The Executive Committee remained largely divided on the project and so became a 'benign observer', rather than driving progress throughout the organisation and addressing the strategic issues which occurred.

Although the RDs were not actively blocking the system, their own reports conveyed disinterest and limited involvement. The RDs were not invited to the main review meetings and consequently felt alienated from the process which the Head Office IS staff were trying to drive. Head Office were not experienced in major project management and so this project was well beyond their capabilities, even though the Regional IS people had been transferred to central control.

In reality, the Regional Directors were enormously influential in the business so any reorganisation following the IS implementation would need their support, regardless of any diminished power.

Kotter's Eight-Step Change Model

John Kotter has been a major academic influence on the practice of making major change. He estimates a 70% failure rate in change initiatives of this nature. Certain types of projects, such as cultural change initiatives, lean and other manufacturing processes, seem particularly vulnerable to poor outcomes. If organisations are honest with themselves, then they will find that budgets have exceeded, timetables extended, and functionality limited, all of which require significant subsequent investment to achieve the initial objectives.

Such concerns influence financial investors such as Private Equity who are reluctant to head into major schemes unless the returns are substantial, visible, and rapidly achieved. Whilst their investment horizon is more limited than public companies, they are also highly aware of the risks in major projects.

Kotter's eight-step process has resonated with many and has developed much support over the many years it has been in operation. The main elements are as follows:

1. **Create a sense of urgency.**
2. **Build a guiding coalition.**
3. **Form a strategic vision.**
4. **Communicate strongly.**
5. **Enable action by removing barriers and empower action.**
6. **Generate short-term wins.**
7. **Sustain acceleration.**
8. **Institute change.**

By far the most demanding and difficult to achieve is a sense of urgency. This needs real leadership, which starts with showing up and being clear you are committed to the project. Top leaders must manage their diaries through delegation to ensure they have time to demonstrate their strong commitment by attending important meetings. As some say 'showing up is 90% of leadership' and, whilst not entirely true, does offer a significant, visible support.

In many organisations, most of the non-customer faced staff are insulated from the harsh realities of the market place. Bringing the realities of the outside world home to employees and indeed top management is crucial. Data collected from the market on performance, customer satisfaction, product performance comparisons, market share changes, and competitor initiatives are often buried if lacking a positive message. In most businesses, candour creates a sense of realism that can be helpful in motivating change. Arranging speakers from outside such as academics, experts, customers, and suppliers may well have sobering messages to present. Kotter's book *A Sense of Urgency* develops this theme.

Reflections

- In our example was there a clear motivation communicated?
- Who provided the change impetus and handled barriers to progress?
- Were there short-term wins and clear milestones?
- Did the project ensure that change was instituted did the organisation develop in ways to support its vision?

Kotter's eight-step process is based on analyses of hundreds of companies, including Ford and British Airways. Whilst a few of the companies that Kotter studied did succeed, many (such as Eastern Airlines) failed miserably. The ones that succeeded, Kotter argues, followed a long process similar to the Lewin change model of unfreeze, change, and refreeze.

Despite Kotter breaking change down into specific steps, he notes that change is seldom as linear as any model might suggest. Still, he provides an excellent way to think about organisational change.

Ingredients of Success (Fig. 5.2)

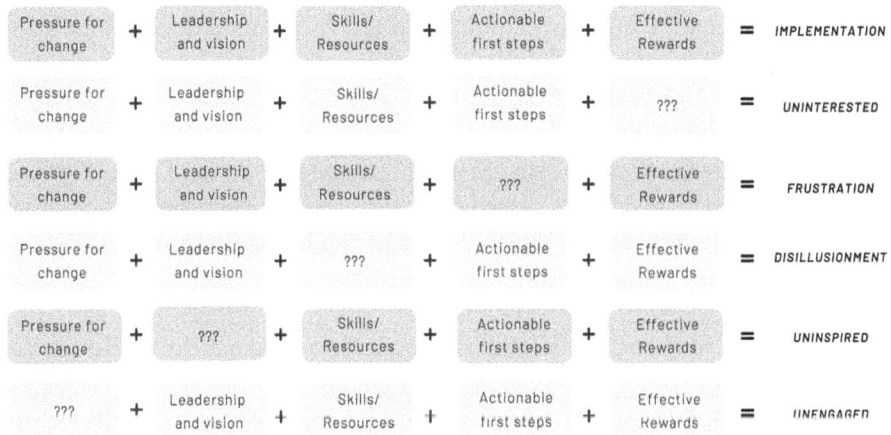

Fig. 5.2 Ingredients of success. An adaptation from the work of Kotters' and Knoster (1991)

Pressure for Change

This is one of the biggest barriers to change and it is the reason that most successful organisations (i.e. Nokia, Kodak, Blockbuster) fail, being unable to create the internal impetus that might overcome complacency and disengagement. As Kotter notes, change won't happen unless at least 75% of a company's management believes they can't survive without change. In order for change to happen, leaders need to be able to create pressure for change and maintain that pressure over the long haul.

Leadership and Vision

One of the primary constraints common in organisations is the need for leadership to instil the right leadership style and a vision that inspires organisational renewal. As a leader of change, it is your task to convince people of its importance. A successful leader will take time to create a compelling vision of the future, shared, and articulated in a way that appeals to all. Leaders do this through clear goals, a well-articulated plan, and carefully identified 'quick wins'.

When articulating such a vision, a leader might encounter two points of resistance:

1. Employees resistant to dramatic change that deviates from the established norms
2. Innovative employees and independent thinkers may have individual views of what strategic objectives should be. A misaligned vision potentially demotivates employees, with negative consequences.

To this end, successful transformational leaders must take time to provide meaning and empower employees (Kotter, 2008). Role modelling, vision setting, and empowering staff all serve to inspire and energise employees (Quintana et al., 2015).

One scholar of change, Jay Conger, says that there are a number of myths when it comes to persuading people:

1. **that the most effective approach is the hard sell, persuading with logic and enthusiasm.**
2. **that persuasion is a one-way street, telling others what they should do.**
3. **that persuaders succeed on their first try.**
4. **that compromise is unnecessary.**

5. **that success is the result of a good argument alone.**

What really makes vision persuasive is something quite different. First, build your own credibility. Why should they listen to you? Second, find common ground—show that the outcomes that you want are shared. Third, make sure you have evidence to back up your claims, not just facts and figures but stories as well, and last but by far least, **communicate meaningfully and consistently**.

Successful leaders of transformation projects spend considerable time communicating their vision, reinforcing its importance and the leader's commitment to the transformation project (Kotter, 2008). Leaders with vision create excitement amongst followers, thus unleashing positive energy. Kotter explains that the presence of vision is one of the differences between management and leadership. Goleman's leadership definition also includes the 'visionary' style, in creating a positive climate for change.

Skills and Resources

It is not uncommon for organisations to lack the right skills and resources required for implementing change initiatives. This is often because they require new ways of thinking, a shift in organisational culture, and the need for leaders to invest time, resources, and energy in helping the workforce to develop a new skillset. Without this the workforce may suffer from disillusionment.

Actionable First Steps

Defining the first steps in the change process is as difficult as defining the projects nature and scope. However, being able to define the very first few actionable steps and give clear direction is critical. Leaders also need to explain their plans for implementation and show some progress at each stage in order to avoid frustration.

Effective Rewards

This is all about motivation—how do you motivate your people to engage in the change process? Work out how you're going to get people who are used to old habits to try and move towards new modes of working. This is difficult because people typically stick with established routines and old habits, reinforced by expectations and social pressures. You may be able to convince one person that change is needed, but if everything around that person reinforces the old pattern, it will be ineffective. Change is hard, so providing effective rewards and incentives can help to sustain motivation.

> **Reflection**
>
> Think about a recent change that you had to implement.
> How can reflecting on the 'ingredients of success' help you to enhance your approach to change?

References

Avolio, B. J., Waldman, D. A., & Yammarino, F. J. (1991). Leading in the 1990s: The four I's of transformational leadership. *Journal of European Industrial Training, 15*, 9–16.

Bartunek, J. M. (2004). Toxic emotions at work: How compassionate managers handle pain and conflict. *The Academy of Management Review, 22*, 141–144.

Bartunek, J. M., Rousseau, D. M., Rudolph, J. W., & DePalma, J. A. (2006). On the receiving end: Sensemaking, emotion, and assessments of an organizational change initiated by others. *The Journal of Applied Behavioral Science, 42*(2), 182–206.

Bass, B. M., & Steidlmeier, P. (1999). Ethics, character, and authentic transformational leadership behavior. *The Leadership Quarterly, 10*(2), 181–217.

Bolden, R., Williams, R., & O'regan, N. (2021). Leading to achieve social change: An interview with Ruth Hunt, former Chief Executive Officer of Stonewall. *Journal of Management Inquiry, 30*(1), 91–97.

Bruch, H., & Vogel, B. (2011). *Fully charged: How great leaders boost their organization's energy and ignite high performance*. Harvard Business Press.

Croft, C., McGivern, G., Currie, G., Lockett, A., & Spyridonidis, D. (2021). Unified divergence and the development of collective leadership. *Journal of Management Studies*. 59 (2), 460–488.

Ewenstein, B., Smith, W., & Sologar, A. (2015). *Changing change management*. Retrieved from https://www.mckinsey.com/featured-insights/leadership/changing-change-management [Accessed March 2021].

Gowing, N., & Langdon, C. (2016). Want to lead? Then tear up the rulebook. *The World Today, 72*(3), 12–16.

Handscomb, C., & Thaker, S. (2018). *Activate agility: Five avenues to success*. McKinsey & Company.

Hollander, E. P. (1992). The essential interdependence of leadership and followership. *Current Directions in Psychological Science, 1*(2), 71–75.

Kahn, W. A. (1990). Psychological conditions of personal engagement and disengagement at work. *Academy of Management Journal, 33*(4), 692–724.

Keller, S., Meaney, M., & Pung, C. (2010). What successful transformations share. *McKinsey Quarterly*, 1–3.

Knoster, T. (1991). Factors in managing complex change. Material presentation at TASH conference, The Association for People with Severe Disabilities, Washington, DC.

Kotter, J. P. (2008). *Force for change: How leadership differs from management*. Simon and Schuster.

Kotter, J. P., & Rathgeber, H. (2006). *Our iceberg is melting: Changing and succeeding under any conditions*. Macmillan.

Kübler-Ross, E. (1973). *On death and dying*. Routledge.

Lasrado, F., & Kassem, R. (2020). Let's get everyone involved! The effects of transformational leadership and organizational culture on organizational excellence. *International Journal of Quality & Reliability Management, 38*, 169–194.

Lewin, K. (1947). Group decision and social change. *Readings in Social Psychology, 3*(1), 197–211.

Northouse, P. G. (2021). *Leadership: Theory and practice*. Sage publications.

Quintana, T. A., Park, S., & Cabrera, Y. A. (2015). Assessing the effects of leadership styles on employees' outcomes in international luxury hotels. *Journal of Business Ethics, 129*(2), 469–489.

Reeves, M., & Pueschel, L. (2015). Die another day: What leaders can do about the shrinking life expectancy of corporations. *BCG Perspectives, 2*.

Vaid, A. (2022). Human Centred Change, Warwick Business School, Executive MBA notes, March 2022.

Wischnevsky, J. D., & Damanpour, F. (2006). Organizational transformation and performance: An examination of three perspectives. *Journal of Managerial Issues*, 104–128.

6

Creating the Capacity for Strategic Leadership

2020 was a year that no one will forget, a year that change found us all, and for leaders, the greatest test of adaptability yet encountered. Adaptation in a world still full of ambiguity and uncertainty is the focus of this chapter. Every day is important in creating a positive, lasting legacy, no matter where on the VUCA spectrum you may find yourself.

> **The aim of this chapter is to help readers address the following questions:**
>
> What is strategic leadership?
> What is the changing context of strategic leadership?
> What are the key leadership skills required for strategic leaders?

This chapter addresses both the concept of strategic leadership and the personal attributes that a developing leader needs in order to be effective. Whilst drawing on theory throughout, it is augmented by examples of practical applications and the steps that leaders need to take in order to embark on major strategic change during periods of crisis.

What is Strategic Leadership?

An organisation's board needs to have one eye consistently on the future. If they fail to craft an effective strategy, then they will be unable to grow or even remain in their competitive market.

© The Author(s), under exclusive license to Springer Nature Switzerland AG 2022
J. Colley, D. Spyridonidis, *Unprecedented Leadership*, Palgrave Executive Essentials,
https://doi.org/10.1007/978-3-030-93486-6_6

Some semblances of the future are likely to continue recent trajectories, for example, the shrinkage of city centre shopping due to internet trade. In turn, large stores are left empty, and subsequently turned into discount format stores with minimal online presence. The result is a greater price sensitivity for consumers, able to buy branded products significantly cheaper and in convenient locations. Will this trend continue? In theory the city centre market will become saturated with such discounters, but boards of all retailers must formulate their own suitable strategies for all likely scenarios.

Inevitably, any strategy must take into account the available resources and capabilities of a business and how these can be developed to support future strategy. These capabilities are invariably tied up with culture and values.

Pound Stores Versus John Lewis

Consider the culture of a pound store business: Whilst it hopes to acquire trade from the middle market supermarkets and convenience stores, its predominant competition is other discounters. Hence every cost must be minimised to hit the price point and show a profit. This includes everything from rent, payroll, and management to purchasing and store presentation. The business culture and values therefore will be intent on lower staff numbers, and a reduced payroll bill.

Contrast this culture with that of John Lewis, a business built on their high-touch service levels supported by staff training and ability to develop expensive, well-located, and attractive stores. The culture and values of these organisations are clearly polarised and in no way interchangeable.

Frequently, firms seeking growth stray from their core knowledge when making acquisitions. A recent example referred to earlier in this book is Sainsbury's purchase of Argos, the catalogue-based online discounter with city centre stores carrying a wide stock. Sainsbury's is an up-market grocery supermarket in well-located, large attractive premises usually in the better suburbs. Argos caters to people with more limited spending capacity and usually occupies premises in lower rent parts of city centres. It does not sell groceries but has a large range of almost anything else from electrical to furniture. The two firms have different strategies, cultures, values, and competences. The rationale for the deal is that Sainsbury's wishes to develop its non-grocery and online offerings. Vastly different cultures, values, and customers mean the chances of a successful alliance are low.

Reflections

Practical Strategic Leadership

Think of an organisation with a well-defined culture: What are the implications of the company culture for its leadership?

Let's see some examples of organisations with a well-defined culture:

- **Amazon** claims to place innovation (invention) at the heart of its culture. It's always 'Day 1' and there's always more to do, a higher point to reach. This concept gives rise to a relentless pace as a task is almost never complete. From a leadership perspective, I imagine one challenge is the extra focus required to manage wellbeing and avoid the burn-out of those team members at the heart of that invention who, fully invested in the culture, may never truly switch off. In turn, they would then have high, possibly even unrealistic, expectations of those in conventional roles—warehouse pickers expected to produce extraordinary pick efficiency, drivers making higher than normal levels of delivery per hour, and so on.
- **Starbucks** has created an internal culture that fits its world expansion plan through inclusion, diversity, equity, and valuation for accessibility. This culture doesn't stop at the employees' borders but extends to their customers by including a culture of warmth and belonging. They also invest in their employees by offering learning opportunities to develop skills, further their careers and help their young people achieve their personal and professional goals.
- The travel company **Skyscanner** supports and encourages personal development, has a no blame culture with regular reflections to improve ways of working and share learning. According to reports by removing the fear of failure, Skyscanner has created an environment where things can be achieved quickly. Experimentation is seen as a positive, even when things don't work out. It's by experimenting with lots of different ideas that the company has been able to achieve its rapid growth. I could also see a risk, as mentioned by Dale and others in similar type organisations; this approach could increase risk if not managed and made visible. It's a balance between flexibility for employees to develop projects and that of the organisation to meet internal and external requirements.
- **Patagonia** is noted for having a family-centred culture. In order to maintain that culture, they recruit individuals based on passion points (such as

a love of the outdoors) and works through informal networks to maintain this culture. The organisational vision and mission that places the environment's sustainability at its core (even at the expense of profit) is such that it requires likeminded individuals who are team players to work at the organisation. They do invest in their staff in order to equip them to make bold business decisions which have a positive environmental impact. The blend of passion, family, and purpose has allowed them to remain at the forefront of sustainable business practices. Patagonia is an interesting company in that it defines its reason for being very much around relaxation and leisure as can be seen on their our-footprint and activism webpage.

- **Google**, founded in 1998, has a net worth of $1 trillion. Google's culture is claimed to be flexible where employees are encouraged to work when they like and how they like. The company not only takes work from the employees but also provides them with an opportunity to coach each other in key business skills such as public speaking, management, and orientation as well as extra-curricular activities like kickboxing. It is inspiring that Google has acquired such a respectable status on the global platform in such a short span of time. Trust is at the core of what makes Google's company culture so successful. In fact, one of the biggest challenges of creating a positive culture is moving away from a top-down style of management that sees people as inherently untrustworthy. Instead, why not make people accountable and then give them the resources and freedom they need to get the job done.

In a nutshell, strategic leaders steer people towards the achievement of a shared vision. One way or another, it typically involves significant amounts of change. As most leaders will tell you, it's one thing devising a strategy, and quite another implementing it. The leadership part of this process is usually 90% of the issue and where the most time is lost. So what elements are needed for success?

Involvement and the power of persuasion or 'influencing skills' are key to implementation. You need to be able to involve the team in decision making elements in order to increase the chances of implementing change successfully.

Establish decent values and ethics in the business. Poor ethics will always catch up with you. We need only reflect on some of the major scandals of previous years such as the Volkswagen, BP, Wirecard, and many banking problems to see that poor ethical standards will usually catch up with you, and that need instilling from Day one.

Strategic leaders are faced with a paradox: people inherently do not like change, favouring stability and certainty by nature. However, businesses need to adapt to evolving contextual circumstances in order to gain or maintain a competitive advantage or simply to survive. This discussion is continued by Vakola (2013) who pointed out that 'change initiatives may not produce intended results because recipients are simply not ready'. Holt et al. (2007) suggest that an organisation's 'readiness' for change can be influenced by the staff believing that the changes are necessary, can be implemented and supported by leadership, and will be organisationally (and personally) beneficial. If individual staff do not appear to see the need or the benefit of adopting new strategies, is an indicator that an organisation is not ready for change, for example one that is more digitally enabled.

Higgs and Rowland (2005) discuss three distinctive leadership behaviours: 'shaping behaviour', 'framing change', and 'creating capacity'. Of these three behaviours, they suggest only the first is fully addressed. Through town halls and leadership communications the clear longterm vision may have been shaped by the leadership, but is often lacking in subsequently 'framing' and 'creating capacity'. That is, staff are *aware* of the vision, but are unable to translate this into tangible or practicable actions, nor see how it can be operationalised through their day-to-day job roles. They therefore struggle to see the personal or organisational value.

The framing aspect therefore is inherently in communication between first line people managers and their own managers. It can be all too easy for first line managers to create a 'them and us' mentality between front line staff (of which they would see themselves) and 'the leadership', meaning those above. This is all the more the case given the emergence of the 'player-manager' types who, rather than being pure people managers, split their time between managing and performing the same function as their staff.

The term 'player-manager' was coined in recognising those sports people that attempt to manage their team, whilst simultaneously playing on the pitch themselves. Heifetz and Heifetz (1994) point this out by describing a number of leadership tasks that result in effective change being implemented. They stress that managers need to 'get on the balcony', that is to say that they need take a step back and consider the business from the balcony or 'helicopter view', thereby allowing themselves time to apply 'critical' and 'strategic' thinking. This is certainly an area that most organisations could improve on, however, it is also one that would be supported by the third behaviour described by Higgs and Rowland (2005), in which managers need to 'create capacity'. Sometimes it is very easy to get so caught up in the day-to-day operations that both staff and people managers don't feel like they have a chance to stop, take a step back, and consider the bigger picture. It is only then that they can ask whether the methods being employed are the most efficient way of working, or if there might be another way that would better utilise the resources to create capacity.

What is the Changing Context of Strategic Leadership?

What is the leadership thinking required in today's environment? This is not a time for business as usual, but for business unusual (Goddard & Eccles, 2012).

We have faced a serious pandemic, maybe the biggest crisis since World War II. We're dealing with both a health crisis and an economic crisis. I would also call it a humanitarian crisis. We need to think about not only the world in which we find ourselves, but also the world that we want to build as we emerge from this crisis. These are tough times for leaders. Many businesses struggle to survive. Business operating models have had to be changed and ways of working have needed to be adapted to the new 'norm'. Overwhelming emotions and the fear of uncertainty have had a massive impact on my thinking as a strategic leader. Since early 2020, the 'situation' can be described as a world in which we must be prepared to deal with constant evolution and change.

The pandemic has obviously raised a very interesting question as so many organisations have had to pivot dramatically in such a short span of time. Over the last year, organisations have done amazing things in terms of how quickly they've been able to change and how agile they have been. But I think the more interesting question has to do with when the pandemic is over, to what extent can we maintain this level of agility in normal times. This is a context that requires strategic leadership more than ever. Below I summarise several other issues related to strategic leadership that will require more attention.

(a) Digitisation

Digitisation has enormous ramifications for jobs, business models, and how knowledge is distributed. It is far more difficult knowing what is true and what isn't in terms of 'fake' news. How human transactions take place and how data is gathered and indeed how we communicate. You can feel the ramifications of how digitisation has shifted in the sense of where value lies and where knowledge resides. These are often called 'wicked problems' or 'complex adaptive problems' because they have not previously been faced and are requiring us to think more deeply than before.

(b) Adaptive leadership

Leaders usually pride themselves on being excellent problem solvers. Preparing a business to face a volatile, complex future cannot be solved simply by instating the right process or upgrading to better technology. Nimbleness, and the capacity of an organisation to respond quickly and fluidly, have become critical. Heifetz and Linsky provide us with a useful metaphor for the art of strategic leadership. They describe it as the ability to keep moving 'back and forth from the balcony to the dance floor over and over again throughout the days, weeks, months, and years' (Heifetz & Linsky, 2002). It requires not being consumed by everyday tactical and operational work, but rather continually scanning the horizon and shaping the future, course correcting, and adapting during the journey. Adaptive leadership is about a leader creating an environment for followers to have confidence to address the challenges being faced (Northouse, 2018). Challenges can be broken down into technical and adaptive challenges. Technical challenges are more easily identified with known root causes and solutions. However, adaptive challenges are complex with root causes and solutions that are difficult to identify (Northouse, 2018).

(c) Resilience

Resilience is far more important than the ability to simply return to the status quo after a setback. It includes 'an expanded ability to keep pace with and even create new opportunities' (Legnick-Hall et al., 2011). This ability to take two steps forward after being forced back a pace is crucial for maintaining progress. It is important to note that this is not a static attribute that some organisations have and some do not; it is a 'path-dependent, latent set of capabilities' that give the organisation the capacity to 'anticipate and adjust to their environment' (Ortiz & Bansal, 2016). The principles of strategic leadership, building organisational resilience and agility have, in my opinion, never felt so significant, or urgent. Change is inevitable, and we must embrace rather than fear it. Moreover, we must become comfortable with ambiguity and learn to work effectively and innovatively within its bounds. Changing the organisational mindset to one of strategic learning, with a feedback loop, rather than the outdated annual cycle of strategic planning is key.

Personal resilience is essential, but organisational resilience is of prime importance. An organisation's ability to respond and recover from a crisis demonstrates its resilience. This resilience relies on three factors—leadership and culture, networks and relationships and organisational energy (Bruch & Vogel, 2011). The resilience response framework (Bhamra et al., 2011) highlights that a response to a threat tends to be reactive, yet feeds into the longer term organisational learning.

Externally, the leader's aim should be to strengthen the firm's digital and physical network and relationships, such that sufficient support is available when the firm is experiencing a crisis. With the increasing magnitude of volatility and ambiguity, the firm's resilience needs to be underpinned by a dynamic and flexible risk management approach.

Ortiz and Bansal (2016) believe that resilience allows individuals and organisations to bounce back from shocks, whilst creating the ability to adjust, avoid, and anticipate them. Leaders need to demonstrate resilience to their team and encourage them not to give up at the first sign of adversity. In driving change it is important to champion ideas personally, whilst also recruiting champions to drive initiates forward. Without resilience, leading through adversity and challenge will not yield results.

Finally, resilience is the 'capacity to survive in crisis' linking leadership, networks, and organisational energy, whilst also being able to 'thrive in a world of uncertainty and ambiguity'. In the whirlpool of 2020, maintaining resilience amidst business closures, government furloughing, redundancies and personal wellbeing, means bouncing back from challenges. By demonstrating to those you lead how to recover from setbacks, you will be encouraging them not just to survive uncertainty and ambiguity, but to embrace and learn to thrive on it both as a team and as individuals.

Reflections

- Consider how many new insights are talked about in your organisation?
- What are you talking about in a normal management meeting?
- What's on the agenda of your management meetings?
- What would be the one or two things at the top of the list?

Most commonly people will talk about day-to-day business as usual, discussing figures and historical data. The inertia that often causes leaders to cling on to outdated beliefs and principles can be resolved by periodic introspection and reviews. Context analysis might highlight that the old paradigms no longer hold and require new ones. It is critical that while attending to today, one needs to make preparation for tomorrow. The balance between 'Control' and 'Learning' with the purpose being the connector (Goddard & Eccles, 2012) is critical, and there should be sufficient attention to the current situation and exploration of the future, through experimentation and scenario planning.

Goddard and Eccles (2012, p. 103) found that executives 'fear that turbulence, uncertainty and discontinuity have become permanent features of the managerial landscape; customers are more discerning, shareholders are more impatient, competitors are more aggressive, and employees are more demanding'. However, when it comes to explaining what has caused this, most refer to external factors and are 'unlikely to claim that they themselves are responsible' (Goddard and Eccles, 2012, p. 104). Therefore, is there a perception that uncertainty is increasing, when in reality it has always been there? Perhaps there is more of a need for leaders and organisations to accept that they are part of the problem and responsible for fixing it (Goddard & Eccles, 2012).

As shown with the recent global pandemic, those organisations surviving are those that had a long-term vision and purpose with employees aligned or who have the flexibility to adapt their business model and focus in order to survive. This comes back to the need, not only for purpose and diversity but more importantly alignment across the organisation and diversity throughout.

What are the Key Leadership Skills Required for Strategic Leaders?

Almost invariably those who we view as having achieved extraordinary things are driven by a sense of *purpose* and a corresponding *mission*. In pursuing their respective missions, when confronted with *complexity and unpredictability* they are able to *find a way* to succeed. Extraordinary achievements are often a lifelong or career defining pursuit, and for many the *mission is never complete, restlessly pursuing further change*. These people understand the *right time to act*, and *which battles to fight*, and they are keen and *curious observers of both the world around them and themselves*. They are keen to share their story and *share their learning with others*.

This section draws on observations of individuals who have achieved things which their peers, or wider society, have deemed 'extraordinary'. I have attempted to correlate some of these observations with literature from the field of strategic leadership, leadership, and other fields, and also the personal writings of some of these individuals.

Purpose

Drive, fuelled by a strong sense of purpose, is essential in extraordinary achievers. For some, this is instilled as a work ethic or competitivity inherited from parents or other influential figures from their youth or formative years. For others it can be from witnessing or experiencing an event or an injustice. Very often this purpose is implicit—not calculated or determined, but inherently felt and understood. Popular media is awash with texts on 'finding your purpose', which suggests that, while many wish to find one, it is unlikely that a true, felt, purpose can be artificially created. A desire to prove worth can also lead to extraordinary achievement, particularly in the fields of endurance and elite sports. Perhaps precisely because of the absence of purpose, the need to prove worth can lead to extraordinary achievement (Beaumont, 2019; Healey, 2010).

The Mission: Setting a North Star

In forming a mission, we begin to see parallels between extraordinary achievers and the Strategic Leadership literature. Strong strategic leaders are acknowledged for their ability to successfully navigate, and even thrive in chaos, creating wealth in times of high volatility, uncertainty, and chaos (Akrofi, 2019).

If a mission is not naturally forthcoming, then the creation of a 'North Star' can be a powerful substitute. While the North Star could be considered a vision, both extraordinary achievers and strong strategic leaders realise that they cannot make the journey alone, rather, that by creating the right environment for those around them to thrive, the mission is more likely to succeed. This requires both visionary and managerial ability, and a willingness to offer autonomy and protection to those around them, as highlighted by both Rowe and guidance in transformational and transactional leadership (Vera & Crossan, 2004).

Navigating Complexity and Unpredictability

Literature relating to the strategic leaders ability to navigate and even thrive during uncertain times is delineated by an ability to anticipate, challenge, and interpret chaotic environments (Schoemaker et al., 2013), as well as configure and leverage organisations, or those around them in pursuit of a mission (Hitt & Ireland, 2002). Achi and Berger (2015) discuss the importance of non-linear and systems thinking, and the ability to take multiple perspectives on a problem.

It is proposed that the 'North Star' effect is at the centre of this ability for both extraordinary individuals and strong strategic leaders to capitalise on uncertainty. Much as a ship in turbulent waters will make small deviations from its course, speed up, slow down, or take on water, if it is guided by a clear direction and a sense of the crew each knowing their roles, it is more likely to ultimately reach its destination ahead of other, less fortunate vessels.

By affording autonomy, protection, and trust, strong strategic leaders and extraordinary individuals alike create a support team that is empowered to make decisions in the best interests of the mission, even in the absence of process. Suarez and Montes (2020) speak about the three types of processes apparent in an organisation, namely routines (scripted actions), heuristics (employing the rule of thumb), and improvisation (spontaneous and ad-hoc efforts). Rowe states that 'influencing employees to voluntarily make decisions that enhance the organisation is the most important part of strategic leadership'. This is especially true when being guided by heuristics and improvisation, elements to which the 'North Star' approach is particularly applicable.

Innovate

The importance of unconventional and non-linear thinking in strategic leadership is noted by a number of authors. It is not surprising that extraordinary achievers are able to find a way through challenge and adversity, either by viewing a problem from multiple perspectives, or by drawing on elements from unconventional on non-traditional sources (Walsh, 2013). These individuals are able to 'legitimise close opportunities' and 'reconceptualize the historical identity' (Gavetti, 2011) of their organisation, or their circumstance, to find a way to succeed when conventional wisdom fails, and others may fall foul of common pitfalls and historic thinking (Pfeffer & Sutton, 2006).

It is also evident that these individuals see organisations, or the world around them, not as mechanistic systems that function with repeatability and predictability irrespective of time or context, but as a semi-sentient hybrid, which can generate wildly different results from similar stimuli.

The Mission is Never 'Complete'

Josephs and Joiner (2006) and Rooke and Torbert (2005) propose a model for the 'action logic' of leaders when considering leadership agility. The action logic is defined as the dominant belief system that underpins actions taken when faced with a specific choice. Both models report that almost three quarters of leaders have action logics in the expert stage, where leaders' actions are broadly defined by being the source of a solution, or the achiever stage where they judge success by a traditional range of performance metrics and rewards, such as task completion, sales, profit, and growth.

That the 'conventional' stages of development, expert, and achiever are dominant in most companies is understandable, for predictable reasons, but strategic leadership literature and the action logics of extraordinary individuals suggest that uncertainty may be better served by those with post achiever action logics. For example, Mintzberg (1994) discusses the importance of not over-planning and leaving some room for strategy to evolve. Similarly, Rowe highlights the importance of emergent strategy on succeeding in volatile times.

Restlessness

It is evident that strategic leaders, and extraordinary accomplishments alike, are the product of a restless and intolerant of the status quo. The cause for this can be readily linked to the driving force of purpose. It is universally highlighted in strategic leadership literature that those who lead organisations through turbulent waters are not only able to embrace change and uncertainty, but are also intolerant of stagnating.

This can manifest itself in strong managerial skills, hyper-competitivity, and extremely high standards, such as the GE era under Jack Welch. Rowe is clear that good strategic leaders must have both visionary and managerial abilities, and that a visionary leader alone, without managerial abilities or an equivalent team, may cause more damage in volatile times than a purely managerial leader who follows existing process, however misguided this may be. While high achievers are often seen as visionary, they also have a high degree of actuation and expect high standards of others.

It is also evident that this restlessness for change promotes or prioritises a culture of exploratory innovation, both in business, such as WL Gore (Jansen et al., 2009; Hamel, 2007).

Act at the Right Time

It is important to note that restlessness does not equate to recklessness. The importance of timing is highlighted in the literature and observed in those who have achieved the extraordinary, in the political (Thatcher, 2013), sporting (Froome, 2015), and business (Welch) fields.

Tichy and Sharman (1993) propose a three-phase process of awakening, envisioning, and re-architecting a strategic mission, with different traits required at each phase. Vera and Crossan highlight the difference in pace and propagation of learning within individuals, groups, and organisations. Both in business and outside, picking the 'kairotic moment' at 'strategic inflection points' when actions can unleash the most organisational energy within your team or strike the biggest blow to your competitors is an important ability (Boal & Hooijberg, 2001; Bartunek & Necochea, 2000; Bruch & Ghoshal, 2003).

Know Which Battles to Fight

Along with timing, but certainly less explored by the literature, is the ability to be resilient after setbacks and defeats. While driven individuals are clearly capable of conflict (Thatcher, Welch, Healey), there is sense in knowing when to fight and when to regroup. Perhaps the 'North Star' effect moderates the impact of detrimental events, or the ability to embrace chaos allows strong strategic leaders to see unexpected events as an opportunity, but it is clear that extraordinary achievers exhibit great resilience in adversity. Sonnenfeld highlights the ability to recruit others, prove your mettle, and discover one's heroic mission as factors for success in overcoming adversity.

Lessons from the elite sport and crisis management world suggest that practising to deal with unpredictable events and regularly simulating failure could lead to improved outcomes and increased resilience when encountered for real. Kaplan et al. (2020) discuss Kahnemnan's (2011) model of system one and two thinking, and observe that practising system two thinking can improve one's capacity to bounce back after a setback.

Be Curious About the World

We have discussed the importance of seeing the world as non-linear, the ability to embrace chaos and pursue exploratory innovations. The literature strongly supports the observation that both strong strategic leaders and extraordinary achievers are curious and committed to learning.

It is clear from recent global events that the role of signal analysis is increasingly important as both a competitive edge and as a signpost to inform emergent strategy or crisis management.

Analysis of performance data has fuelled extraordinary achievement in elite sports for some time (Walsh), but it is still surprisingly under-utilised in many companies. Kozyrkov (2020) discusses the additional clarity that signal analysis can provide during uncertainty. In the same way that they are aware of strategic inflection points, it is evident that strategic leaders and extraordinary achievers are able to leverage technological inflection points in pursuit of their mission.

Be Curious About Yourself

Another trait of the extraordinary is that they have a passion for and commitment to learning and are often highly self-aware, if not also (although not always) highly emotionally intelligent. Achi and Berger state that 'in a complex world we're better served by leaders with humility, a [...] sense of their own limitations, [...] curiosity and an orientation to learning and development'. Many of the traits identified so far are exhibited by the emotionally intelligent (Goleman, 2005).

Strategic leaders and those who achieve the extraordinary are able to combine this self-awareness with their own restlessness to create a sense of urgency across their peers and ensure that a whole organisation, or team, is able to contribute effectively to the pursuit of the mission, not just the individual themselves.

Share Learning

While Kotter suggests that 'institutionalizing a leadership-centred culture is the ultimate act of leadership', Davies and Davies (2004) and Rowe highlight wisdom and the ability to influence others as key tenets of strategic leadership. Davies and Davies and Kotter (1990) both also emphasise the need to provide opportunities and coaching to new leaders in order to cement a leadership-centred culture.

It is clearly evident that the desire to share learning and creating a culture of support and coaching is a sign of strategic leadership in business and this trait is no less prevalent in other extraordinary achievers. Some use a flair for business and a charismatic storytelling ability to maximise returns on their thoughts and memoirs (Welch, Healey) and others relish the opportunity to defend a legacy or share their side of the story (Thatcher). However, many extraordinary achievers seem content merely to share their experiences with others purely because the information exchange may be beneficial to individuals or society. Returning briefly to the theory of action logics, it is noted that the most evolved action logics portray an almost spiritual wisdom and desire to share knowledge.

Paradox Mindset

Most leaders who have been successful in driving change over the last decade often say to me 'why do we need to change if it's working?' Too often leaders are reactive, keen to maintain the status quo and embrace conformity and comfort; they only change structures and procedures when problems occur, rather than being proactive and creating the future they would like to be part of. History is littered with the relics of companies who carried on doing what they were good at as the world changed around them—Kodak, Blockbuster, Nokia, Woolworths, Xerox to name but a few. These were not bad companies; they just failed to embrace uncertainty and paradox.

In this world of rapid change, political volatility, demographic changes and 5G set to drive the fourth industrial revolution, this is a dangerous position to take. As a society we are facing 'grand challenges'—a move to clean growth in the era of climate change, an ageing population across much of the developed world, the emergence of AI and the Internet of Things, and new mobility with the development of autonomous vehicles.

Keith Grint famously defined wicked problems as complex with 'no clear relationship between cause and effect' and often intractable. But the grand challenges of society are like wicked problems on steroids. Climate change, for instance, cannot be solved by one heroic leader. It needs many leaders from many organisations working together as part of a system. The leaders of the next decade will have to lead differently if they are not only to tackle these environmental forces and grand challenges, but also to build a growing and profitable business, especially as these external pressures are creating paradoxes for leaders who have traditionally focused only on corporate goals.

Leaders don't like paradoxes because it creates uncertainty. They want a clear plan ahead, however the next decade will reward those leaders who are capable of working with paradox and its accompanying uncertainties. Instead of 'either/or' thinking they need to accept both options. Indeed, they will need a passion for paradox. Elements of these issues overlap the more extensive consideration given in Alan Matcham's 'Paradoxes in Executive Development' to follow, but here are five to address in brief.

The Paradox of Fast and Slow

As the pace of change gets ever faster and we suffer from information overload, it is important that leaders stop and be still. They need to find time in their routine to step away to reflect and challenge their assumptions, routines, and biases.

Most leaders have lost the ability to stop and think because they are obsessed with the pace of change. This means they don't actually challenge the way things are being done. They are too comfortable with their ideas and their status. But leaders need to have the curiosity and courage to challenge their assumptions and be able to adapt to the changing environment.

Leaders who can add value are those that can stand still and think what needs to be done, they embrace change by experimenting with new ideas whilst still providing 'business as usual'.

Amazon's first chief science officer Andreas Weigend recently revealed the tech giant's obsession with experimentation in an organisation, so it is ready and able to leverage its AI capability. Weigend said: 'Jeff [Bezos] has this great belief in experimentation—of; "you know we don't know what will happen here, but let's try something out, see what we can measure and be very clear from the start what are the metrics that define success". We did thousands of experiments and found out all kinds of things about human behaviour'.

The Paradox of Today and Tomorrow

In the 2020s, leaders need to embrace a shift from years of accumulated wisdom in a single individual discipline, to the ability to access, interpret, and contextualise insights provided by machines.

Two decades ago, leadership was very individual, but now that we are in a networked and interdependent society, leaders need to re-think how they practise.

The other important challenge is that we need talent in areas where we have no history. Look at the Internet of Things, look at AI, and so on. All of this creates new challenges for leadership and requires new and different thinking for leadership development.

This is the paradox of today and tomorrow. Do you train your staff for today or tomorrow? If you develop them for the challenges of today, you might not a have future because you are not ready for tomorrow's challenges (think about Kodak, Nokia, etc.). Conversely, if you train them for tomorrow, you may lose sight of what is happening in the present. Leaders need to embrace this conundrum and develop systems that can train staff for both today and tomorrow.

The Paradox of Purpose

Leaders develop their mission, vision, and strategy around corporate purpose. Creating shareholder value, increasing market share, and creating a competitive advantage are all part of that purpose.

But in the next decade leaders will need to think about their organisation's bigger purpose, how it affects and improves society. This may be a paradox alongside the corporate purpose, but it cannot be ignored.

Consumers and workers are demanding that businesses have a social purpose. When Paul Polman was CEO at Unilever, he aligned its corporate purpose with a broader societal purpose to reduce the company's impact on the environment. This paradox must be encouraged by leaders, and in so doing they will gain a competitive advantage.

The Paradox of Leaders Without Answers

If leaders think they are suffering information overload now, they have seen nothing yet. The advent of 5G will see all companies become data firms, with all products and objects connected to the internet as the Internet of Things becomes a reality. This technological overload will force leaders to face another paradox.

They may be experts in their field, but they will not have all the answers. In fact, the leaders' role is not to provide answers, but to be a catalyst for change.

Most of the answers will come from the bottom of the organisation, from those interacting with the data. Thus, leaders need to build the right relationships so that those sitting lower on the hierarchy can provide input into the decisions and solutions of the company.

Any mature organisation has more than ten hierarchies, but how many add value? In the digitised world, hierarchies do not play a part. Leaders need to make sure everybody has a voice, bringing ideas and problems to the surface.

Becoming a catalyst for change involves a mind-shift for leaders and means embracing the human aspects of leadership—the ability to embrace humility, compassion, and humanity.

You might have incredibly powerful technology, but if there's no empathy and no humanity in the way it's presented to the people who engage with it, there's no point having an incredibly powerful technological capability.

They need to realise that leadership is not a technical role. It is a human role and should focus on developing the right relationships, invest in the wellbeing of employees, and develop the self, through reflective practice and self-awareness.

The Paradox of the Self and the Community

Changing their mindset and becoming a catalyst will require leaders to take time out so they can focus on self-improvement. As Indra Nooyi, CEO of PepsiCo, said: 'Just because you are CEO, don't think you have landed. You must continually increase your learning, the way you think, and the way you approach the organisation. I've never forgotten that'.

But to tackle the grand challenges of the next decade will also mean working with others. Take the challenge of an ageing society that is putting pressure on a hospital's resources and costs: the hospital CEO may have a very different corporate purpose from that of a pharmaceutical company CEO, but they may well have a common societal purpose, so that these organisations can work together along with others on this grand challenge.

Indeed, tackling this issue will require the pharma companies, medical technology firms, the Government's department of health, and many other stakeholders to work together.

Leaders need to build the capacity for collective leadership in the ecosystem while also thinking about their self-development to tackle these grand challenges. Environmental sustainability, for example, is becoming a key challenge. We see how companies like Puma, Unilever, Patagonia, Lush, and others have not only changed how they do business but have also tried to engage with customers and the industry, to build a relationship with their broader ecosystem.

Reflection

- What other paradoxical tensions do you have to navigate when thinking about the future of your organisation?

References

Achi, Z., & Berger, J. G. (2015). Delighting in the possible. *McKinsey Quarterly*, March 2015, pp. 1–8.

Akrofi, S. (2019). *Value creation through executive development*. Routledge.

Bartunek, J., & Necochea, P. (2000). Old insights and new times. Kairos, Inca Cosmology and their contribution to contemporary management inquiry. *Journal of Management Inquiry, 9*, 103–113.

Beaumont, M. (2019). *Around the world in 80 Days: My world record breaking adventure*. Corgi.

Bhamra, R., Dani, S., & Burnard, K. (2011). Resilience: the concept, a literature review and future directions. *International journal of production research, 49*(18), 5375–5393.

Boal, K. B., & Hooijberg, R. (2001). Strategic leadership research: Moving on. *Leadership Quarterly, 11*(4), 515–549.

Bruch, H., & Ghoshal, S. (2003). Unleashing organizational energy. *MIT Sloan Management Review, 45*(1), 45–51.

Bruch, H., & Vogel, B. (2011). *Fully charged: How great leaders boost their organization's energy and ignite high performance*. Harvard Business Press.

Davies, B. J., & Davies, B. (2004). Strategic leadership. *School Leadership & Management, 24*(1), 29–38.

Froome, C. (2015). *Chris Froome: The autobiography*. Penguin.

Gavetti, G. (2011). The new psychology of strategic leadership. *Harvard Business Review, 89*(7/8), 118–125.

Goddard, J., & Eccles, T. (2012). *Uncommon sense, common nonsense: Why some organisations consistently outperform others*. Profile Books.

Goleman, D. (2005). *Emotional intelligence* (10th ed.). Bantam.

Hamel, G. (2007). *The future of management*. Harvard Business School.

Healey, A. (2010). *Me and my mouth: The Austin Healey story*. Monday Books.

Heifetz, R. A., & Heifetz, R. (1994). *Leadership without easy answers* (Vol. 465). Harvard University Press.

Heifetz, R. A., & Linsky, M. (2002). A survival guide for leaders. *Harvard business review, 80*(6), 65–74.

Higgs, M., & Rowland, D. (2005). All changes great and small: Exploring approaches to change and its leadership. *Journal of change management, 5*(2), 121–151.

Hitt, M. A., & Ireland, R. D. (2002). The essence of strategic leadership: Managing human and social capital. *Journal of Leadership & Organisational Studies, 9*(1), 3–14.

Holt, D. T., Armenakis, A. A., Feild, H. S., & Harris, S. G. (2007). Readiness for organizational change: The systematic development of a scale. *The Journal of applied behavioral science, 43*(2), 232–255.

Jansen, J., Vera, D., & Crossan, M. (2009). Strategic leadership for exploration and exploitation: The moderating role of environmental dynamism. *Leadership Quarterly, 20*(1), 5–18.

Josephs, S. A., & Joiner, W. B. (2006). *Leadership agility: Five levels of mastery for anticipating and initiating change.* Wiley.

Kahneman, D. (2011). *Thinking fast and slow.* Penguin.

Kaplan, R. S., Leonard, H. B., & Mikes, A. (2020). The risks you can't foresee. *Harvard Business Review, 98*(6), 40–46.

Kotter, J. P. (1990). What leaders really do. *Harvard Business Review, 68*(3), 103–111.

Kozyrkov, C. (2020). To recognize risks earlier, invest in analytics. *Harvard Business Review, 98*(6), 53–57.

Lengnick-Hall, C. A., Beck, T. E., & Lengnick-Hall, M. L. (2011). Developing a capacity for organizational resilience through strategic human resource management. *Human resource management review, 21*(3), 243–255.

Mintzberg, H. (1994). Rethinking strategic planning part I: Pitfalls and fallacies. *Long range planning, 27*(3), 12–21.

Northouse, P. G. (2018). *Leadership: Theory and practice.* Sage publications.

Ortiz-de-Mandojana, N., & Bansal, P. (2016). The long-term benefits of organizational resilience through sustainable business practices. *Strategic Management Journal, 37*(8), 1615–1631.

Pfeffer, J., & Sutton, R. I. (2006). *Hard facts, dangerous half-truths, and total nonsense: Profiting from evidence-based management.* Harvard Business Press.

Rooke, D., & Torbert, W. R. (2005). *Seven transformations of leadership.* Boston, MA.

Schoemaker, P. J., Krupp, S., & Howland, S. (2013). Strategic leadership: The essential skills. *Harvard business review, 91*(1), 131–134.

Suarez, F. F., & Montes, J. S. (2020). Building organizational resilience. *Harvard Business Review, 2020,* 47–52.

Thatcher, M. (2013). Supranational neo-liberalization: The EU's regulatory model of economic markets. *Resilient liberalism in Europe's political economy,* 171–200.

Tichy, T. & Sharman, S. (1993). *Control your destiny or someone else will* (New York, Doubleday).

Vakola, M. (2013). Multilevel readiness to organizational change: A conceptual approach. *Journal of change management, 13*(1), 96–109.

Vera, D., & Crossan, M. (2004). Strategic leadership and organizational learning. *Academy of management review, 29*(2), 222–240.

Walsh, F. (2013). Community-based practice applications of a family resilience framework. In *Handbook of family resilience* (pp. 65–82). Springer, New York, NY.

7

Responsible Leadership and Sustainability

Leading during turbulent times requires skills and approaches that have wide-reaching applications beyond that of the global COVID-19 pandemic. The crises of the past have shown us this much; from the banking crash of 2008 to the VW emissions scandal, we have emerged with more awareness of how behaviour shapes business. The worldwide economic damage of the banking crisis is still being felt today, undermining consumer trust in corporations, their leaders, and the huge rewards given to CEOs, sometimes despite poor performance. To this we could add a catalogue of other events that have caused and continue to cause enormous damage to businesses and stakeholders alike.

In this cultural climate there is an increasing demand for leaders who are mature, ethical, and responsible—not just for the outcomes of their own activities, but for those of others as well. It has been argued that millennials are growing ever more ethically aware. Indeed, research by Global Tolerance in 2015 suggested that 62% of millennials wish to engage with organisations that have a positive societal effect, whilst 53% felt they would be prepared to work more if they felt they could make a difference to the lives of others. In short, the present generation are emerging as more aware and inclined to respect ethical and moral standards than their predecessors.

Job seekers, particularly millennials (Leveson & Joiner, 2014), are factoring Corporate Social Responsibility (CSR) into determining who they work for, and in turn, organisations can use their CSR profile to enhance their desirability to prospective candidates (Greening & Turban, 2000). In high-employment economies around the world, issues relating to CSR are taking on greater importance as they compete for top talent. Until, that is, the COVID-related job losses began.

© The Author(s), under exclusive license to Springer Nature Switzerland AG 2022
J. Colley, D. Spyridonidis, *Unprecedented Leadership*, Palgrave Executive Essentials,
https://doi.org/10.1007/978-3-030-93486-6_7

We have come a long way since Friedman's (1970) expansive statement that maximising shareholder value was the primary purpose of an organisation. Society has changed, led in part by the values of younger generations, who have realised that our descendants must prepare to live in times of limited resources. This push from society is responsible for change in the attitudes of corporations. Consequently, more and more companies are including long-term sustainability plans in their strategy, as well as including CSR initiatives in their annual reports. Twenty-first century corporations have to enhance and foster a climate that supports ethical and moral standards, and for this to happen, responsible leadership is needed.

Consequently, talking about ethics and morals within organisations is just one means of appealing to and retaining talent; it also improves employee engagement and satisfaction. In addition, organisations need to think about their customer base; strong CSR can become a source of competitive advantage, and to realise this, their leaders need to understand and practice responsible leadership.

The aim of this chapter is to:

- Familiarise the reader with the need for responsible leadership, what it means, and its implications.
- Encourage readers to engage with the debate as to limits to corporate social responsibility.
- Understand current models of responsible leadership and subsequently apply these to real business cases.
- For readers to consider and develop their own views on responsible leadership and how it can be practised in different contexts.

As with previous chapters, we will engage with both recent theory and case studies that encourage the reader to engage meaningfully with the concept and practise of responsible leadership.

Defining Responsible Leadership: A Link to the Self

Leadership is defined as the 'process of influencing an organisation in its efforts towards achieving an aim or goal' (Northouse, 2018). A responsible leader must also be an effective leader. An ineffective leader will be severely limited in their capacity to guide his or her organisation towards achieving any of its overarching goals. The converse, however, is not necessarily true, we need only look to historic figures, such as Hitler, Stalin, Saddam Hussein, and Genghis Khan, whose now hugely controversial leadership style could be described as effective, but far from 'responsible'.

Authentic and Responsible Leadership

To refine it to a modern standard of 'responsible' we must add further traits and behaviours to the defining characteristics associated with effective leaders. Responsible leadership starts with being responsible to the self, to lead authentically, upholding ethical and moral stances. A responsible leader requires exceptional awareness of both self and others. A fundamental necessity is to understand their own personal purpose and values, and align these to the organisation's goals.

Although some research treats the authentic leader and responsible leader as two mutually exclusive styles, one could argue that authenticity is a requirement of responsibility and hence a point of overlap. Values, ethics, and authenticity are all dimensions discussed as being supplementary to provide a more rounded view of what responsibility represents in the context of leadership (Freeman & Auster, 2011). Authenticity is regarded as a key tenet of the effective leader—having a personal passion for the organisational purpose and vision is likely to greatly aid the perception of an authentic leader. It is much easier, and less energy-consuming, to propagate a persona that is in line with your own internal values and passions than to 'fake it' when communicating widely. Perhaps even more critically, we expect organisations and their leaders to actually act (George & Sims, 2007) in accordance with these values.

Ethics and Responsible Leadership

Responsible leadership can be best understood as 'ethical leadership' or 'effective leadership'; that is to say, leadership that takes other contributors, such as employees, communities, customers, and environments, into account in critical and ethical decision making. Many diverse personal qualities contribute to the development of ethical leadership—drive, commitment, selflessness, courage, honesty, creativity, and adaptability are all characteristics on which effective and responsible leadership can be built, especially within the banking sector. Some of these will be defined and referred to both in the course of this chapter and the book as a whole.

Integrity

Integrity is foremost in developing responsible leadership. According to the Cambridge English Dictionary, integrity is 'the quality of being honest and having strong moral principles'. Just as Dwight D. Eisenhower, former president of the US, emphasised, 'the supreme quality for leadership is unquestionably integrity. Without it, no real success is possible'. One of the main reasons why this attribute outweighs other leadership character traits is that whether he or she can effectively motivate others is based on a trusting relationship—something fundamental to achieving a common goal. A recent survey by Williams has revealed that a large number of employees feel they would be unwilling to be led if they do not believe their leader to be trustworthy. If their leader behaves appropriately and appears morally correct, they feel more reassured that they themselves will be fairly and equally treated. It follows therefore that leaders demonstrating decency and integrity in their practise will also increase their employees' motivation and productivity; trust in a leader encourages a corporation to develop in a healthy, sustainable way.

Passion, Optimism, and Responsible Leadership

Passion and optimism are less teachable but essential aspects of responsible leadership. Ultimately they are the driving force behind a team and must therefore be reflected in leader behaviour. Energy and enthusiasm inspire a positive team, one more likely, in turn, to invest their dedication towards reaching a shared goal. More importantly, these personal qualities are the essential fortitude required if, or perhaps when, leaders must tackle unexpected obstacles and times of difficulty. In short, a passionate leader can be a powerful one.

Vision, Values, Purpose, and Personal Commitment in Responsible Leadership

An effective and responsible leader needs to ascertain an organisation's core purpose and go on to formulate a vision of how it is to be delivered. This is a redundant vision however unless other members of the organisation both share and understand the thinking behind it. This is the leader's responsibility to communicate this amongst the team and stakeholders alike. A leader's ability to convey and progress towards an organisational code should, in work at least, subsume the personal and disparate values that might otherwise result in conflict. A leader should also engage stakeholders in these shared purposes, attaining and motivating commitment towards the achievement of hopefully sustainable results.

To describe a leader as 'responsible' assumes that the values, purpose, and passion of the organisation guided by such a leader will contribute positively to the operational and social environment. It is also likely that responsible leaders are more engaged and invested in the success of their organisations due to an alignment of values and purpose. In this situation, the leaders themselves have the potential to reap greater engagement and job satisfaction in discharging their duties. In some ways, this has the potential to create a virtuous circle; increased leader engagement and satisfaction leading to greater passion and clarity of vision in the organisation's purpose, itself hopefully driving stakeholder engagement, alignment, and success. Drawing these concepts together, Pless (2007) defines responsible leadership as a 'values-based and thorough ethical principles-driven relationship between leaders and stakeholders who are connected through a shared sense of meaning and purpose through which they raise one another to higher levels of motivation and commitment for achieving sustainable values creation and social change'.

Critiquing Personal Leadership

Responsible leaders engage with their wider stakeholder group in order to ascertain and promote the organisation's common purpose, communicating that this should be long term in nature. Waldman and Galvin (2008) argue that omitting 'responsibility' from the dimensions of previously established leadership theories undermines the effective capability of the leader. Considering this, all leaders ought to be frequently self-critiquing not only their level of responsible leadership but that demonstrated by the organisation. At the corporate level, effective leadership encourages a strong and positive relationship, employee engagement, and satisfaction—all of which are critical to any form of success. The key indicators that all strong leaders should be looking for are not just profit and sales, but overall productivity, consumer satisfaction, employee retention, loyalty and an environment of supportive team collaboration (Harter et al., 2002).

The Bottom Line: Financial, Social, and Environmental Performance

Responsible leadership also refers to the management of an organisation's relations with numerous stakeholder interests, all while contributing to what has been called 'the triple bottom line of financial, social, and environmental performance' (Voegtlin & Scherer, 2017).

Responsible leadership necessarily overlaps with both ethical behaviour and CSR (Maak & Pless, 2006; Voegtlin & Scherer, 2017). It requires sensitivity to actions that concern a broad set of stakeholders, from employees, customers, contractors, to the environment, society, and forthcoming generations. Some of the definitions above align 'other' stakeholders to shareholders but imply shareholders remain dominant. Others explicitly call out 'for future generations', implying a deeper and longer term view of leadership actions. All, however, understand responsible leadership to be a far-reaching and sustainable approach that has a clear purpose beyond traditional boardroom strategy. Only in recent years have we begun to recognise that social, community, and environmental responsibility can support reputation, build positive relationships with colleagues and customers, and ultimately support business growth. The Unilever case study later in this chapter will explore and clarify this further.

This hypothesis is widely accepted as valid and becomes even more appropriate in the VUCA (volatile, uncertain, complex, ambiguous) world where leaders need to be able to effectively negotiate siuations both ambiguous and complex. This is defined well by Voegtlin and Scherer (2017), who state that 'the aim is not only to do the best for the firm, but also to aspire to be a general force for good that generates positive change'.

Corporate Social Responsibility

Corporate social responsibility (CSR) is assuming a position of greater influence in organisations. This refers to strategies put in place to mitigate the impact on the environment in which an organisation operates. This is a significant role of a responsible leader who is expected to have the capacity to conduct research and understand issues relating to sustainability, climate change, gender issues, and investment in both the local operating environment and globally. It needs to be integrated as part of the values and purpose of the organisation. Responsible leadership should be able to assign values to CSR not necessarily in terms of financial numbers, but in terms of what the organisation stands to benefit in regard to reputation, regulatory and social endorsements, and competitive advantages.

Whilst several definitions of CSR exist (e.g. Marrewijk, 2003), most offer balanced and multi-factorial approaches to social, ecological, and financial considerations. In order to be considered responsible, a leader and organisation have to conduct research and analysis and make the results the backbone of their CSR approach.

Climate change is a major topic never far from the media cycle, or modern *zeitgeist* and, as such, environmental sustainability is regularly at the heart of considerations as to when corporations and leaders are judged to be 'responsible' or otherwise.

In order for CSR, particularly strategic CSR to be successful, the role of a responsible leader is essential. CSR can be developed by organisational members and external stakeholders, however when senior leadership support is lacking or, as is often the case, divided, it won't be integrated into the values and long-term strategy of the organisation and is thus less likely to be successful (Haski-Leventhal, 2018). Strong corporate responsibility benefits the organisation's long-term sustainability, as well as attracting non-speculative investors and committed employees.

Thus, responsible leadership is a matter not just of self-governance (the 'Me'), nor of the organisation (the 'We'), but of responsible business practise across the larger ecosystem of investors, consumers, competitors, regulators, and other interested parties (the 'Us').

Why is Responsible Leadership Important in Today's Society?

As consumers acquire more awareness of the impact organisations can have on supply chains, they are also increasingly influenced by factors such as a brand's environmentally responsible reputation. Many organisations have demonstrated the positive impact of CSR development programmes—hence a responsible leadership approach could potentially generate a competitive advantage in the marketplace.

We live in a capitalist society that prizes capital gains in which corporate leaders focus on generating shareholder returns at the expense of other stakeholders. The consequences of this have been widely and deeply felt. There is however a rising tide calling for responsible leadership at all levels, which is increasingly hard to ignore. Responsible leadership calls for an alignment of purpose, people, profit, and the planet. During recent years, we have witnessed the global economy experience a sustained period of growth (prior to COVID-19). However, multitudes of people and communities have not benefited, even when they were involved in the value chain/inequality. During this period, environmental threats have also intensified. Few business leaders and the leaders of Western nations have managed to pursue lucrative growth in alignment with positive societal and ecological effects, although pledges abound (remember the Paris 15 agreement). In other words, a responsible leader aims to embrace sustainability through their corporate actions, which encompass concerns for all stakeholders.

Case Study: Responsible Leadership at Lush and AIB

The cosmetics company Lush offers a good case of responsible leadership, whereby ethically sourced products define their corporate purpose. Additionally, the company also contributes annually to human rights associations. Lush's operations are sustainable and cater to all stakeholders. Shareholders benefit from sustainable profits, as the company differentiates itself by treating its employees well and offering customers trusted, good quality products. Meanwhile, the charity work and environmentally friendly operations support the community and future generations.

Another example comes from the banking sector. Allied Irish Banks PLC is one of the four main high street banks in Ireland. In AIB, Colin Hunt acknowledges that 'being CEO of AIB brings both responsibility and opportunity to make a difference to our customers, colleagues, communities and other stakeholders'. Sustainability is a core part of its purpose, which is to support its clients to realise their ambitions. The company's sustainability report with its title alone 'We Pledge to Do More' demonstrates a long-term commitment to their values.

Governance structures in AIB include a Sustainable Business Advisory Committee reporting to the Board, with an Executive Committee member sponsorship for sustainability reporting to the CEO. Traditionally a leader could be deemed successful by delivering profit or shareholder return without concern for how that return was created. This has changed and a responsible leader needs to link how the return is generated to their purpose. AIB's success is linked to sustainability, with a €5 billion climate action endowment offered primarily for climate-connected products over the next few years. The 2019 sustainability report provides further evidence of the importance of a responsible leadership approach directly addressing climate change, stating 'Climate change is one of the greatest challenges of our time, and the role of finance to support the transition to a low-carbon economy cannot be understated or underestimated'. In the conclusion of its 2019 sustainability report, AIB recognised this collective effort so that the bank continues to deliver shared value that benefits everybody.

The Role of Central Banks in Responsible Leadership

Central banks lie at the core of the financial system and in the recent years of economic, financial, and lately, pandemic turbulence, their leadership has been tested in new, often unexpected ways. In the words of Peter Drucker, 'rank does not confer privilege or give power, it imposes responsibility'. During the last decade, central banks played a leading role in many countries creating credibility and performing with confidence for the financial markets. Central banks had to take new measures to fulfil their primary responsibility for price stability in their respective economies while keeping the balances with various stakeholder groups and achieving prosperity.

Companies who do not focus on their staff, the communities they serve and the environment, are unlikely to survive in today's culture. There is evidence that companies able to successfully embed a responsible leadership approach often experience a competitive advantage. Research by Shook et al. (2020, p. 10) shows that organisations that align innovation with sustainability and reliable relations outpace their competitors. The triple aim of individuals, environment, and profit can be shown to produce far better returns over the long term than a narrower focus on only returning profits to shareholders.

Responsible leadership however is difficult in an era of constant change and uncertainty, when leaders must still deliver in the interests of stakeholders. A prime example of change in current financial operations is the strong push for automation; machine learning and Artificial Intelligence are technologies that are changing how finance operates. The traditional finance skills are quickly shifting to non-traditional tools, and the unprecedented pandemic has acted to accelerate the development of automation, particularly for the purpose of communication.

Responsible leadership is all the more of a concern for multinational corporates. As past events show, large financial firms are susceptible to misconduct and regulatory breaches. Despite establishing responsible leadership to help control and mitigate these events from happening, there are still difficulties and limitations in 'too big to fail' or 'too big to manage' organisations. Investment banks like J.P. Morgan have enormously increased their controls department throughout the past few years in order to monitor operations within the bank, however it may take some time and effective management to connect operating standards across borders.

The Challenges of Responsible Leadership

Key challenges with which developing leaders often struggle are discussed in the next section. These include:

- Managing complexity in a time of ongoing change and uncertainty
- Managing multiple stakeholders
- Managing over a longer term horizon
- Self-management

Combined, these four areas encompass the formidable challenge of responsible leadership. We intend to provide options that a responsible leader might adopt to ensure these are comprehensively addressed.

Voegtlin and Scherer (2017) highlight the fact that responsible leaders must be able and willing to handle environmental, financial and community concerns concurrently, and this includes exhibiting consistent behaviours in their actions and choices.

An example detailed in AIB's Sustainability Report is an initiative called 'culture conversations'. This was launched in 2019 to engage personnel from across its hierarchy in the diagnostic stage of the project. Around 800 employees participated, and the outcomes suggested that the organisation needed to focus particularly on areas such as collaboration, trust, accountability, and positive spirit. The outputs have been translated into a new set of cultural values, two examples being 'One Team' and 'Reduce Complexity'.

The extent to which leaders are responsible for the impact their organisations have on the wider world is a source of ongoing debate. The last two decades particularly have demonstrated the accelerated damage organisations potentially have on society and the environment. Consequences of the banking crisis are still felt in many countries, whilst issues such as the VW emissions scandal have attracted large bodies of opposition. In their fall out we are left with questions as to which organisations and businesses should be held responsible for their impact, particularly regarding complex and ambiguous issues such as climate change. This has resulted for some time in tension between civil society and businesses in terms of responsible conduct in their local and global community.

Responsible Leadership in the Business World

As a leader in an organisation, how far does one's responsibility extend? From a stakeholder perspective, how far do leaders' responsibilities extend towards the wider community? Whilst engaging in this debate we must also consider the highly controversial idea that this isn't really the role of the leader at all and his or her responsibility is expressly to the shareholders and employees.

Pursuing this line of enquiry, we must ask whether a CEO is responsible for everything that happens in his or her organisation? In a crisis climate—volatile, complex, unpredictable, and ambiguous—who should be held responsible for any unintended but negative consequences of business activity?

Case Study: Pacific Gas and Electric

Pacific Gas and Electric (P G & E), the Californian electricity provider, filed for bankruptcy protection in January 2019, after evidence emerged that power lines owned and maintained by the company might have been responsible for igniting catastrophic forest fires. The probability of unpredictable wildfires has increased in California in recent years, almost certainly as a result of the changes to weather patterns related to climate change. Lawsuits have been filed against P G & E alleging that poor maintenance and lack of infrastructural investment meant that power cables malfunctioned, creating sparks that started the fires.

Questions to consider

- As a power company, do they have sole responsibility for maintenance issues that could be the proximal cause of fires?
- How far are they responsible for weather conditions that may derive from excessive use of carbon fuels?
- Could a broader perspective that included their responsibility to stakeholders have saved P G & E from this situation?

Reflection Points

- The power company almost certainly has responsibilities to address the periodic maintenance issues believed to be the immediate cause of the forest fires. The weather conditions, it might be argued, could have been mitigated through the longer term use of clean and renewable energy. Based on the available information, we are inclined to think that Pacific Gas and Electric ignored its responsibilities to the community at large and, in doing so, resulted in damage to life, property, and environment.
- A key component of responsible leadership is sustainability, and an organisation's impact on the environment and society. Had P G & E embraced a responsible approach to leadership that focused on the shared goals and purpose of all its stakeholders, it might have achieved a more positive outcome.
- P G & E was liable because their neglect of maintenance breached regulatory requirements. There was a clear causal link between the unmonitored power lines and the ignition of the fires. The causal link between these particular fires and climate change is obviously more difficult to prove and P G & E became the obvious culprit to indemnify all losses suffered. This is what makes corporate life so challenging in current business culture: the difficulty of being implicated in wider adverse events whilst mitigating the most probable risks.

Models of Responsible Leadership

Maak and Pless (2006) present a theory of responsible leadership which concerns a number of roles and behaviour types relating both to responsible leadership and to other theories of leadership, such as that of Goleman (2000). While it provides a useful and comprehensive framework for reflection and analysis, it has been criticised as too complex for practical use.

Maak and Pless's model is relational in nature. It focuses on how responsible leaders make and build relationships with different stakeholders by adopting a stakeholder perspective. They lay out a theory illustrating some of the roles they suggest a responsible leader needs to adopt. Together, these roles build what they refer to as a 'gestalt for responsible leadership', meaning a collection of separate roles which, taken together, create a leadership model that ensures they act and behave responsibly.

Breaking this theory down further, they delineate the stakeholder groups they make reference to, which include citizens, family, employees and direct reports, customers, board members, other stakeholders, suppliers, peers, and future generations. Their suggestion is that these are *all* stakeholders who a responsible leader should be building relationships with in line with their relational model.

They go on to examine the characteristics and qualities that responsible leaders need to display in doing this, which they loosely group beneath subheadings:

- The **visionary**: the leader makes a vision of the future integral to his actions of the present.
- The **servant** facilitates all possibilities and builds loyal relationships.
- The **steward** is responsible for the longer term sustainability of the organisational structure.
- The **citizen** adopts the perspective of one beholden to and responsible for a society's citizens.

Mark and Pless also outline activities associated with these roles. The visionary, for example, as storyteller and enabler, casts an image of the future that will motivate a team. The servant might act as a coach, facilitating and supporting people in those relationships. The steward is the architect, creating the boundaries, systems, and processes, which will ensure that the enterprise remains responsible and sustainable into the future. The citizen is a change agent, intent not just on obeying laws, but also thinking about beneficial change initiatives for civil society and perhaps even political engagement.

The unifying factor in Maak and Pless's work is the **shared** concept of a responsible leader, that weaves relationships. Thinking in network terms, how do you build relationships not just within your organisation or business, but within the wider world? How do you communicate to relevant stakeholders the impact of your own organisation and its activities?

Voegtlin et al. (2019) revisit and simplify Maak and Pless's model into three key roles:

- **Expert**
  Leaders as experts show direction intended to deliver organisational strategic goals.

- **Facilitator**
  Leaders as facilitators display behaviour which motivates, integrates, and cares for employees.
- **Citizen**
  Leaders as citizens concerns him or herself with secondary stakeholders, emphasises the greater good, and pursues the creation of long-term value for societies.

They make a distinction between primary and secondary stakeholders, the first being fundamental to the endurance of the organisation, such as employees and customers, whilst the secondary stakeholders include third-party bodies such as local communities, NGOs, and groups representing wider social concerns; the result ensures a contextually diverse perspective of an organisation's impact.

Whilst this simpler model may seem easier to grasp and implement, the roles described are more typically managerial as opposed to leadership. Nor does this version include important areas originally outlined by Maak and Pless, such as the visionary, storyteller, or change agent. Maak and Pless acknowledge the complexity of responsible leadership and emphasise the need for ambidexterity and a 'both/and' approach to resolving the paradoxes encountered when attempting to behave responsibly towards different groups.

This view resonates with Adam Smith's 'invisible hand' on two key points:

1. Society needs to make sure business leaders are aware of market failures, for example situations when value and price diverge. It may be argued, however, that with the advance of technology, market failures will take up greater resources.
2. Business leaders need to be more aware that a fundamental precedent of capitalism is an embedded growth obligation. This has led to offshoring, the gimmick economy (for example, iPhones being released every other year), globalisation, M&A activity, and other strategies to maintain growth. Either businesses will find new and creative ways to create growth, or the system will reach a point of implosion (as any system that grows exponentially will periodically collapse). One clear problem with the current economic model is that, although GDP has risen, median income levels have broadly stagnated. In effect, wealth creation has not been equally distributed and the so called 'trickle down effect' has made minimal difference.

We, as a society, should appreciate that a rising tide lifts all boats, but should we try to move away from this consumer-led model and demand more from our business leaders?

Reflection Point

Opponents of the stakeholder view challenge this idea of responsible leadership:

- 'In a free enterprise, private property system, a corporate executive is in effect an employee of the owners of the business. He has direct responsibility to his employers. That responsibility is to conduct the business in accordance with their desires, which generally will be to make as much money as possible while conforming to the basic rules of the society, both those embodied in law and those embodied in social custom' (Milton Friedman).
- 'By becoming more efficient and more profitable, it makes businesses better for the community' (Douglas Daft—CEO Coca-Cola). 'I baulk at the proposition that a firm's "stakeholders" ought to control the property of the shareholders' (Thurman Rogers CEO of Cypress Semiconductor).

Do you think this view of a business leader's responsibility is valid?

System Leadership

Peter Senge and others (2015) propose a model that goes beyond these already discussed. It situates leaders within complex dynamic systems and, like Maak and Pless, see an essential function of responsible leadership as one of collaboration and co-creating solutions to complex problems.

They outline three capabilities to be exhibited by good leadership:

- **The capacity to make sense of the bigger picture**
  In a complex situation, humans tend to focus on the elements most visible in front of them. The ability to see the larger picture is essential to building a mutual understanding of the situation.
- **The ability to foster reflection and generative conversations**
  Critical reflection is necessary to enable alternative points of view to be heard and alternative realities to be considered.
- **The ability to embrace collective focus for proactive thinking**
  This shift involves proactively challenging the present status quo to inspire new thinking and approaches.

Senge and his co-authors offer a number of practical tools for leading change from this perspective in their article 'The Dawn of System Leadership' (citation).

This view of responsible leadership emphasises collaboration and co-creation, and goes further in seeing the responsible leader as one who is engaged in creating the conditions for creative problem-solving in complex systems.

Case Study: Unilever—Paul Polman—Championing Sustainability and Responsible Capitalism

For this case, we can apply more recent critiques of responsible leadership. The models already discussed are largely management rather than leadership centric. Whilst the two undoubtedly share on the majority of points, certain elements require different roles and approaches.

They suggest that leaders have a responsibility to the greater good and should keep the concepts of people and planet firmly in mind when making business decisions. It is the leader whose business governance will be the ultimate decider, motivator, and negotiator of complex power politics, whilst attempting to assimilate differing views on morality across cultures.

Paul Polman, CEO of Unilever from 2008 to 2018, is an example of a leader who fully embraced such challenges. In 2010, Polman introduced the Unilever Sustainable Living Plan with the goal of doubling revenue, while halving the company's environmental impact by 2020.

His leadership style and approach incorporate elements of both the 'visionary' and 'architect' roles of Maak and Pless's model, and to some he represents an image of charismatic leadership. He certainly appears to be authentically motivated in his pursuit of responsible and sustainable business, that aligned with the UN Sustainability Goals.

Polman recognised that to shift the company towards the resultant values he sought, he would have to encourage change in the behaviour of his primary stakeholders, shareholders, suppliers, and, most importantly, customers.

From the outset he used passionate rhetoric to broadcast a clear and consistent vision for the sustainable business he was trying to achieve. He also established practical constraints on how business was to be conducted and the behaviours that he expected to see. This approach resonates both with the creative approach to leadership and that of the military where orders are formulated in terms of a 'main intent' and acknowledges that responsible leadership in Unilever's case involved extensive change throughout the larger company system.

Responsible Leaders as a Force for Sustainable Change (Linked with Leading Teams and Organisations)

There is a growing movement amongst business leaders to take responsibility for problems beyond the remit of their operation. They must exhibit an increasing awareness of the impact their organisation may have and their ability to effect positive change. This underlying ethos is motivating them to use their business to drive sustainable change. Sustainable activities consider the social and environmental factors alongside driving financial performance.

Certain business leaders are now recognised favourably, having revisited the purpose of their organisation, then recognised and introduced means of developing more sustainable business practice. A global example would be the aforementioned Paul Polman, the former CEO of Unilever. He spent the past decade ensuring sustainability lay at the heart of Unilever's corporate strategy, and implemented impressive and transparent change at a scale of its €50bn turnover organisation, impacting 100,000 direct employees, two million people across their supply chain and over two billion consumers.

Polman believed that a responsible purpose would drive top- and bottom-line growth. By driving action on the social and environmental aspects of Unilever's business, through their 2009 strategy, 'The Compass', he put forward the vision to grow the business and reduce the environmental impact by half by 2020. This purpose focuses on enhancing people, profit, and planet aspects associated directly with their operation.

Polman went further than just reviewing how his organisation operates. He set in motion an ethical, purpose-driven culture throughout the organisation, creating financial and reputational results and applied his vision across Unilever's value chain to create a viable long-term business. This vision resonates well with modern consumers, and Unilever brands with a responsible purpose have benefited, growing over 30% faster than traditional brands.

The embedded sustainability messages were also a key factor with shareholders who rejected an attempted takeover from Kraft-Heinz in 2017. Polman has stuck to his vision and, since stepping down in January 2019, is using his position to advocate responsible business practices in other political and corporate organisations. Alan Jope, Unilever's new CEO, has taken this approach forward.

Paul Polman is regarded as a responsible leader by industry experts and academics. During his time as CEO, the reputation and credibility of Unilever increased significantly and made Unilever one of the world's most preferred employers (Chakroborty, 2016). In addition, Polman also helped to form bodies such as the Consumer Goods Forum. Revenue and profits also performed positively, with sales growing by 19% and profits more than doubling during his tenure.

Another noteworthy example of a responsible leader is Emmanuel Faber, the CEO of Danone who has set Danone's 2030 ambition to create long-term sustainable value at all levels of the organisation. He is aware of external matters associated with people and the planet, and he has committed to making internal changes to address these.

Faber is committed to gender equality, and when he took over as the CEO in 2014, he created a gender-balanced executive team and gave equal paternity leave. To further demonstrate his example of responsible leadership, he turned Danone's US operations into a certified B corporation, which denotes companies that hold themselves accountable for balancing profit and the planet. As well as their responsibility for profit, such corporations are also responsible for reflecting how their decisions impact their employees, clients, contractors, society, and the environment.

From a climate change viewpoint, providers of non-renewable energy are beginning to take responsibility for the wider implications of their business actions. Centrica, the global oil, and gas services provider launched its responsible business strategy in April 2019 called 'Ambition 2030'. To be a responsible leader at Centrica means having a commitment to reducing the environmental impact and increasing the social impact at a global scale through their business activities.

Centrica's 'Ambition 2030' focuses on enabling their customers to use energy more sustainably, reduce their emissions by 25%, and enable a decarbonised energy system. The responsible business ambitions in Centrica's document set out 15 goals that embrace, amongst other things, sustainability. In terms of its impact on the society angle, Centrica is committing to building a workforce of the future.

The world is facing numerous unprecedented challenges. Shook et al. (2020) highlight challenges such as climate change, technological advancement, and consumer expectations. The recent primary leadership focus of return on shareholder value can ignore how this return is achieved, manifesting itself in an increased risk of destruction to the environment. New technology can be deployed without appropriate prior understanding of the impact. To ignore this change in consumer expectation puts a company at risk in terms of sustainability and the ability to attract future talent.

A leadership approach focused only on shareholder return is not aligned to the future needs of the globe and the sustainability of organisations. Therefore, a different approach is required. Responsible leadership is an important approach to counter these challenges. It displays an emotional intelligence that recognises the inability of any one person, company, or country to solve the issues at hand alone. It is reliant on multiple stakeholders working together on a shared purpose that is not singularly focused on financial returns.

There is evidence that senior leaders are recognising the challenge and adapting a responsible leadership approach. We can see this by comparing the 2019 and 2020 annual letter to customers by Larry Fink CEO of Blackrock. In 2019, he said his 'overriding duty was to make customers money'. In 2020, his letter to CEOs stated that 'climate change is different from any other economic financial crisis'. In the letter, he announced that sustainability will be at the heart of investment decisions.

These examples reflect an acknowledgement that the leadership approach that worked previously will not resolve the challenges we face in the future and that responsible leadership is required to address the challenges.

1. Influencing Responsible Action

If a leader is someone who influences others to create action, then to be a responsible leader is about using influence to create responsible action. Responsible action focuses on solving crises that are not solely internal to the organisation but affect us all, and then acting to prevent and limit the externalities associated with the business. The examples of Polman with Unilever, Faber with Danone, and Centrica's Ambition 2030 demonstrate that a responsible leader takes responsibility for their organisation. They take responsibility for environmental challenges and act to create a positive impact on society.

When determining how to be a responsible leader, it's important to note that there are similarities in their approach. They emphasise vision whilst holding an awareness of the wider impact of their business—not just profit. They listen to the concerns of their people and of society. This is evidenced in their long-term commitments to change. Using their position of power in their organisation they ensure the organisation addresses these issues, whilst recognising the long-term commitment involved. The Compass vision led Polman to develop a 10-year plan to transform Unilever's operation; Faber has made his US operation legally responsible for profit and the planet (this is an indefinite time commitment) and Centrica's Ambition 2030 highlights a move from short-termism to embedding responsible action over the longer term.

After examining examples of what responsible leaders do, its practise can be summarised as leaving the organisation, the environment, and society in a better place than when you found it. Responsible leadership reflects the impact your business makes on all these levels.

The purpose of responsible leadership is to commit to the sustainability of your actions, build trust and reduce the negative externalities associated with your operating activities. Responsible leadership could be considered good for business as it builds a positive reputation with customers and employees and may well attract new customers who value what you value. In addition it attracts and retains talented employees who are committed to your purpose.

The way consumers view the world is changing. The availability of information increases the risk of business practices being exposed, both for positive and negative practise. The speed of media communication means poor behaviour is widely communicated and can soon 'go viral'. Such transmission of company actions do or can have a positive effect to spread your brand image and retain consumer confidence and trust.

Case Study: Iceland's Palm Oil Campaign

As part of their Christmas marketing campaign in 2018, the large food retailer Iceland targeted unethical sourcing practices associated with obtaining palm oil. The campaign highlighted deforestation and the subsequent loss of animal habitats solely caused by unethical sourcing strategies.

This marketing campaign built positive brand awareness for Iceland, by associating them with environmental issues that society is concerned with. On the basis of this association alone, customers felt their buying habits made an implicit contribution to the common cause, and ethical practise more broadly. This is a good example of the power of corporate influence.

Unilever too has proven that profitable growth and cost reduction aren't necessarily mutually exclusive, and that simply by benefiting the environment and demonstrating responsible practise on a global level can have positive implications for consumers. To become a responsible leader, one should take responsibility for problems that belong to no one, but impact many, if not all of us.

Reflection Points

- What examples of responsible leadership have you observed or participated in?
- Are you a responsible leader? Is your approach consistent in the context of responsible leadership?

References

Chakroborty, B. (2016). *Championing sustainability and responsible capitalism.* Paul Polman at Unilever IBS Centre for Management Research.

Freeman, R., & Auster, E. (2011). Values, authenticity, and responsible leadership. *Journal of Business Ethics, 98*, 15–23.

Friedman, M. (1970). A theoretical framework for monetary analysis. *Journal of Political Economy, 78*(2), 193–238.

George, P., & Sims, P. (2007). *True north: Discover your authentic leadership.* Jossey-Bass.

Goleman, D. (2000). Leadership that gets results. *Harvard Business Review, 78*, 78–90.

Greening, D. W., & Turban, D. B. (2000). Corporate social performance as a competitive advantage in attracting a quality workforce. *Business and Society, 39*, 254–280.

Harter, J. K., Schmidt, F. L., & Hayes, T. L. (2002). Business-unit-level relationship between employee satisfaction, employee engagement, and business outcomes: A meta-analysis. *Journal of Applied Psychology, 87*(2), 268.

Haski-Leventhal, D. (2018). *Strategic Corporate Social responsibility: Tools and theories for responsible management*. Sage.

Leveson, L., & Joiner, T. (2014). Exploring corporate social responsibility values of millennial job-seeking students. *Education & Training, 56*, 21–34.

Maak, T., & Pless, N. (Eds.). (2006). *Responsible leadership*. Routledge.

Marrewijk, M. (2003). Concepts and definitions of CSR and corporate sustainability. *Journal of Business Ethics, 44*, 95–105.

Northouse, P. (2018). *Leadership: Theory and practice*. Sage.

Pless, N. M. (2007). Understanding responsible leadership: Role identity and motivational drivers. *Journal of Business Ethics, 74*(4), 437–456.

Senge, P., Hamilton, H., & Kania, J. (2015). The dawn of system leadership. *Stanford Social Innovation Review, 13*(Winter), 27–33.

Shook, E., Lacy, P., Monck, A., & Dutton, J. (2020). *Seeking new leadership: Responsible leadership for a sustainable and equitable world*. Forum of Young Global Leaders, Global Shapers Community and Accenture.

Voegtlin, C., & Scherer, A. G. (2017). Responsible innovation and the innovation of responsibility: Governing sustainable development in a globalized world. *Journal of Business Ethics, 143*(2), 227–243.

Voegtlin, C., Frisch, C., Walther, A., & Schwab, P. (2019). Theoretical development and empirical examination of a three-roles model of responsible leadership. *Journal of Business Ethics, 156*(1), 1–21.

Waldman, D., & Galvin, B. M. (2008). Alternative perspectives of responsible leadership. *Organizational Dynamics, 37*(15), 327–341.

Part IV

Communication, Education, and Coaching—Tools for Leading During Crisis

Recommended Reading for 'Communication, Education, and Coaching—Tools for Leading During Crisis'

Cowan, D. (2017). *Strategic internal communication* (2nd ed.). Kogan Page Ltd.

Goddard, J., & Eccles, T. (2012). *Uncommon sense, common nonsense: Why some organisations consistently outperform others*. Profile Books.

Groysberg B., & Slind, M. (2012). *Talk, Inc.: How trusted leaders use conversation to power their organizations*. Harvard Business Review Press.

Heifetz, R. A., Heifetz, R., Grashow, A., & Linsky, M. (2009). *The practice of adaptive leadership: Tools and tactics for changing your organization and the world*. Harvard Business Press.

Morgan, G. (1999). *Images de l'organisation*. Presses Université Laval.

Pfeffer, J., & Sutton, R. I. (2006). *Hard facts, dangerous half-truths, and total nonsense: Profiting from evidence-based management*. Harvard Business Press.

Pfeffer, J. (2018). *Dying for a paycheck: How modern management harms employee health and company performance—And what we can do about it*. Harper Business.

8

The Purpose and Power of Leadership Communication

Tim Wray

In a world of extraordinary change and heightened uncertainty, organisational leaders are faced with two core challenges. The first is to remind the organisation of what remains constant, such as purpose, values, and culture. These provide stability and meaning amid turbulence and change, while also sparking the engagement, energy, and creativity of employees at all levels. Leaders need to persuasively remind their team of these anchors, often reinterpreting and reframing them in order to continue making sense in a changing context. Secondly, leaders need to build the agile capabilities required to respond to continuous change in an organisation, including strategic sensing—generating and sharing market and customer insights across the organisation—and enabling collaborative working across the boundaries of the organisation to act on these insights.

In a VUCA world, both leadership and organisational communication have never been more important; sitting at the nexus between strategy formulation and strategy execution, both remain in a constant state of flux. Leadership communication is not just about how leaders convey messages, but critically how they engage employees at all levels of the organisation, including those with formal and informal authority. The leader's task is to create an organisation-wide conversation that is continually evolving the strategic posture of the organisation and how it is to be implemented. This chapter will explore how leaders initiate and sustain this conversation.

J. Colley, D. Spyridonidis, *Unprecedented Leadership*, Palgrave Executive Essentials,
https://doi.org/10.1007/978-3-030-93486-6_8

This chapter will seek to help you answer the following questions:

- What is the purpose of leadership communication in the face of uncertainty?
- How do leaders define organisational reality?
- How is leadership communication processed in the informal networks of an organisation?
- What attributes and skills do leaders need to be more effective communicators?
- How does organisational communication support agility?

What Is the Purpose of Leadership Communication?

When I have asked senior leaders across a range of sectors why they invest their scarce time in communication, I receive a range of answers. The chief people officer of a global software business described to me her organisation's hierarchy of objectives when it comes to internal communications. At the most basic level, communication is about the dissemination of general information that people should know, for example, the company's latest set of results. At the next level up, people need to have the information necessary to do their job effectively. The next two levels contain what could be described as 'higher order objectives'. The first is to share with people the purpose and values of the organisation, explaining what we are about and what we stand for in the world. The second is to connect people to one another and forge a sense of community. These higher order objectives encapsulate the experience of what it is like to belong to this organisation and are often communicated through actions as well as words. For example, the chief people officer described the statements made by the company and the actions it took in response to the death of George Floyd in the US and the subsequent events. She described the communications of the company as intentional, with a very clear purpose of defining its stand on an important global issue. Having a point of view on real-world events, rather than simply rising above the debate, is a departure for the company and not without controversy. However, as the global economy begins to recover from the pandemic, and the war for talent heats up again, a clear definition of the company's purpose and values, and the experience of belonging to its global community, is an important differentiator in the marketplace.

Ensuring there is strategic clarity and alignment within an organisation is another important reason why leaders need to invest significant time in communication. Alignment is crucial if you want the efforts of all your people focused on delivering your strategic goals. Much research suggests the greatest challenge is not strategy formulation, but rather strategy execution. The Chief Information Officer (CIO) of a major retail bank discussed the communication process he uses with his team and wider division to achieve alignment. Every quarter, he spends two days with his direct reports. The time is split into three sections: first, he will spend extended time sharing his own perspective on the strategic landscape, reflecting on anything in the wider environment or within the organisation that has changed during the preceding three months; second, team members have the opportunity to replay what they heard and ask for clarifications; finally, once there is clarity and agreement on what has been said, they will have the opportunity to challenge, discuss and share their own ideas. Having role modelled this approach, the CIO then tasks the individuals with replicating this process with their own teams. What was interesting to me was the extent of the preparation that the CIO invested ahead of the quarterly communication event, sometimes stretching into days. He emphasised to me that if he wanted clarity and alignment within his team, then he needed his own thinking to be razor sharp. Other leaders have remarked to me in the past that the need to communicate with others was a means of gaining clarity in their own minds.

This same CIO made another interesting observation about the purpose of leadership communication. He described his ability to create strategic clarity and alignment of action as limited largely to his direct reports. Their responsibility was to translate this for their own teams, thus cascading alignment down through the organisation. However, he viewed communicating the culture to its several thousand employees as a key part of his job as leader. Much of this is achieved through actions, not words. Leaders shape the culture through what they pay attention to—for example, what measures of performance they consistently highlight, what behaviours surface under pressure, what guides their decision making over scarce resources, what they reward, who they promote, and how they role model certain values and behaviours (Schein & Schein, 2019).

A further reason for investing in communication is to achieve higher levels of employee engagement. The MacLeod Report, commissioned by the UK government, identified four drivers of engagement. The first is a strong strategic narrative, that clearly articulates the purpose and vision of the organisation, and the journey the organisation is on. The second driver, engaging managers, works to combat the old maxim 'people join organisations, but they leave managers'. Engaging managers provides clarity around role expectation as well as constructive feedback and coaching to enable the individual to reach their full potential. A third driver is integrity, meaning there is little or no gap between the espoused values of the organisation, captured in various company publications, and what is lived out in practice by leaders at all levels. The fourth driver of engagement is employee voice. Of course, giving employees voice means leaders learning to listen! Listening does not necessarily mean agreeing with every view expressed or acting on every idea offered, but it does mean acting on some things and ensuring that employees feel they have been heard. I will return to this idea of the listening leader later in this chapter.

When we consider Macleod's four drivers of engagement, communication permeates every single one. However, it is important to note that this does not mean old style, one-way corporate communication, but rather a fully engaged and ongoing organisational conversation. This is even more important when so much of the context in which the organisation operates is constantly and rapidly changing. I discuss how leaders generate and sustain this conversation in the next section.

Defining the Organisation's Reality

While all the things we have discussed so far are important, communication is the essence of leadership and should take up much, if not most, of the leader's time. Karl Weick (1995) in his seminal work on sensemaking in organisations puts it this way, 'One message for practitioners is that what is real is more up for grabs than they realize … managers need to author, examine, and critique realities thought to be in place. They cannot take those realities for granted or assume they are obvious to anyone else'. Max de Pree, the former CEO of Herman Miller, is famously quoted as saying the 'the first responsibility of a leader is defining reality'; this becomes even more important when the environment in which the organisation operates is characterised by heightened uncertainty and complexity. The task of communication is in fact the challenge of managing and making sense out of complex and confusing situations. We step into a leadership role when we do this.

Creating a strategic narrative is exactly this. Ancel (2012) describes a strategic narrative as essentially an imagined future, one that 'sets the stage by interpreting the relevant history and current conditions. It defines the challenges to be addressed, and it describes how those challenges will be met'. The power of a strategic narrative is that it 'establishes the fundamental understandings that let people find their place, becoming part of the story and taking right actions in the face of a changing environment'.

During the global pandemic, Michael O'Leary, the Group Chief Executive of Ryanair, boldly declared that the clean-out of the airline industry presented real opportunity: 'The real seismic change from Covid will be the growth opportunities across Europe. They are much greater than after the financial crisis or 9/11' (FT 27/12/20). O'Leary re-framed and re-defined the reality for the key stakeholders in his business. Sensemaking and sensegiving in this way enable the organisation to step forward amid uncertainty with confidence and purpose—it can stabilise the organisation in a time of crisis.

If leaders are in the business of defining reality, it does raise the question as to whose interests they have in mind. In another seminal definition of sensemaking, Gioia and Chittipeddi (1991) describe it as a process whereby leaders 'influence the sensemaking and meaning construction of others toward a preferred redefinition of organisational reality'. In other words, leaders have a worldview and through the communication process seek to influence others to embrace this.

For those who may have misgivings about this perspective on leadership communication and its Orwellian undertones (which others may happily embrace it) I would add three additional insights. Firstly, my mantra to many senior leaders is there is no such thing as no communication. Often leaders hold back, particularly in times of uncertainty, waiting for the moment when they can speak with certainty, conveying only facts. Typically, this strategy simply leaves a vacuum that will be rapidly filled by the sensemaking of others. What leaders need to grasp is that everything is a communication. Even the act of not communicating will be interpreted and imbued with meaning by others. Organisational life is like the unfolding drama on a stage, where every action, as well as every word, is observed and integrated into the interpretive process. The choice for leaders is not *whether* to communicate or not, but simply if they wish to *actively manage the meaning* that their words and actions convey.

A second important point for leaders to understand is that they are not the only ones seeking to manage meaning. Other actors, sometimes deliberately and consciously, sometimes unconsciously, will contribute to how those around them make sense of the organisation's reality. Cowan (2017) describes how the intended narrative of organisational leaders is often met by the emergence of a counter narrative, both of which then contend to become the dominant narrative. This counter narrative can be constructed and driven by formal stakeholders or simply by influencers in the informal communication networks of the organisation, a powerful force that savvy leaders will tap into—more about this later.

The final point I would make is that what removes the sensemaking process from the realms of manipulation is the willingness of leaders to have their own version of reality, their own truth, challenged, informed, and shaped by the input of others. In other words, the communication process becomes a true dialogue. In this way, leaders create a dynamic, collective organisational conversation, one that can evolve to address emergent challenges and opportunities and integrate fresh insights and learning from the organisation's experience. What is most interesting are the ingredients, such as authenticity and trust, that create the conditions where this conversation can thrive, as well as the communication channels, including social platforms that enable it. We will return to this point shortly.

Language and symbolism are key sensemaking devices. I spent the first ten years of my career working for a national telecom's supplier, migrating from being a monopoly provider to operating in a fully liberalised and highly competitive marketplace. One of the most important changes we brought about was replacing the word 'subscriber', with the word 'customer'. This single change in the use of language encapsulated the entirety of the journey the organisation was on. Another example that demonstrates the power of symbolism in sensemaking can be seen in a gift given to Pope Francis. Shortly after his election in 2013, he received a 1984 Renault 4 from a priest in northern Italy. He began using it to drive himself around the Vatican and the vehicle soon came to serve as a potent symbol of his message of humility and simplicity.

All of this points to communication as the essence of the leader's role. Not all leaders understand this. I have had several conversations over the years cajoling and encouraging some to invest more of their time connecting and communicating, challenging them to put communication at the top of the 'to do list' rather than on the 'nice things to do if I have time list! I remember one interaction intending to persuade a senior executive in a large telco to spend more time communicating, gained the response 'what else would I be doing!' He understood that as a leader, communication is the job; this is all the more true in circumstances of great uncertainty and rapid change.

Reflection

- How much of your leadership time is invested in communicating?
- How do you respond to Max de Pree's view that 'the first responsibility of a leader is defining reality'?

Understanding the Dynamics of Organisational Communication

If communication is a critical component of what a leader does, then understanding the dynamics of organisational communication is essential. Many leaders I have worked with indulge in event-driven, 'tick-box' communication. For example, the town hall meeting to kick-off the latest change initiative takes place and can be crossed off as complete on the Gantt chart. In fact, what has happened is the communication process has just begun. I like the metaphor of throwing a rock into a pond. Once the rock hits the water it sends ripples out in every direction. Similarly, the communication that has landed will now begin to be processed by the informal communication networks of the organisation, and often reworked, reframed, and interpreted to mean different things. These informal networks represent the collective and informal sensemaking and sensegiving processes of an organisation.

The CEO's carefully crafted presentation at the town hall meeting represents the official narrative. It will describe how the top team views the organisation's operating environment, what are the key threats and opportunities, the nature of competition and how the organisation needs to think, act, and behave to succeed. However no sooner has the message landed, then sitting around tables at break time the question will be posed to local leaders, and other informal influencers, 'What do you think, what does this mean?' So begins the process of interpretation, where the rational logic of the executive team meets the emotional reality of peoples' experience and feelings. Often, this process happens out of earshot of the leaders whose logic is now the focus of sustained scrutiny.

If the CEO's message represents the official narrative, and we accept that within the informal networks of the organisation this will be reworked or indeed directly challenged with a counter narrative, surely leaders need to know how to influence this process to ensure the official narrative survives intact to become the dominant narrative? Leaders need to go beyond formal organisational charts to understand the informal interactions that shape beliefs within an organisation.

There are two aspects of informal networks that are key. The first relates to structural dimensions such as centrality, which identifies the actors in a network that have the greatest density of connections and therefore the most opportunity to influence. Another structural feature relates to strong and weak ties. We often focus more on the former—strong ties are characterised as those with whom we have regular and meaningful interaction such as family, friends, or work colleagues. The basic premise is that people are most likely to be influenced by and come to agree with those with whom they have frequent interaction (in network terms, are more strongly tied). In this way informal communication networks could be viewed as a constraining factor, driving people towards conformity in their attitudes, beliefs, and behaviours. Weak ties, in contrast, might be simply acquaintances, people we meet occasionally. However, the importance of weak ties is that they provide a bridge to other networks. From a communications perspective, people with weak ties can connect across organisational silos and boundaries to accelerate the diffusion of a particular narrative.

The second aspect considers the nature of the relationship that binds a network together. Informal networks that construct and propagate a particular narrative are more likely to be based on affective relationships, such as trust and friendship, in contrast to more task-related networks. A few years ago, I conducted research in a large retail bank. The bank had been through two mergers in the previous decade, and, despite the passage of time, employees would often speak about a colleague with reference to the bank they had initially joined. My research focused on the question of what social network people turned to in organisations in times of heightened uncertainty to make sense of what was going on. If people adopted a particular narrative, how did they access it in the first instance and with whom did they process this? There were some more obvious explanations, for example proximity plays a part. Simply put people are more likely to interact with those physically close to them and easily accessed, such as colleagues in their bank branch. Other explanations were more intriguing. One significant network of relationships that surfaced included people who had joined the bank at the same time and shared the initial weeks of training and induction together. Deep bonds were forged during this shared experience, and decades later people remained in touch. The group had followed different career paths and trajectories and as a result were geographically dispersed and located at different levels and functions within the bank. However, the strength of the network was such that it provided opportunities to gain a range of perspectives and gather insight from several sources, later processed and integrated into an emergent narrative.

What are the practical implications of all of this for leaders? Firstly, recognising that there are many actors at all levels of an organisation engaged in sensemaking who will influence what emerges as the dominant narrative of the organisation. Secondly, understanding that many of these actors enjoy high levels of trust and credibility within informal communication networks, that can be highly persuasive. Thirdly, understanding the power of the social influence that drives conformity of attitudes and beliefs. The famous experiments conducted by Solomon Asch in the 1950s vividly demonstrated the power of social influence that results in a change of behaviour or belief to fit in with a group. There are two types of social conformity—a desire to 'fit in' or be liked (normative) and a desire to be correct (informational). In the context of organisational communication, both operate as a gravitational pull, causing people to align with the dominant narrative within their informal communication network. During periods of heightened uncertainty or ambiguity, while people will listen to what senior leaders say, they will turn quickly to their own personal networks to both interpret and corroborate this. So, the real implication for leaders is to recognise the limitations of their own communication reach and influence, and to harness the power of these informal communication networks. Identifying key influencers at all levels of the organisation and investing time in their understanding of your message is key.

Communication Strategies

In my work around organisational communication over the last two decades, I have observed three core philosophies that translate into distinct communication strategies. While communication technologies and platforms have radically changed, if the core philosophy remains intact, the intent behind the communication strategy is the same.

The first approach is governed by **a control mindset**, characterised by carefully crafted messages, stage managed events, and top-down communication that seeks to sell the strategy and persuade the rest of the organisation of the logic and wisdom of managerial approach. Large amounts of time spent packaging the message and little time spent in real dialogue with employees are signs that this tell-and-sell strategy is in play. Even opportunities for input are managed with 'questions' for the senior team hand-picked and advised in advance to avoid anyone going off message. Most town hall meetings I have attended follow this format. Groysberg and Slind (2012) have described this as the old model of corporate communication; however, it remains surprisingly robust in many organisations, or at least continues to coexist alongside strategies aimed at greater levels of engagement. Of course, this approach offers certain benefits, providing consistency of message as well as speed when you need to communicate something quickly to the organisation. So, there are certain contexts where this model of communication may be the best choice. However, regardless of how correct the logic may be, the trade-offs remain. The belief that the message can be controlled is an illusion. The less input that others have at the point of delivery of the communication, the greater the likelihood that the narrative will be reworked in the informal communication networks already discussed, with every chance that an alternative narrative will emerge.

The second communication strategy is one designed to **engage employees** and create and sustain an organisational conversation around its purpose, values, and strategic priorities. It is important from the outset to say that this is not a rudderless approach, where the conversation is free form and shaped by the whims of the moment. Rather, there is an intentionality in how leaders frame the conversation and identify the themes for discussion and exploration. Leaders talk *with* employees, not to them; listening is a key skill. Conversation then flows across the organisation, connecting colleagues and peers, as well as closing the gap between leaders and employees. In this way, strategy emerges from a cross-organisational conversation.

This conversation can be enabled in many ways. I have supported several executive teams in the design and implementation of face-to-face workshops that set out to engage the organisation in a strategic conversation. Mostly these have been small, around twenty people, which allowed for maximum participation. However, processes such as Future Search, developed by Marvin Weisbord and Sandra Janoff (2010), can bring together up to 100 people in a room or indeed hundreds in parallel rooms. Future Search seeks to bring together a microcosm of the whole system, connecting people across the boundaries of the organisation, and discovering both the common ground and energy to forge new futures together. The principles behind the approach have been tested and proven over three decades.

Murray (2014) describes three parts to powerful conversations—process, themes, and skills. Process refers to how the conversation takes place, how it is enabled, and whether it results in the desired outcomes like increased organisational agility. The second consideration for leaders has to do with themes, more precisely with whether you have framed the conversation correctly, so that it is focused on the right issues and informed by the right content. Finally, powerful conversations require leaders to have the skills required to generate high-quality interactions.

In recent years, social media platforms like Workplace and Yammer have provided a potent tool to connect people across an organisation, mobilising communities of action around strategic priorities, informing and shaping both the dialogue and consequent actions. Bradley and McDonald (2011) describe the emergence of the social organisation and the potential for mass collaboration. They make the point that this does not happen by itself, rather leaders must 'actively nurture mass collaboration around a compelling purpose that is both meaningful to the participants and produces value for the enterprise'. A leader of a global function in a large facilities business spoke to me about the use of digital media platforms within the organisation to test and pilot new ideas and emerging strategic priorities. The company uses social media and mobile platforms to connect and engage a global workforce of several hundred thousand in a discussion around key strategic themes. One conversation around diversity and inclusion prompted some 10,000 comments and replies. Similarly, the Chief People Officer of a software firm with a global footprint described the pervasive use of digital channels in their communication strategy. She went on to outline how the business had used these platforms to engage the whole organisation in a conversation about its values, and how the data and insights this generated continue to be used some time after the conclusion of the initiative.

There is a critical point of intersection here between communication and organisational strategy. When organisations operate under conditions of uncertainty and complexity—and its increasingly difficult to point to organisations for whom this is not true—then strategy formulation can no longer be the preserve of the top team. When strategy evolves through a dynamic process of experimentation, discovery, and learning, rather than a static planning process, opens up the strategy dialogue as a capability in its own right. Yves Doz (2020) and Christian Stadler (2020) are among the leading strategic thinkers who urge organisations to adopt this approach. Doz (2020) argues that, in contrast to a debate where one side seeks to convince others of the merit of their viewpoint, a strategic dialogue with both internal and external stakeholders sharpens strategic sensitivity as participants surface and consider issues, assumptions, and underlying frames. The outcome is deeper insight and the capacity to co-create a better and more innovative solution.

The third communication strategy I continue to see in use, although it is in decline, is the **political approach**. Here leaders withhold information until necessary and when confronted by rumours, they stick tightly to the party line. Secrecy and control are often the implicit values of those who embrace this approach. My favourite mantra, mentioned earlier, that there is no such thing as no communication, applies here again. I recall working on a large-scale change project where I was a member of a change team being supported by external consultants. At the kick-off meeting, one of the consultants shared a timeline outlining the communication activity to the wider organisation that was to start some months into the project. It was emphasised that no communication about the project should be shared before this date. I asked if anyone knew we were meeting that day? This was an off-site meeting, so I imagined that someone else had been involved in booking the room. What had they been told about the purpose of the meeting? How many of those present in the room had shared with colleagues they would be out of the office for two days and had they said anything about why? My point was that everyone in the organisation would already be working with fragments of information, speaking to others in their network to make sense of this, and developing a narrative that would explain what was going on. Any communication vacuum will always be filled and by the time the formal communication starts you are already battling an established narrative.

Of course, there are times when leaders are compelled not to share information, such as the rules governing the disclosure of price-sensitive information for companies listed on stock markets. However, as a rule secrecy is over-rated and can even result in self-inflicted damage. In a recent *Forbes* article, Christian Stadler (2021) identifies the obsession with secrecy as one of the three fault lines in the failed launch of a European Super League in the world of soccer. He argues that strategies most often fail because they are not well executed, and people who are not consulted during the development of a new strategy will most likely resist new strategic initiatives. Many of the most important stakeholders in this project, including managers, players, and fans, were kept completely in the dark. Not surprisingly, when the project was finally announced statements from all three roundly condemned the initiative.

Reflection

- As a leader, is your approach to communication focused on the delivery of carefully crafted messages or generating an organisational conversation?
- What changes do you need to make to how you communicate, in order to engage more effectively?

Effective Leadership Communication

Without doubt, organisations today operate continually under conditions characterised by volatility, uncertainty, complexity, and ambiguity. However, the global pandemic provided a period during which the gauge was turned to high on each of these. In my conversations with top executives, communication surfaces time and again as a critical leadership capability during times that present extraordinary and unprecedented challenges.

I have spoken with leaders from a range of sectors including technology, banking and finance, global facilities management, and public service bodies about how they approached communication during the global pandemic. Several themes and principles emerged that I believe are applicable not just for times of deep crisis, but also provide insights for how leaders communicate with real impact every day, when we operate in a world that is turbulent and constantly changing.

Authentic Communication

Nearly every leader I spoke to about communicating through the pandemic talked about the importance of authenticity, of being real and genuine and creating connections on a human level. Even after more than a decade of intense debate and discussion by practitioners and experts on leadership, the concept of leadership authenticity remains somewhat ill-defined. It is explored in more depth elsewhere in this book, but it is worth commenting on here, as leaders and followers alike consistently link an individual's authenticity to their impact as a communicator. Even if someone is not a polished public speaker, they will have impact if their audience experience them as open and honest, speaking from the heart and meaning what they say.

George and Sims have identified five building blocks of authenticity.

1. **Clarity of purpose**, or as one leader expressed it to me, being clear on the why? Sometimes this can be what Lynda Gratton of London Business School has described as an igniting purpose, one that inspires and mobilises an organisation. Paul Polman, the former chief executive of Unilever, famously challenged the organisation with an ambitious Sustainable Living Plan which aimed to double its growth, halve its environmental impact, and triple its social impact. This was the catalyst that sparked the creativity of employees and resulted in a surge of innovative projects.
2. **Understanding and living your values**. I am impressed by leaders who have clearly thought deeply about their values and can readily articulate them and talk about how their values impact their leadership in real ways. One leader I spoke with described the importance of family as one of his values. What was interesting was how he extended this to his workforce of 2500 employees, interpreting it as a feeling of belonging, of being 'inside the circle'.

3. **Relationships built on accessibility** both physically and emotionally, meaning being open and honest with those around you, including expressing vulnerability.
4. **Resilience in tough times** that is grounded in your purpose and values. One of the most powerful examples I have come across is Maryam Bibi, founder of Khwendo Kor, an organisation based in the remote and undeveloped areas of north-west Pakistan, that seeks to improve the education, health, and economic wellbeing of women and their children. Despite sometimes violent opposition, Maryam has continued to build the organisation, propelled forward by her sense of mission, purpose, and values.
5. **Compassion** characterised by empathy and action to meet the needs of others. Empathy creates a connection with others and demonstrates how the leader shares their hopes and fears.

Several leaders I spoke with shared small, practical examples, of how they had conveyed or demonstrated authenticity when communicating throughout the period of the global pandemic. Simply turning up—being accessible—is the first requirement. Related to this was the intensity of communication, meaning both the pace and regularity with which communication takes place. Many spoke about the need to respond rapidly to a fast-changing situation, where lockdowns and stay at home orders meant transitioning to remote working overnight. For others, the reverse challenge presented itself, in reassuring a team of essential workers that their work environment would be as safe as possible.

In both scenarios, the need to respond quickly, inevitably meant tolerating uncertainty and ambiguity in communication. A key to building trust is to be open about what you know and what you do not know. I have worked with several leadership teams over the years, who held back on communicating until they had answers to most questions that might arise. As I have repeated several times in this chapter, there is no such thing as *no* communication. If you choose not to say anything the vacuum will be filled by greater uncertainty. Even outside of major crises and events like the pandemic, the constancy of change and the pace at which change happens, means that leaders need to embrace ambiguity and be comfortable communicating before they necessarily have the full picture or definitive answers. Uncertainty can destabilise a situation, but Rock points out that relatively minor actions can mitigate against this, for example, simply providing a specific date when people will know more information.

One final point is that, as the intensity of communication increases, the need for leaders to invest more of their time and to be attentive to the conversations they start also increases. One leader described how her company initiated an organisation wide conversation around the theme of 'Black Lives Matter', sparked by the murder and aftermath of George Floyd in May 2020. This involved a series of town hall meetings and online discussions. She described the intensity of feeling that was generated and the deep reflection that took place at all levels of the business. Several employees reached out to her personally to share their experiences and perspectives, and she made the point that many of these messages needed a quick response, so she sat up for several hours, over several nights, ensuring that people who had taken the step to share their story were responded to and felt heard. If you want people to engage with you, then being too busy to engage with them will not cut it!

One interesting observation that was made related to the setting for communications during the pandemic. Most leaders found themselves conducting town hall sessions from their own home, with all the distractions and intrusions that go with domestic life on display. In most instances, this window into their everyday lives presented the leader in a more human light, made them more relatable and created a connection that made their communication more impactful. While the post pandemic setting may revert to more corporate surroundings, the key insight is that making a connection with people on a personal level, that reveals something of the *real* you, provides the foundation of powerful and impactful leadership communication.

Sharing your own personal story is a way to build connection and empathy. One senior leader I spoke to described how he had participated in an online town hall meeting during the pandemic. At the halfway break, he reviewed some of the comments and feedback. This suggested the conversation to date had been overly focused on the state of the business and had failed to reflect or connect with peoples' lived experience at that moment. After the break, he acknowledged the comments and decided to share his own experience of being prevented from attending the funeral of a very close family member. It was an experience shared by several people on the call and struck a chord that everyone was in this together.

The Art of Listening

Of course, before you can demonstrate empathy, you first need to listen. When it comes to communication, particularly during times of uncertainty and crisis, active listening is a key leadership skill. Stephen R. Covey is credited with one of my favourite wall slogans—'Most people don't listen with the intent to understand; they listen with the intent to reply'. In contrast great communicators are, in fact, great listeners. They resist the urge to interrupt and ensure instead that individuals and groups feel listened to. Listening is more than simply hearing; it is also about demonstrating understanding and empathy. A helpful model I came across several years ago captures the art of active listening. The first step is to **listen**, which means blocking out all distractions and providing the individual or group in front of you with your full attention and focus. Secondly, make sure your **body language**, including eye contact or simply nodding your head, conveys to those speaking to you that you are in listening mode. Thirdly, **explore further** what you are hearing, to ensure your interpretation is correct. This might involve asking questions to access the underlying meaning of what is being said. Fourthly, **reflect to the speaker** what you have heard. This involves the skill of paraphrasing, capturing the essence of what has been said and providing further clarification. Finally, **summarise the conversation** and the outcomes. Murray describes a 'listening contract', in which only when employees are convinced that they are being listened to and that their views matter are they ready to listen themselves. Of course, one of the most tangible ways a leader can demonstrate they are listening is to respond and take action to resolve an issue that has been raised. When operating in a VUCA context leaders do not have all the answers; recognising that others have insights that you do not and enabling them to elucidate these are key to effective communication. As such, active listening becomes a critical leadership skill.

Avoiding Corporate Speak

A simple step towards more authentic communication is to avoid using corporate speak or a carefully crafted script, and instead use your own words. One chief executive complained to me that she was regularly presented with draft communications that simply did not reflect the words she would use or her more informal and conversational style. It is important to note that being unscripted is not the same as being unprepared. It is possible, indeed desirable, to put considerable thought and preparation into what you want to say, while still delivering the message in your own words. Another example that was shared with me was leaving the microphones unmuted as leaders chatted informally before the commencement of an online town hall meeting. Those connecting to the meeting get a glimpse behind the curtain, they over-hear 'the conversation before the conversation', something the listener tends to perceive as more spontaneous and real than what takes place once the meet-ing has formally begun.

The Power of Stories

One way of avoiding corporate speak and connecting with people on a more emotional level is to use stories as a vehicle for communication. In contrast to yet another power-point presentation, stories engage people, requiring them to use their imagination, creating in their own mind the film reel of what they are hearing. Stories combine words and images to powerful effect, ensuring that the key messages are recalled long after their telling. One video clip I have shared with many of my executive classes captures President Barack Obama recounting the story of his encounter with a woman in Greenwood South Carolina during his 2008 presidential election campaign. This woman is famous for her chant, 'Fired up! Ready to go!'—something she does at every meeting she attends which prompts everyone in the room to repeat the chant back to her! Sometimes this will go on for several minutes. When Obama tells the story, he shares how the energy generated in the room by this woman transformed his own demeanour on the day and indeed left him feeling fired up and ready to go! Towards the end, Obama explains the meaning of this story—that if one voice can change a room, then one voice can change a city. If one voice can change a city, then one voice can change a state. If one voice can change a state, then one voice can change a nation! The powerful truth at the heart of the story is one of empowerment, that change starts with one voice, one person, and that person can be you.

While the story as Obama relates it delivers a powerful message, it also works for him in several other ways. He speaks about waking up and feeling tired and grumpy, something we can all relate to! With this simple insight, he conveys vulnerability and creates a human connection. His humour is self-deprecating, demonstrates self-awareness and implies that his feet are firmly on the ground despite his elevated status. As he goes on, the story's central character is dressed in a big church hat and in some iterations even has a gold tooth. The scene is of a dark, half-empty community hall, on a damp day with the rain pouring down and an umbrella that does not work. Our minds instantly create the image in our head as a lasting and memorable imprint long after the story is told. Too often some of those executives that have sat in my classes will meet me and shout fired up, ready to go! It is an important reminder that communication is not an exercise in rational explanation. It is fundamentally about making a connection on an emotional level and about how stories, well told, can move people in a way that facts, statistics, and bullet points never can. Of course, the combination of stories and facts, one connecting with the brain, the other the heart, is particularly powerful.

Murray helpfully identifies four types of stories for organisational leaders: the **'who you are'** story that reveals something of the leader; the **'future'** story that provides insights about the future and motivates and inspires people towards realisation of the vision; the **'values at work'** story that vividly illustrates how the company values, too often only written on the sides of pens and the back of business cards, are brought to life in real and meaningful ways; and finally the **'customer'** story that connects the organisation to the difference it makes in the lives of those who use its products and services, providing meaning and purpose.

To link to a key theme in this chapter, stories are only impactful if they are authentic—you cannot just make them up. Ideally, they will be drawn from the leader's own lived experience. Note that being authentic does not mean you cannot or should not practice telling your story. Gareth Jones who was a renowned author and expert on leadership, and with whom I had the pleasure of working on many occasions, used to describe leadership as 'being yourself, more, with skill'. As he loved to point out, too many people overlooked the last two key words—with skill! Practice makes perfect and this is certainly true when telling a story.

Consistency of Words and Actions

Consistency of words and actions provides powerful, visible evidence of authentic leadership. I met with the chief executive of a vital public service, many of whose employees were required to attend the workplace during the pandemic. She described spending a lot of her time speaking to employees and reminding them of the importance of their work to the public and placing the need to be physically present in this context, particularly at this time of crisis. Critically she turned up in the public offices and buildings where her staff were required to be present, clearly demonstrating that she was not asking anyone to do something she would not do herself.

Developing Digital Media Skills

One final observation is the now ubiquitous presence and use of digital tools to drive communication. Of course, during the pandemic, online platforms enabled most organisations to simply keep the show on the road, by facilitating operational communication and co-ordination. However, even before this exceptional circumstance occurred, organisational leaders were already turning to digital media and social platforms to exercise strategic leadership and enable them to connect with and engage employees. All the leaders I spoke with referenced extensive use of collaborative social media platforms within their organisation such as Yammer or Workplace from Facebook, combining this with use of external social media including Twitter, Instagram, and TikTok.

Digital communication tools accelerate the trend towards self-organised discourse in organisations, where conversations extend across business units, functional silos, and geographical boundaries, promoting global teamwork and collaboration. All of this tilts the balance of strategic initiative away from the traditional top-down dynamic towards one that is more bottom-up and organic, amplifying the knowledge and insights of employees at all levels of the organisation. In a complex and fast-moving world, the ability of a leader to be a catalyst, curator, and orchestrator of organisational conversations that capture strategic insights and shape strategic decisions and actions becomes a critical organisational capability and a source of competitive advantage.

To embrace this shift, leaders need to become comfortable with several things. Firstly, becoming their own content creator and editor. One thing that happened during the global pandemic was that leaders were literally left *with* their own devices and *to* their own devices! Stripped of the immediate support of their communications and IT departments, many leaders learned how to shoot and edit material such as a video blog. This real-time communication provides an opportunity for leaders to share what is on their mind at any time, enlivening the communication by re-counting stories of their interactions and experiences throughout the day or week, sharing insights that have emerged from these, and inviting comment and input from people at all levels across the organisation.

Allied to this is a willingness to adapt to an era where the rules of the old corporate communication model, such as a finely honed message, professional production values and most importantly control over how the message lands and circulates, no longer prevail. Instead, leaders need to be satisfied with 'good enough' and be aware that what they produce can be re-packaged and re-purposed, almost at will by others. Earlier in this chapter I discussed the importance of communication networks. The emergence of social media only serves to increase the importance of this point. Knowing who the informal influencers are throughout an organisation and cultivating and growing a group of followers on social media platforms who can spread and reinforce the message become key success factors. Another point I made earlier was that when leaders communicate, the communication process has just begun, not ended. A 'tick box', event-driven mentality to communication can generate a sentiment of 'glad that's over', when something like a town hall has been completed. Of course, the conversation has just begun, and this is even more true when leaders make use of social media tools. What is generated is a dynamic conversation, characterised by interaction where employees engage in the discussion not only with organisational leaders but with each other.

Leaders can often be wary of social media, concerned about loss of control and how things they say can be taken out of context or mis-quoted. They may well hanker after the tried and trusted methods of old. However, put plainly, that ship has sailed! Leaders have little choice but to embrace digital communications. These platforms and channels provide a mechanism to engage directly with employees at all levels, enabling leaders to powerfully shape the organisational discourse as well as tapping into the insights and knowledge that exist there to inform and shape strategy. That provides any organisation with a real edge as it seeks to create value for stakeholders in a fast-changing world.

Conclusion

Most organisations now operate in contexts that are both complex and uncertain. Leadership and organisational communication sit at the nexus of strategy formulation and implementation. Leaders provoke, stimulate, and challenge the organisation by how they frame the organisational reality. Through engaging communication and by connecting people to one another, they are able to tap into the collective intelligence of the organisation, which then allows them to discover the pathway to future success. This critical organisational capability enables organisations to survive and prosper.

Learning Points

1. In a VUCA world, leadership and organisational communication have never been more important, sitting at the nexus between strategy formulation and strategy execution. The leader's task is to create an organisation wide conversation that is continually evolving the strategic posture of the organisation and how this is implemented.
2. Sharing the purpose, values, and culture of the organisation, achieving strategic clarity and alignment, and achieving high levels of employee engagement are all outcomes of effective leadership communication. However, framing the organisational reality is the primary task.
3. Leaders need to understand the dynamics of organisational communication, that their message can be altered within communication networks and how counter narratives emerge. It is critical for leaders to grasp that when they communicate it is the beginning of a process, not the end.
4. There is no such thing as no communication. What leaders need to grasp is that everything is a communication. Even the act of not communicating will be interpreted and imbued with meaning by others. The choice for leaders is not whether to communicate or not, but simply if they wish to actively manage the meaning that their words and actions convey.
5. Effective communication is enabled by leadership authenticity, listening with the intent to understand not reply, avoiding corporate speak and crafting powerful stories to convey a message. In today's world, it also means embracing digital forms of communication and developing basic digital media skills.

References

Ancel, D. (2012, October/November). Using the strategic narrative process to drive organizational alignment. *Workforce Solutions Review*.

Bradley, A. J., & McDonald, M. P. (2011). *The social organisation*. HBR Press.

Cowan, D. (2017). *Strategic internal communication* (2nd ed.). Kogan Page Ltd.

Doz, Y. (2020). Fostering strategic agility: How individual executives and human resource practices contribute. *Human Resource Management Review, 30*, 100693.

Gioia, D. A., & Chittipeddi, K. (1991). Sensemaking and sensegiving in strategic change initiation. *Strategic Management Journal, 12*, 433–448.

Groysberg, B., & Slind, M. (2012). Leadership is a conversation. *Harvard Business Review*.

Murray, K. (2014). *Communicate to inspire. A guide for leaders*. Kogan Page Ltd.

Schein, E., & Schein, P. (2019). *The corporate culture survival guide* (3rd ed.). Wiley.

Stadler, C. (2020). 3 ways to plot your company's strategy in Covid era and beyond. *Forbes.*

Stadler, C. (2021). 3 strategy lessons from the European Super League Fiasco. *Forbes.*

Weick, K. E. (1995). *Sensemaking in organizations.* Sage.

Weisbord, M., & Janoff, S. (2010). *Future search: Getting the whole system in the room for vision, commitment, and action* (2nd ed.). Berrett-Koehler Publishers.

9

Paradoxes in Executive Development

Alan Matcham

Previous chapters have explored how crises are a demanding test of leadership, and offered advice regarding the nature of a leader's relationship with his or her team. Fear and pressure, we have learned, can at times be felt most acutely by the leader, placing a much greater reliance on the team to collaborate and problem-solve effectively. Hierarchy is of limited value in such circumstances, and cooperation often proceeds more effectively without it. Teams can collaborate to determine the objectives, scope, and ideas for dealing with the crisis—aspects more traditionally associated with the leader. Breaking down traditional boundaries between functions, departments, and dispersed operations, as well as hierarchical inflexibilities are an essential precedent to unleashing the potential of a significantly under-utilised resource—our people.

As more frequent major change becomes necessary to counter volatility and complexity in the markets, industries, and the environment, it is essential that we examine how executive education can best contribute. This chapter explores that question with a focus on the way in which executive education can assist organisation leaders in facing unprecedented challenges.

J. Colley, D. Spyridonidis, *Unprecedented Leadership*, Palgrave Executive Essentials, https://doi.org/10.1007/978-3-030-93486-6_9

This chapter will seek to help you answer the following questions:
- How can executive education create the conditions and mindset for effective and rapid change?
- How can the role of collaboration and challenge be captured and directed?
- What is the role of 'executive education' in breaking down traditional boundaries associated with hierarchies and functional, departmental, and geographic boundaries?
- How can executive education create opportunity out of complexity?

Introduction

As executive development seeks to innovate and move forward, corporate learning professionals and programme designers are faced with several interesting paradoxes. This chapter will focus on five in particular:

1. The problem to solve.
2. The focus on hierarchy.
3. The fixation with leadership.
4. The search for certainty and answers.
5. The obsession with content.

Before exploring these paradoxes, it is worth understanding the context within which Executive Development finds itself today.

The Changing Nature of Executive Education

Amongst the most established business schools, it is hard to identify any significant differentiation in terms of content, design, or delivery. All have excellent faculty and subject expertise, and all operate within similarly well-choreographed and administered pedagogical models.

As suggested by Thomas et al. (2013), the main drivers of executive education within business schools tend to be strongly aligned with rankings, revenues, space occupancy, and faculty utilisation over challenging prevailing wisdom and resolving major organisational challenges and bottlenecks.

At an aggregate level, MBA programmes remain popular, whilst Open Programs appear to be in relative decline. Custom or tailored programmes enjoy a better position, however, all is not well, according to Stefan Stern (2010): '*There is a paradox here. The world remains hungry for MBAs and other accredited management qualifications. Business schools are in demand. And yet many of the most distinguished schools are themselves deeply concerned at what they teach, and the way they teach it.*'

The Returns on Executive Education

In my experience, the aims of many executive education programmes are defined in terms of individual learning outcomes and learner satisfaction. Often, they include generalised requirements to:

- Develop broad leadership capability.
- Increase personal understanding of leadership and strategy.
- Stimulate personal growth.
- Become enthused.
- Strengthen the delegates' role as a change agent.
- Reward the staff to improve retention.
- Expose the delegates to the latest thinking.

Millions of dollars are invested each year on executive education, yet the returns remain hard to define.

The impact of most executive education programmes on individual delegates tend to fall into one of three outcomes:

1. Delegates go back to work with greater enthusiasm and try hard to bring about meaningful change. After a period of time, they get sucked back into traditional ways of working and look upon their experience with merely fond memories.
2. Delegates go back to work with greater enthusiasm and try hard to bring about meaningful change. After a period of time, they realise nothing is really going to change. They have 'crossed the Rubicon', there is no going back and so seek to leave the company for pastures new.
3. Delegates go back to work with greater enthusiasm and try hard to bring about meaningful change. After a period of time, they have had some degree of success but realise the ability to change the organisation goes way beyond their individual efforts and frustration grows.

Organisations, particularly in a climate of austerity, now demand the demonstration of a stronger and more direct relationship between their development investments and the performance of the business. This is a challenge for business schools and requires both the shaping of a new relationship with clients as well as a more effective set of design rules for management education.

Time for a New Contract Between Industry and Academia?

At the beginning of November 2010, The European Foundation for Management Development held a one-day conference in Berlin. In attendance was an impressive collection of academics, including business school deans. The aim was to discuss how to remain relevant and effective and avoid the outcome presaged by one senior corporate executive who commented: *'The relationship between business and the school was a kind of co-alcoholism— each dependent on the other, and not in a good way'*.

As the world of work changes, there is an increasing appetite for a new form of engagement between industry and academia. I received a recent request from a major European organisation that highlights this changing shift of emphasis:

Most of the managers have already been through leadership development programs. They understand how they work, but at the same time, pose a challenge: how do we come up with something new and, more importantly, something with high impact? Firstly, any interventions should contain the following aspects:

- An intimate and safe atmosphere in which to be open about personal development.
- Address mind, body, emotions, and soul. Challenge intellectually and explore emotional Intelligence, health (the corporate athlete) and spirituality.
- Action learning to embed in practice as well as the use of new technology in learning.

Their requirements reflect a growing ground swell in the need for management education to link business education with results, to redress the balance between theory and practice, to focus on the whole person not just the intellect, and finally to move from a traditional set of design rules to something more appropriate.

Time for a More Helpful Set of Design Rules?

All approaches to executive education design are underpinned by a philosophy which guides the pedagogical shape of the learning intervention. Historically, design has been shaped by a philosophy more closely linked to that described in the left-hand column of Fig. 9.1. In the context of shifting client needs, where the nature of our relationship with work is changing and where the relentless tides of change seem to be getting stronger, executive education might be better served if it were guided by the design rules summarised on the right-hand side of Fig. 9.1.

Executive education becomes more about exploring complex challenges than seeking one-size-fits-all answers, more about releasing potential than working harder and more about developing greater originality of thought rather than the acceptance of prevailing wisdom.

Paradox 1—The Problem to Solve

The paradox—Executive development is often seen in isolation of context and is all too often characterised as a set of formulaic personal leadership characteristics that will ensure success in any context. Yet understanding context and the nature of the problem to be solved can be the most helpful guide to set the frame for the type of leadership required.

LESS OF THIS	MORE OF THIS
Teacher and Lecturer	Guide and Facilitator
Content Driven, Passive Taught Experience	Discovery driven active lived experience
Learning Outcomes	Performance outcomes
Pre-defined methodology	Co-creation of methodology
Answers without from "experts"	Answers within from knowing self
Best practice - copying others	Original practice - interpreting signals
Outcomes toward corporate learning objectives	Outcomes toward solving serious corporate problems
Transmission of knowledge	Transference of capability
Theory led	Theory challenged
Inspiration from orthodox places and experts	Inspiration from unorthodox places
Lecture theatres	The real world
Judgment of delegates	Unconditional positive regard
Projects	Experiments and tests
Focus on the person	Focus on the person and context

Fig. 9.1 Old and new design rules

Today's business leaders and corporate learning professionals are so busy that the temptation to reach out for ready made, prescriptive, best practice solutions to complex problems is overwhelming. Universities, business schools, consultants, and gurus earn a healthy living off the back of such demand. Consequentially the bookshelves (or Amazon warehouses) are full of 'how to' advice with some of the more familiar titles including:

- The Seven Habits of Highly Effective People (Stephen R. Covey, 1989).
- Stepping Up: How to Accelerate Your Leadership Potential (Sarah Wood, 2017)
- Leading Transformation: How to Take Charge of your Company's Future (Thomas Zoega Ramsoy, Nathan Furr and Kyle Nel, 2018).
- Pivot Points: Five Decisions Every Successful Leader Must Take (Julia Tang Peters, 2014).
- How to Reposition Today's Business While Creating the Future.
- How to win Friends and Influence People (Dale Carnegie, 1936).

Consequentially this leads to the creation of a form of 'plug and play' leadership culture. There is no doubt we all need help in dealing with the complexity of managing and leading in today's exponentially changing world, but it is important we don't ignore the unique context in which we work or the nature of the challenges we face. In the search for the 'right' leadership model, the nature of the problem to be resolved is underestimated at best and overlooked at worst. When discussing executive development, one of the most important questions to ask is: 'What is the problem to which executive development is the answer?'

One of the more common models of leadership is the need to develop 'ambidexterity'—that almost superhuman breed of person who can focus and deliver short-term operational KPIs (Key Performance Indicators), whilst simultaneously serving as an innovative, dynamic, long-term strategic thinker and visionary creating the business of tomorrow.

Perhaps we expect too much of our leaders in asking them to intellectually, behaviourally, and emotionally bounce between the two contexts of running Business As Usual (BAU) whilst trying to create Business As Unusual (BAUU). In doing so, they often fall short on both the operational as well as transformational goals they pursue.

At the conclusion of any executive development programme, it's wonderful to hear delegates say how enjoyable and insightful the experience has been. However, that is frequently followed by, '*But it's back to the grind tomorrow and it's going to be difficult to find the time and space to implement our new insights'*. This reaction could either be a reflection on the inability to deliver an effective learning experience or a sign of the pressure and tensions facing today's executives. There is a significant and growing body of knowledge, along with anecdotal evidence reported in mainstream media that points towards increasing levels of work-related stress, mental illness, anxiety, burnout, and lack of engagement—in short, all is not well emotionally.

Figure 9.2 is an abbreviated excerpt from a genuine role profile of a senior executive within a European-based multinational corporation highlighting the seemingly contradictory demands placed on their business leaders.

On the face of it, the individual profile objectives and behavioural characteristics seem perfectly reasonable. My argument is not with the individual profile requirements but with the way they are bundled into one role profile.

- How well does tolerating failure sit with stretch targets?
- How well does taking smart risks sit with leaner ways of working?
- How well does challenging the status quo sit with operational excellence?
- How well does accelerating change sit with performing beyond expectation?

Goddard and Eccles (2013) explain there are two dominant contexts executives inhabit to greater or lesser degrees—the context of dealing with today (business as usual) versus the context of creating tomorrow (business as

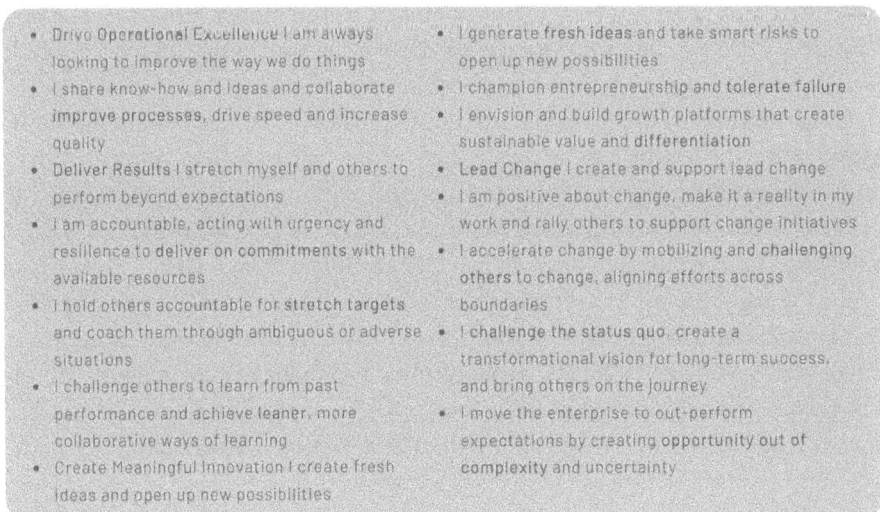

- Drive Operational Excellence I am always looking to improve the way we do things
- I share know-how and ideas and collaborate improve processes, drive speed and increase quality
- Deliver Results I stretch myself and others to perform beyond expectations
- I am accountable, acting with urgency and resilience to deliver on commitments with the available resources
- I hold others accountable for stretch targets and coach them through ambiguous or adverse situations
- I challenge others to learn from past performance and achieve leaner, more collaborative ways of learning
- Create Meaningful Innovation I create fresh ideas and open up new possibilities

- I generate fresh ideas and take smart risks to open up new possibilities
- I champion entrepreneurship and tolerate failure
- I envision and build growth platforms that create sustainable value and differentiation
- Lead Change I create and support lead change
- I am positive about change, make it a reality in my work and rally others to support change initiatives
- I accelerate change by mobilizing and challenging others to change, aligning efforts across boundaries
- I challenge the status quo, create a transformational vision for long-term success, and bring others on the journey
- I move the enterprise to out-perform expectations by creating opportunity out of complexity and uncertainty

Fig. 9.2 Role profile for senior executive

BUSINESS AS USUAL
OPERATIONAL
NARRATIVE

BUSINESS AS UNUSUAL
EXPLORATION
NARRATIVE

What are the targets?

What are the questions to ask?

How do we measure them?

How do we generate ideas?

What do we get in reward for their
achievement?

Can we test the ideas through
experimentation?

Common &
Shared
Purpose

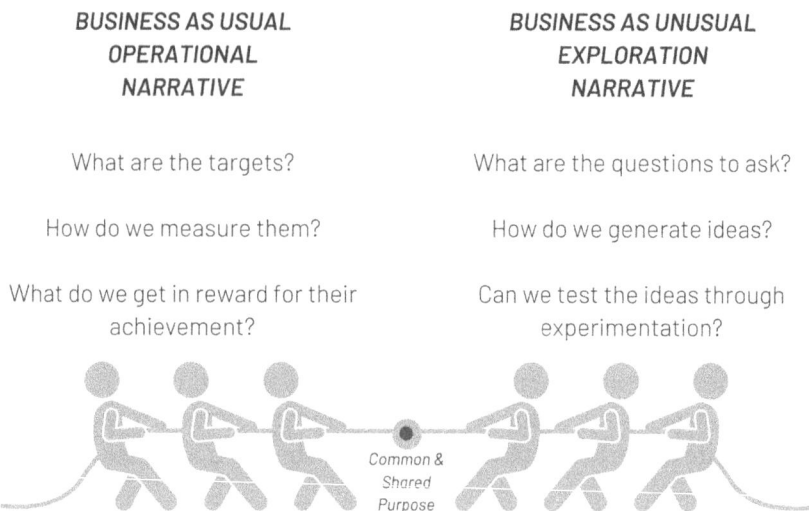

Fig. 9.3 Business as usual/business as unusual

unusual). This thinking is visualised in Fig. 9.3. Its simplicity belies its significance in helping unpick why leaders often fall short in finding the right balance to deal with the challenges they face.

The two contrasting but complimentary worlds, connected through a common and shared purpose, provide the paradigms to both operate an existing business model and reinvent the business model in the face of an exponentially changing world. You could describe the operating side as aspiring to a 'well-oiled machine', and the exploration side as the model for 'out of the box' thinking. Therein lies the essence of many fundamental differences which leaders are finding hard, if not impossible, to reconcile.

Organisations want their executives to transform, be more strategic, more agile, more innovative, more adaptable, more collaborative, more inspiring and differentiated. All are characteristics the exploration side are designed to achieve. However, having asked many delegates, '*Where do you spend most of your time on a day by day, week by week or month by month basis?*' The answer is always the same no matter what the industry—'*We try hard to find the time to innovate and change but constantly get sucked back into business as usual*'. In effect the priorities, rewards, recognition, and behavioural triggers of the operating side regularly over-ride those of the exploration side. This often means leaders frequently find themselves in a vicious 'no win' circle.

Causes of Tension and Trade-offs

Focusing on today's issues is only half the story, and not enough to build an organisation with the capability to respond to complex, often unknown, challenges. History is littered with organisations that have been outmanoeuvred and out thought by those competing for the same space. From the point of view of the business, the ability to navigate the tides of change and thrive over the long term depend on a different set of capabilities and skills to those required in the achievement of more immediate goals.

Of the many tensions and trade-offs between these two paradigms Fig. 9.4 highlights some of the main ones.

The Mindset and Learning Logic

The predominant mindset of running most organisations on a day-to-day basis is, *'We run this business as efficiently as possible, we know what we do, and we'll do it better than anyone else by achieving our KPIs. We need to defend our position in the market and fight all competition that threatens us'*.

The culture is one of implementing against clear guidelines, targets, and rules with limited tolerance or scope for ideas that go against the grain of

Generates Money (hopefully)	Spend Money (short term)
Dominant Mindset - Protect the business model	Dominant Mindset - Challenge the business model
Strategy - Linear extrapolation from the past	Strategy - Future thinking backwards
Challenges - Solutions are known from previous experience	Challenges - Solutions unknown requiring experimentation
Engagement - Compliance and diligence dominate	Engagement - Initiative and creativity are essential
Competitors - Known	Competitors - Unknown
What is Valued - Alignment, consistency, diligence	What is Valued - Original thinking and creativity
Leadership - Authority based on hierarchy	Leadership - Authority based on the ability to engage others
Recruitment - Industry knowledge and expertise	Recruitment - Diverse and not embedded in industry orthodoxy
Measures of Success - Contractual compliance and hitting targets	Measures of Success - Generation of new insights, ideas and options

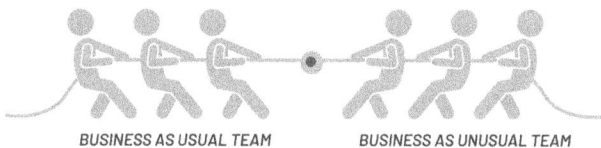

BUSINESS AS USUAL TEAM   BUSINESS AS UNUSUAL TEAM

Fig. 9.4   Tensions and trade-offs

prevailing wisdom. The learning logic is, in effect, a single loop process and broad acceptance of known strategies and assumptions.

The opposite is the case when it comes to leading a group with a mindset dedicated to challenging, new ideas, and experiments. Building a business for the future means: '*everything is challenged. From the assumptions we make about who are our competition to how value is generated, we need to relentlessly try new ideas, experiment, and learn through failure. In doing so, we will stand a better chance of creating competitive advantage. If we don't do it, someone else will*'.

The learning logic is double loop where prevailing wisdom and assumptions are challenged. If leadership is to be ambidextrous, to challenge underlying assumptions one minute, then be asked to implement a corporate standard approach the next requires almost saintly skills and can be a cause of much anxiety for many leaders.

Leadership and the Problem to Be Solved

For many aspects of running 'business as usual', the problems to solve are those intended to incrementally improve what is done already. The conversation can become dominated by best practice and the implementation of the known solutions around established problems.

In the case of unpicking the challenges posed by an uncertain future, the nature of the problem is significantly more ambiguous, uncertain, and far from clear. How to respond to climate change? What are the impacts of emerging technologies? How will consumer profiles shift? Who will be our competition? The resultant implications for style of leadership are profound.

You cannot cost cut your way out of complexity. Leadership's value is based in adopting a highly collaborative, trusting, and facilitative approach, creating the environment for innovative practices and ideas to flourish. Writers such as Ronald Heifetz call this 'Adaptive Leadership'. Less is more in the sense of letting people have the freedom, autonomy, and ability to make decisions in a space where mistakes are expected as part of the process. Any notion of leadership control becomes a function of the individual's approach to building trust and respect, not their role, title, or rank.

The work of Heifetz et al. (2009) and Grint (n.d.) brings into stark relief the importance of understanding and clarifying the problem to be solved before doing anything else. From this, the appropriate leadership approach makes much more sense. Figure 9.5 demonstrates how a 'formulaic' approach to leadership and its development, irrespective of context, is ill-conceived.

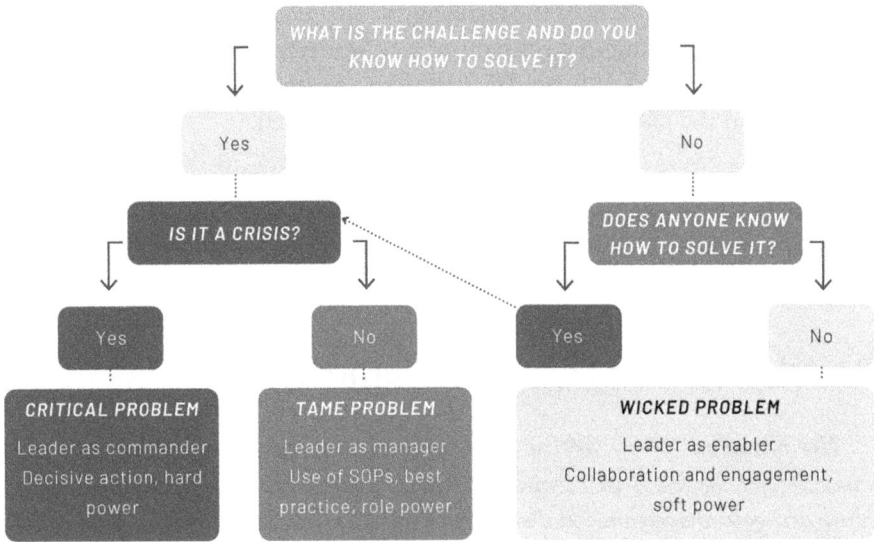

Fig. 9.5 Formulaic approach to leadership and its development

If the problem to solve is a critical one, where life could be at risk with a need for immediate and decisive action, then probably being an experienced, knowledgeable, and skilled dictator would work very well. If it is a problem of a tame or technical nature and you have had experience resolving it previously and there are known solutions, then the leadership role is more about following process and procedure. Finally, if the problem you face is wicked, complex, and adaptive with no known solution, then leadership style favours a collaborative, engaging, and facilitative approach to harness the diversity of talent and perspectives available. The real problem occurs when styles get mixed up with problems—you cannot solve a complex problem by following process or dictatorship and you cannot solve a critical life-threatening problem through endless collaborative meetings.

Whatever the problem and whatever the appropriate leadership style adopted, a shared problem galvanises effort and sharpens the mind like no other issue. It clarifies the nature of the leadership required and what it takes to resolve it.

Three Top Tips

- Understand the context you are working in, as that will help explain and resolve the tensions between seemingly conflicting interests.

- Understand the nature of the challenge or challenges to be resolved because they are a significant determinant of how leadership adds value.
- Avoid one-size-fits-all formulaic solutions, particularly in relation to leadership and the nature of the problem to be resolved.

A business is a community of people working together to create value for other people—customers, team members, shareholders and communities. (John Mackey, Founder and CEO, Whole Foods Market)

Paradox 2—The Focus on Hierarchy

The paradox—*We work in multi-layered, cross-functional teams and communities yet we learn in hierarchies and role-based silos. Organisations consistently struggle to overcome challenges such as silo mentality, trust, collaboration, diversity of thought, innovation and agility so why not have cross functional teams as part of the construct of the learning experience?*

There is an almost unquestioned belief that differing layers of seniority require differing levels of insight and knowledge into how organisations, markets, and people work. This often taken for granted principle behind custom or open executive development programmes takes high potentials and senior managers from the organisation and puts them into discrete cohorts full of people like themselves. We develop executives based on their position in the hierarchy, yet back in the workplace people spend much of their working lives immersed and engaged with teams and communities across the business.

Following Brexit, politicians and business commentators across Europe proclaimed regularly and vociferously that "*markets don't like uncertainty!*" This may well be the case but, whether they like it or not, we live in a far from certain world. Uncertainty is becoming the norm; both governments and business leaders would be better served to think more about how best they can work with, and through complexity, rather than trying to make it go away. Forward thinkers such as Professor Nick Barker at Tomorrowtoday, Professor Ian Goldin at Oxford and Anton Musgrave at FutureWorld spend their careers analysing major global trends and conclude that volatile, uncertain, complex, and ambiguous (VUCA) conditions will become more common not less, occur faster not slower, and have greater impact on the way we live and work.

I'm not saying hierarchically oriented leadership development has no place; it has. But given the nature of the challenges faced by most organisations,

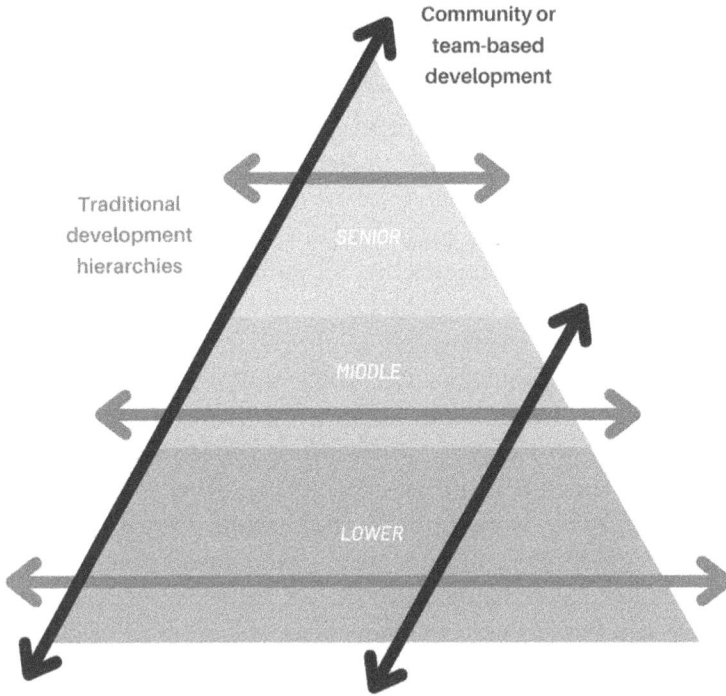

Fig. 9.6   Rebalancing the executive development effort

Fig. 9.6 shows how the executive development effort can be rebalanced from the 'elite' in the hierarchy to cross functional teams and communities, involving all those who do the work, learning together to combat shared business challenges.

A cross-functional community or team is a group of colleagues who share a common aim and are interdependent in the achievement of that aim. They may well be from within the same organisation or include suppliers and partners involved in the collective endeavour. These groups are not to be confused with intact teams of functional specialists such as executive teams, IT, accounts, operations, marketing, sales or finance. They are instead people from across the business, encompassing all functions. The glue that holds them together is a shared business-wide challenge (or opportunity), the type of challenge with no obvious solution, requiring significant amounts of creativity, collaboration, diversity, and perspective.

It is reassuring to hear Heads of Talent Development express their views on the business challenges their talent strategies need to address. The conversations I have been a party to go along the following lines: '*We need to transform the culture of our business and design interventions that enable our leaders to break down silos, collaborate more, improve agility, creativity, engagement, inno-vation, responsiveness and ultimately productivity'*. This is of course perfectly sensible and in a VUCA world few would disagree. The *ends* are consistent yet the *means* in terms of executive development remain stubbornly fixed on developing individual leaders held together only by their similar level of seniority within the hierarchy.

The work of Gratton and Scott (2016) indicates that people and their working life are changing dramatically. Social media trends tell us people are better connected, they collaborate and network more easily, are generally better educated, technically literate, more informed, and have access to unprecedented amounts of information. More of the workforce are 'born digital' and brought up valuing freedom and autonomy over being managed and led. They prefer discussion over prescriptive direction, creativity over process, volunteerism over conscription, and meritocracy over length of service. They are extremely comfortable working in multiple teams, virtual or otherwise; a VUCA world sits more easily with them. These broad observations hold a central truth about our changing world. We are seeing the emergence of a labour force that has less need to be managed and led by a hierarchical elite whose development occurs independently of the broader team or community working relationship.

Why Do We Persist in Developing Leaders in Isolation?

It is right to support any individual who wishes to develop their leadership capability. I have invested many years of my life in designing and delivering leadership programmes for companies around the world. I am, however, of the opinion that delivering learning experiences in a hierarchical model unintentionally creates a disconnect between what is learnt by an elite cohort and what changes back in the workplace. It reinforces the difference between leaders and the led and can build further barriers between those 'that know' and those that 'don't know'.

The work of Pfeffer and Sutton (2006) highlights some of the myths that sustain this hierarchically oriented model of development. They emanate in part from military history and have become embedded into management thinking through the industrial revolution. They are now starting to be seen as increasingly unhelpful in a time of different employee expectations and capabilities, a time of more complex challenges, a time of less dependence and deference towards seniors and authority.

Four commonly held myths include:

- *Myth 1—Leaders are essential.* Self-organising and self-regulating groups and communities of people do not need one leader. Different individuals rise to the challenge supported by colleagues in a common bond or cause. There are many examples of this exemplified by the Dutch healthcare supplier Buurtzorg.
- *Myth 2—We can control performance through strong leadership.* There are so many variables impacting the creative and dynamic process of running a business. The context we operate in and the principles, processes, and practices we work with have all been seen to have a significantly greater impact on human performance than 'strong leadership'. The work of the late Professor W.E. Deming and latterly Paul Dolan, Professor of Behavioural Economics at the LSE, suggests context is well over 80% responsible for performance particularly when undertaking complex interdependent tasks.
- *Myth 3—People like being managed and leaders motivate people.* Organisational health Index research by McKinsey & Company back in October 2013 suggests most senior people and leaders have an over inflated view of their importance, impact, and influence on others in getting work done. It is also well documented that a significant proportion of people who leave organisations do so because of a poor relationship with their boss not because of the organisation. For many leaders doing nothing is not a natural option; bosses find it difficult to just get out of the way.
- *Myth 4—Leadership is all about the individual.* Organisations are communities of people, not collections of human resources. What Professor Henry Mintzberg feels required is greater 'communityship'. It cannot just be about the individual and their unique talents; it is about the release of potential from the entire group and their collective 'leadership' contribution to a cause worth serving. Leadership needs to evolve into becoming a corporate capability not something resident in the few.

If these myths persist, executive development will continue to be structured along traditional lines and hierarchical structures. My contention is that these myths are just that, not absolute facts of life that are true all the time under all conditions. They might hold some truth some of the time but increasingly less so, particularly in a VUCA world. The time has come for a new approach to challenge these myths with one that supports a more team and community-based approach to developing leadership capability.

The Benefits of Cross-functional Team/ Community-based Development

By taking a cross-organisational/cross-functional slice of people and developing them as a cohesive cohort, there are significant benefits that can accrue which include:

- *Breaking down silos and stimulating collaboration*—One of the most common issues in all large organisations is the 'silo mentality'. Bringing cross-functional teams together defuses and reframes this mentality.
- *Building mutual respect, trust, and understanding*—A shared intellectual and emotional experience, if executed well, builds close bonds and ties. Effective learning requires personal disclosure and taking risks which cannot normally be achieved in the working environment.
- *Replicates the real world*—It becomes much easier and quicker to translate from the intervention to the workplace. The learning that takes place in many development programmes has a very short half-life beyond the programme. People get sucked back into the prevailing culture of day-to-day work and find it very difficult to put new insights into practice. Having all the key players together establishing new norms greatly increases the chances of success.
- *Diversity and perspective*—One of the keys to improving creativity and innovation is diversity of thought, values, and experience. The resolution of complex adaptive challenges will not emanate from a group of likeminded individuals. Constructing a learning experience with people from a variety of backgrounds within and across the business adds to the richness of the debate and hence options available.
- *Opportunity to work on genuine shared challenges*—This is the glue that bonds teams and communities. Having a common focus is one of the most powerful ways of translating new insights into positive change and reduces the rhetoric/reality gap often found in many development programmes. The gap between what is said and what is done narrows if the team collectively learn by doing.
- *Reframes the nature of and responsibility for leadership*—Bringing together cross-functional, interdependent teams allows the opportunity for leadership to be understood and practiced by everyone, not just the most senior people. Opening up to new ways of thinking requires leadership, the courage to speak up requires leadership, the organisation of activity requires leadership, and the creation of new solutions requires leadership. This has a chance to come from the many, not the few.

Case Study: Experimental Development Programme

During 2020, I was engaged to deliver an experimental programme involving 21 delegates from five different organisations. The delegates were drawn from different levels of seniority and ranged from departmental heads of multinational corporations to champions of the rights of minority groups.

The key things they had in common were:

- A mandate to lead and enable 'change'.
- A thirst for learning, but knowledge that they needed further help and support.
- A curiosity about what others were doing and thinking.
- An intrinsic sense of purpose and motivation towards the impact they could make.

Mainly due to COVID-19, this experimental programme was delivered online over a period of nine months and contained a combination of online seminars, 1:1 development dialogues and virtual action learning set sessions. Over the life of the programme, a deep level of intellectual intimacy was attained between all those involved allowing trust, respect, and collaboration to thrive. The myth that delivering online cannot replicate the face-to-face experience was shown to be a half-truth at best.

The outcomes delighted all those involved and include:

- Learning from each other by being exposed to many different perspectives and hierarchical positions.
- Feeling connected and not alone by realising they had so much in common.
- Making real change by understanding how to influence without line authority.
- Realising seniority is not that relevant in the pursuit of knowledge and enablement of change.
- A collective shift in thinking from 'What do I want to do' to 'Who do I want to be'.

Three Top Tips

1. If your organisation wrestles with a silo mentality, agility, responsiveness, innovation, and lack of cross-border collaboration, then look to include all the main players in your development efforts. Draw from partners both within and outside the organisation.
2. Make explicit and challenge the prevailing wisdom and assumptions that shape the nature of your approach to executive development. You may well find they are unhelpful or obsolete.
3. Listen carefully to the voice of the new generation of employees, particularly what they value, how they work, and what they need from an employer. They have been brought up in a different context to that of previous and current leadership.

> Leadership is focused on the individual. What we need is communityship. Organisations are communities of people not collections of human resources. (Henry Mintzberg)

Paradox 3—The Fixation with Leadership

The paradox—*There are a plethora of books, articles, videos, and blogs on leadership. At the last count, a mind boggling 2,500,000,000 results for "leadership" on Google. Many are authored by commentators, sports professionals, academics, former captains of industry or business leaders. Yet it is very hard to believe that people are born with an overwhelming desire to be led or managed by another individual. It is difficult to find anything written on leadership by those who spent a lifetime being led and managed.*

Henry Mintzberg (2009) suggests that we are in danger of being over-led and over-managed as a working population. What is proposed is a rebalancing from developing individual capability, towards developing 'context architects'—people who create meaning and purpose at work and the conditions for colleagues to flourish. Mintzberg comments that leadership and management are indivisible. *'You can't have a leader who doesn't manage because they won't know what's going on and you can't have a manager who doesn't lead because that would be demoralising'.*

A New Context

Most commentators agree that modern leaderships roots were established during the industrial revolution, reinforced by generations of societal norms ingrained with a deference to authority and servitude towards hierarchy. These forces have undoubtedly contributed to a post-industrial fixation with the 'leader and the led' model, coupled with a dominant paradigm based on efficiency—in effect, 'how do we get more from our people'.

Explicitly or implicitly the legacy of such a fixation remains within many of today's organisations and is visible within organisational charts, role profiles, audible through corporate language and experienced through bureaucracy. Whilst there are many great organisations trying to develop a more enlightened leadership approach there is still a deep seated, often unconscious belief within many of the business elites that the use of authority and imposition of control over subordinates is the main tool for mobilising work.

What Is Leadership's Value Today?

Leadership's value is often justified by stating it provides direction, motivation, decision making, resources, information, control, vision, and strategy. The trouble is that these value points are now under severe threat from a society that is more educated, has access to more information, more communication tools, more ideas, more connectivity, and creative experiences than ever before. I hesitate to label this population as Generation X, Y, or even Z because it is not just about the internet generation.

The ability of people to look after their own affairs, manage their own lives, make their own decisions is constantly underestimated by business leaders and managers.

Case Study: Drachten

Drachten is a small town in the Netherlands which, over time, became crowded, congested, and unpleasant to be in. It was crammed with traffic management signage: no entry, stop, directions, cross here, no parking, one way, speed restrictions, and so on.

To make the town environment more attractive, a more pleasant place to live, work, and visit, and after lengthy debate, the council decided to remove all the traffic management signage. The outcry from many leading local dignitaries was anticipated—*"There will be an increase in accidents, death on the road, control will be lost, chaos and carnage will ensue!"*

The reality was completely the opposite. There was a decrease in accidents, a compliance with speed limits and an increase in wellbeing. Why was this? Responsibility for behaviour was transferred from the traffic management signage to the citizens and visitors. Over time people took more care, became more cautious and respectful of others. They demonstrated they were perfectly capable of managing their lives without being told where to go, when to stop, and what to do.

In short, leadership and management came from within and between people, not externally imposed.

Academics call the Drachten experience an example of a self-organising system. What was once thought fanciful is now a reality. We are seeing the emergence of a global population that is increasingly self-confident, willing, and able to be:

* *Self-managed* in terms of how group/team decisions are made, and resources allocated. Control is exercised through consensus and transparency not by imposition.

- *Self-motivated* in terms of what they do and why they do it. Research studies over the years suggest people tend to leave bosses not organisations because they are treated as human resources rather than resourceful humans.
- *Self-directed* in terms of setting their own goals and priorities. As humans, we tend to expect more from ourselves, setting tougher and more demanding targets than others do.
- *Self-oriented* in terms of their learning and development. Steven Pinker (2019) makes the case for human progress and societies being more educated than ever been. Self-actualisation increasingly comes about as a consequence of finding your own purpose, meaning, and belonging.
- *Self-assured* in terms of independence of thought, contributing to debates, and not having ideas imposed.

Jules Goddard (2006), Fellow at London Business School, makes the point that deference towards all forms of authority and the institutions they represent is diminishing as is the sense of servitude towards hierarchy. People are looking for a greater sense of meaning (purpose), a sense of self (identity), and affiliation (belonging) in their life, which are not fulfilled through corporate life or indeed many of the traditional institutions in society that historically have been provided by organisations or movements such as the church.

What Does This Mean?

Many organisational agendas and hence executive development objectives are focused on some form of transformation as organisations seek to become more collaborative, agile, innovative, digitally savvy, adaptive, and creative.

The response to developing these capabilities is unlikely to be found in a 'leader and the led' model but in a new performance paradigm based on: 'How do we inspire people so that they give their talents and efforts willingly?' We are in a new context and leaderships' challenge is to reposition its value proposition if it is to remain relevant and impactful.

In the face of this shift, leadership's opportunity to establish its contemporary value is threefold:

1. **The creation of meaning and purpose**

This is not to be confused with the communication of corporate values, mission statements or corporate social responsibility initiatives. It is the requirement of leadership to provide a deeper sense of meaning as to why work is important and how it can support a greater sense of individual and collective identity.

W. L. Gore is recognised as one of the most sought-after companies in the world to work for. They are a non-hierarchical organisation based more on a lattice network of relationship with no traditional role titles other than associate. They embrace the changing nature of leadership. If someone wants to hold a meeting and nobody turns up, then the matter is deemed not that important. However, if people do turn up, then the matter is deemed 'important', consequentially the meeting host is likely to become the de-facto leader if things move forward.

2. The creation of context

The work of Dr. W.E. Deming in relation to quality and continuous improvement plus the work of Daniel Kahneman and the Behavioural Economics movement remind us that contextual conditions are over 80% responsible for driving performance, not the well-intentioned and often 'heroic' efforts of individuals and their leaders. This alone should inform executive development professionals to rethink where to focus the executive programme effort when it comes to improving performance.

By any measure, the internet is the most powerful example of context providing a liberating and enabling space on a global scale. It has truly changed everything. Never before have people had access to so much information, the use of so many creative tools and are able to freely express their point of view without having to be told, have direction, or set targets.

Organisations find it hard to transform because the change in paradigm from leader as master to leadership as enabler is too big a jump. It was only when HCL Technologies, one of the world's leading software service's companies, was on the brink of collapse did they invert the pyramid and implement their 'Employee first, Customer second' philosophy making all managers and leaders answerable to employees.

3. The creation of a new leadership paradigm

Goddard and Eccles (2013) conclude that *'Ordinary people in extra ordinary organisations consistently outperform extra ordinary people in ordinary organisations'*. Not seeing leadership as a set of personal characteristics imbued within specific individuals but as an organisational capability within the collective talents of everyone.

This means avoiding building organisations and teams that are dependent upon the heroic actions of the few in favour of building an organisation or team where everyone is capable of great things. Leadership is distributed, and the organisation thrives in the face of personality changes. As a result, share prices don't plummet when a CEO decides to leave.

Case Study: Lithuanian Basketball Team

Basketball is the most popular sport in Lithuania, despite not having any individual world-class players and, for such a small country, it is immensely successful in international tournaments.

Almost irrespective of who is playing, they have developed a system which brings out the best in each player, both individually and collectively. Lithuanian American basketball coaches and players in the 1930s helped the Lithuania men's national basketball team win the last EuroBasket tournaments prior to World War II, in 1937 and 1939, causing a massive impact in Lithuanian society and a basketball popularity spike. Since then, despite Lithuania's small size, with a population of almost 2.9 million, the country's devotion to basketball has made them a formidable force across Europe and internationally.

After the restoration of Lithuanian independence in 1990, the national team was resurrected, with their first official tournament being the 1992 Olympics, where they won a bronze medal. The Lithuanians have since won another two bronzes at the Olympics, a bronze medal at the 2010 FIBA World Championship and five EuroBasket medals, including the country's third title at FIBA EuroBasket 2003 in Sweden.

Three Top Tips

- Think less of leadership as a set of skills imbued within specific individuals and more as a capability across the whole organisation.
- Avoid over emphasising the leadership card and place more faith in people's ability to manage their own circumstances. When they leave work, they manage a plethora of complex situations from personal finance to bringing up families, why should that change when they come to work?
- If you feel you have 'mission critical' employees, then you have consciously or otherwise built weak links into your organisation and not a system that is more resilient and taps into the available collective talent.

As managers most of what we take as fact is not so. It is no more than a naive theory of human behaviour. (Jeffrey Pfeffer)

Paradox 4—The Search for Certainty and Answers

The paradox—*As insight and knowledge grow a realisation dawns that there is so much more to learn and understand—"the more you know the more you realise what you don't know". From certainty emerges uncertainty, from knowing emerges not knowing, more questions and more enquiry. Executive development becomes best served by being a never-ending journey of exploration, not an ad hoc refuelling station for the latest answer.*

Fashions and Fads

The literature on leadership and management development is littered with 'the latest thing', fuelled, in part, by research from institutions and academics across the world. Such fashions and fads are designed to offer business leaders certainty, solutions, hope, and answers to the challenges they face. One minute, it is all about customers, quality, empowerment, and wellbeing, and in the next phase, the focus is on re-engineering, sustainability, resilience, and purpose—the list is seemingly never ending. Commentators such as Richard Pascale have mapped such changes since the 1950s showing that the production of business fads and fashions equates to almost one per year.

What is driving this relentless pursuit of trying to find certainty, the answer or one best way? At one level, it can be seen as part of the healthy overall development of insights through research and a growing appreciation of how the world of work works. Insight builds upon insight, and we start to put pieces of the jigsaw together. At another level, it plays directly into the hands of how we are as humans. Behavioural science, particularly the work of the UK Government Nudge Unit and their MINDSPACE model (n.d.), demonstrate nine generic principles of the human condition. As a species, we like to be liked, we do not like uncertainty, our minds tackle the future by referring to the past and we like to be the same as others.

A Far from Certain Science

Unlike physics where the outcomes of any action are more certain and predictable, the art of leadership and the management of others is a social science with no absolute right answer, no absolute truth, and no absolute right way. Jeffrey Pfeffer (2018) illuminates this as shown in Fig. 9.7, an adaptation from his work to show how leaders often base their decisions on 'naïve theory',

BELEIFS AND ORTHODOXIES COME IN MANY FLAVORS

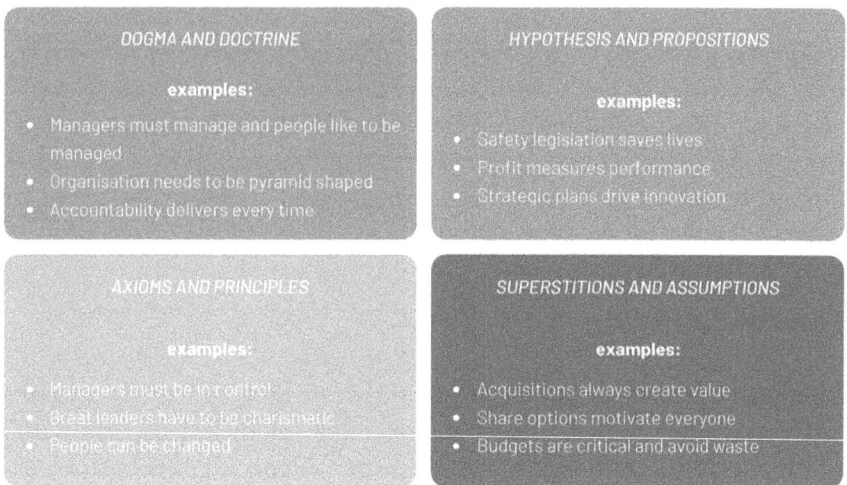

DOGMA AND DOCTRINE

examples:

- Managers must manage and people like to be managed
- Organisation needs to be pyramid shaped
- Accountability delivers every time

HYPOTHESIS AND PROPOSITIONS

examples:

- Safety legislation saves lives
- Profit measures performance
- Strategic plans drive innovation

AXIOMS AND PRINCIPLES

examples:

- Managers must be in control
- Great leaders have to be charismatic
- People can be changed

SUPERSTITIONS AND ASSUMPTIONS

examples:

- Acquisitions always create value
- Share options motivate everyone
- Budgets are critical and avoid waste

Fig. 9.7 Beliefs and orthodoxies come in many flavours

natural bias and beliefs grounded in dogma, axioms, superstition, and hypothesis.

Every leadership team I have worked with has to some degree been influenced by what I refer to as 'the forces of sameness'. These forces are beliefs, norms, and behaviours which feed off our natural desire to follow the crowd, to be the same, to be identified as one of the team, for example:

Best practice—this has become an industry within its own right and based on the principle of 'who is doing the best out there and let's copy them.' In effect, outsourcing one's creativity, innovation, and thinking to keep up with the crowd.

Behavioural norms—we are heavily influenced by the way others behave particularly if it's someone we relate to, trust, and can identify with. It is not unusual for aspiring business leaders to unconsciously adopt the approach of others they admire.

Addiction to consultants—organisations purchase consulting services because they feel they neither have the time or expertise to do it for themselves. The assumption being that purchasing from a consulting firm will provide some guarantee or certainty of outcome. In truth, consulting firms sell the same services to many different clients levelling the playing field as they go.

IT solutions—like consulting, IT firms sell more or less the same solutions to many different organisations such as HRM, supply chain CRM, and finance systems. It is often said that an IT director has never been fired for implementing Oracle, SAP, or Microsoft.

The Value of Business Schools

In the face of this tsunami of bias, fashions, fads, initiatives, and behavioural influences, it is remarkable to think that the strategic *raison d'etre* of most organisations is to be different rather than the same as its competition. Marketing theory tells us competitive advantage via developing a unique selling proposition is crucial to success, yet that requires leaders and leadership to be and think differently not the same.

In this context, the role and value of business schools in developing leaders should not be to proliferate best practice but explore new practice, not to accept orthodoxy but challenge it, not to teach theory but experimentation, not to learn from the mainstream but from the unorthodox. It becomes less about the pursuit of certainty and more about living with uncertainty, the development of a leadership culture which embraces curiosity and doubt in seeking more helpful and innovative ways of thriving in an exponentially changing world.

A key component of developing new perspectives is the ability and willingness to step out of your own shoes and into someone else's, to see the world afresh, to see the world from a new perspective—this is called discovery learning. Albert Szent-Gyorgi, the Nobel prize winning biochemist, calls discovery, '*Seeing what everybody has seen and thinking what nobody has thought.*' It is the relentless search for new insights and perspectives. And once identified, it is then to test new hypothesis and see if they can provide different answers and solutions to the challenges faced.

I have led discovery learning experiences all over the world, a selection of which is given in Fig. 9.8. Each experience was specifically designed to provide a different and unique perspective on a significant corporate challenge.

The principle of discovery is to seek learning in everything and, in doing so, challenge the prevailing orthodoxy in which many leadership teams find themselves mired. It is rare to find innovation and creative thinking stimulated where everyone is aligned, thinking, and behaving in the same way. The challenge for business schools as they create their executive development programmes is to rethink their own value proposition and to not be led by rankings, faculty utilisation, and space occupancy. These will follow if the proposition is right.

DISCOVERY EXPERIENCE	NEW PERSPECTIVE ON...
Junior school in rural China	Challenging and changing the system of learning
Monastery	Reflection and contemplation
IT firm run by disabled people	Overcoming adversity
Flower market in Holland	Rapid decision making and precise process execution
Blind/sight impaired community	Working with all of one's senses
Earth Hour (part of WWF)	Influencing with impact and limited resources
Creating and reciting poetry	Effective communication, confidence building and meaning making
Rowing	Team work and co-ordination
Playing jazz & blues	Creativity, agility, and team work
Prisoner reform group	Changing behaviours and mindsets
Oil company	Innovation at scale

Fig. 9.8 Discovery learning experiences

The Implications for Leadership

It has been said that 'Wise leadership acknowledges the frailty and fallibility of its own judgement'. This is counter intuitive to many schools of thought which espouse a view that leadership needs to have the answers and failure is not an option. Today's operating environment is far from stable and far from predictable making fallibility and frailty an asset as we seek new ideas, new insights, and new ways forward.

Three Top Tips

- In the social science of leadership and management never assume anything is fact and correct all the time.
- In today's operating context, embrace and work with uncertainty; it will prove to be a much more healthy, productive, and enlightening path to follow.
- Commit yourself and your colleagues to seek learning in everything, particularly away from the mainstream. It will build up your personal and collective capability to see the challenges you face from new and diverse perspectives.

The truth is that today's executives are cognitively fit, but emotionally troubled—and in need of help. (Jules Goddard)

Paradox 5—The Obsession with Content

The paradox—Unique executive education content is important, after all there is no learning without theory, but in a world of information overload, demanding performance targets and growing levels of anxiety, leaders increasingly value networking and sharing personal experiences over the injection of yet more content, more concepts, and more models.

The pressure to perform and hit targets, goals, and milestones is felt by everyone in organisational life, not just leadership, and this shows no signs of abating. According to Jeffrey Pfeffer (2018) *'Many decades of research and teaching by both myself and colleagues around the effect of high-commitment, or high-performance work practices on productivity and other dimensions of organisational performance had resulted in little or no positive change. Notwithstanding the publication of numerous books on this topic, workplaces were, if anything, getting worse with less employee engagement and satisfaction and diminished trust in institutional leadership'.*

Edward Segal (2021) refers to a study which includes data from 15,000 leaders and 2102 human resource professionals representing more than 1740 organisations. To summarise:

- Nearly 60% of leaders reported they feel used up at the end of the workday, a strong indicator of burnout.
- Approximately 44% of leaders who feel used up at the end of the day expected to change companies in order to advance.
- 26% expected to leave within the next year.
- Only 20% of surveyed leaders believed they were effective at leading virtually.

Further insights come from an article on the BBC website, 19 November 2019: '*Meetings at work should be seen as a form of "therapy" rather than about decision-making, say researchers*'. Academics from the University of Malmo in Sweden say meetings provide an outlet for people at work to show off their status or to express frustration. Many managers do not know what to do and people like to talk as it helps them find a role.

Case Study

During the height of the COVID-19 pandemic 2020/21, I led an online leadership development programme consisting of 25 delegates from a large European services company. It quickly became apparent just how much pressure the delegates felt under to not just undertake the programme and juggle complex personal issues, including childcare and home schooling, but also to deal with the unrelenting pressure to deliver on their work commitments. Many delegates felt they had no choice but to miss programme sessions because of these conflicting pressures.

As the programme progressed, a survey was undertaken to understand exactly how the delegates were emotionally. The results were concerning yet not surprising with feelings of exhaustion and frustration leading the way. The respondents were asked: 'Think back on your last two weeks of work. How did work make you feel?' They were then asked to choose a maximum of five emotions from a long list to indicate their most frequent emotions. Those emotions with the highest per cent by far turned out to be 'frustrated', 'anxious/worried/fearful', and 'drained/exhausted'.

Allowing for the unique and quite exceptional context COVID-19 created, this was a group of highly talented business leaders at the limit of their tolerance, trying to reconcile seemingly irreconcilable priorities despite best efforts. This, unfortunately, is not uncommon in modern corporate life.

Delegates attending executive development programmes are already often physically and emotionally exhausted, only then be met with a barrage of topic-specific content ranging from strategy to high-performing teams, innovation to agility, and employee engagement to decision making. It is often the case that the delegates undertaking such programmes have already had some form of further education, been on other courses and attended a variety of in-company programmes. On top of all that and thanks to the internet, they now have unprecedented access to a vast range of materials from Ted Talks to journals, from periodicals to papers, and from blogs to books. Just about every topic you can think of which is relevant for leaders to know about is available and accessible. Business executives, in the main, do not suffer from a lack of content; quite the opposite, they can and often do feel overwhelmed by what is available. The value therefore that business schools can bring should not be to add yet more content. They should spend time helping delegates navigate through it but importantly focus time on the emotional dimensions of being a healthy, well-adjusted human being.

The Implications for Executive Development

Increase networking and peer-to-peer conversations—The opportunity to network invariably scores high on feedback sheets. It is recognised that leaders learn more on the job and from each other than in classrooms. Anyone who has taken part in an executive education programme will have noticed that the level of energy, noise, interaction, and conversation rises significantly during the coffee breaks and informal sessions. Once back in the classroom its back to the serious business of learning and content absorption. Trying to apply oneself to what is being taught is an altogether different feel and atmosphere. I have spoken often to my fellow Programme Directors about what lessons we can learn from the coffee breaks. Lesson one is to not over-engineer programmes and build in time and space for emergence. Lesson two is to not lecture delegates; the teacher is best served taking the position of a fellow learner and facilitator. Lesson three is to build in more purposeful coffee breaks, giving the delegates a focus for their conversation. Lesson four is to reverse roles and allow the delegates time to be teachers.

Find time for emotions—Over the years, my colleagues and I have often commented that certain programmes have felt more like therapy sessions than a learning experience. Having a pent-up desire to get things off their chest, have a good moan and offload their frustrations. I have grown to appreciate just how important this is. An essential pre-requisite is to find time and space to give the delegates a 'damn good listening to' before moving forward. In addition, it is helpful to provide delegates with a clear, more academic, understanding of the role of emotions and feelings, particularly in the context of decision making. This combination of informality, timing, and formal understanding can then clear the path for other issues and topics to be explored and discussed.

Release the fear of 'failure'—Fear of failure is a cause of anxiety and stress. Success is rewarded and failure frowned upon in many organisations; yet 'failure' is the essential ingredient to uncovering new insights and the lifeblood of innovation. The late education guru Sir Ken Robinson in one of his many Ted Talks said, *'If you are not prepared to be wrong, you'll never come up with anything original'*. Unfortunately, fear of failure runs deep. From the day we enter school, we are taught there is a right and a wrong answer and the whole education system is based on that premise. Unfortunately, this paradigm then continues into the world of work. A time to break that fear should be integral to an executive development experience by providing a safe place for freedom of thought, freedom of expression, the ability to challenge prevailing wisdom and experiment with new ideas.

Reduce the content—No one doubts the value of great content, that which reveals new insights and perspectives; however, there is a better balance to be found building in more time for delegates to talk about themselves and their context, to share their life experiences, and to realise they are as much a teacher as they are a pupil. The maxim of 'less is more' is increasingly appropriate. In their working life, most of what executives learn is done on the job. One of the most effective tools I have come across to unpick the emotional, experiential, and intellectual journey of delegates is the 'lifelines' model which highlights the main events in someone's life that have shaped who and what they are today. It depends on the delegates as to how much detail they wish to include, but the process invariably leads to a deeper and quicker appreciation of what is really going on with delegates and also helps build trust long before more academic subjects are discussed.

Teach faculty how to teach—My former colleague at London Business School, Jules Goddard comments: *As teachers we lecture far too much. As a result, our students learn far too little*. At the beginning of my Programme Directing career, this came as a bit of a surprise but as the years rolled by, I began to understand the wisdom of his observation.

University lecturers, subject matter experts, and specialists are rarely taught how to teach. Despite that, they end up at the sharp edge of delivering most executive development programmes. These are individuals who, because of having 'unique' insight into a particular subject area, are known for what they know. As such, many have a vested interest in lecturing or telling others what they know rather than engage in debate, questioning, and exploration.

We learn very little from being lectured at and somewhere down the line this seems to have been lost. Confucius summed it up well when he said: '*I hear, and I forget. I see and I remember. I do and I understand*'. It is time to ensure all teachers are taught how to teach executives, how to engage business leaders and how to bridge the divide described by Jeffrey Pfeffer as 'The Knowing-Doing Gap'.

Rethink the learning environment—Behavioural science tells us we are much more creative, more engaged, and more expansive in our thinking if we work in large, well-ventilated open environments versus more enclosed, regimented spaces. It is one of the unconscious 'nudges' all humans respond to which makes us feel more human and more connected.

Universities and business schools invest heavily in physical infrastructure, state of the art classrooms, lecture rooms, and amphitheatres where they ask delegates to sit in uniform rows of seats within often bland, sterile environments. It is almost as though they are designed for control not collaboration with the lecturer being the focal point of attention. Knowingly or otherwise, they accentuate the teacher and the taught, the master and the pupil, those who know and those who do not know. In the world of executive development, this is spectacularly unhelpful and does little to help delegates engage, network, and debate.

Case Study

In 2016, I was working for an independent leadership development company that was primarily made up of freelance experienced programme directors. Traditionally, we delivered programmes on the client site or in hotels around the world. The opportunity arose to design a leadership programme for 26 delegates from a large European-based financial services company. The client wanted it 'to be different'.

All the delegates were UK-based but half of the programme was delivered in The Netherlands. The site we chose was a renovated warehouse next to a canal in central Amsterdam. It was a building constructed in the eighteenth century with all its stunning character preserved. There were rich oak floors scarred with history and a large open-plan space where we could reconfigure the furniture to suit our needs. We could write on the walls, use the latest technology, enjoy the refreshments on hand, and open the windows onto the canal to soak up the atmosphere of this remarkable city.

It was a space that lifted the spirits and engaged everyone, a place of learning the delegates loved. It was different, it was new, it was inspiring. Above all, it was as far away from corporate life as you could get.

The late Professor Sumantra Ghoshal from London Business School sums up the feelings we had in Amsterdam from his own experience: '*I now spend a lot of my time working at INSEAD in the beautiful surroundings of Fontainebleau and when I can I go home I go to see my family and friends in India. When I'm in India, the temperature is high, it's very humid and oppressive and I spend most of my time resting and giving the appearance of not doing much at all. When I go back to work in Fontainebleau, the air is cooler, the environment more pleasant and generally less oppressive, in fact I get up much earlier and jog to the office sometimes. I feel much more alert, bright, and alive in such conditions.*

Interestingly, I am exactly the same person in India as I am in France and yet my whole level of wellbeing and activity is significantly different from one place to the other'.

Three Top Tips

- If you try to make learning a purely intellectual exercise it will fail. Ample time needs to be found for delegates to recharge their emotional batteries.

- The context within which we learn is crucial; there is a direct relationship between the emotional and intellectual engagement of delegates and the space within which it takes pace.
- Teachers and lecturers should not sit outside the learning experience but be an integral part of it just as much as the delegates. In doing so, this enhances learning to build empathy, trust, and mutual understanding.

Summary

Life is full of paradox and the world of executive education is no exception—it simply reflects the nature of life itself. However, an increasing amount is expected from those in positions of influence and leadership today which provides both a challenge and an opportunity for those of us who commission, design, and deliver executive education programmes.

What seems to be evident is that many of the paradoxes I have described can be resolved and reconciled. They do have solutions and they do have alternatives. My contention is that to stay relevant, viable, and valuable, business schools need to reflect deeply on their role in helping delegate organisations fulfil their ambitions and resolve their challenges. That shift in proposition includes:

- Moving from a focus just on the individual to a greater focus on the context.
- Moving from cohorts of 'sameness' to cohorts crossing over hierarchies and functions.
- Moving from leadership as a set of individual skills sets to an overall organisational capability.
- Moving from offering 'how to' solutions to developing originality of thought, greater curiosity, and the capacity to learn continuously.
- Moving from teaching research and case-based content at an intellectual level to conversations which are emotionally enlightening and reassuring.

I offer the above not as either/or choices but as options to rebalance the nature of how executive education can enhance its value. Business schools who have the courage to test and experiment with these propositions could well find they, the delegates, and the organisations they represent will all have significantly more enjoyable, fulfilling, and productive futures.

References

Goddard, J. (2006). Management and moral capital. *Discussion Paper*.

Goddard, J., & Eccles, T. (2013). *Uncommon sense, common nonsense*. IPS.

Gratton, L., & Scott, A. (2016). *The 100-year Life-living and working in an age of longevity*. Bloomsbury Information.

Grint, K. (n.d.). Wicked problems. https://scholar.google.co.uk/scholar?q=keith+gri nt+wicked+problems&hl=en&as_sdt=0&as_vis=1&oi=scholart

Heifetz, R., Grashow, A., & Linsky, M. (2009). *The practice of adaptive leadership*. Harvard Business Press.

MINDSPACE. (n.d.). https://www.bi.team/publications/mindspace/

Mintzberg, H. (2009). Interview for Director magazine.

Pfeffer, J. (2018). *Dying for a paycheck: How modern management harms employee health and company performance—And what we can do about it*. Harper Business.

Pfeffer, J., & Sutton, R. I. (2006). *Hard facts, dangerous half-truths & total nonsense: Profiting from evidence-based management*. Harvard Business Review Press.

Pinker, S. (2019). *Enlightenment now: The case for reason, science, humanism and progress*. Penguin Books.

Segal, E.. (2021, May). *Forbes Magazine*.

Stern, S. (2010, November). Will business schools save—Or destroy—The world?

Thomas, H., Lorange, P., & Sheth, J. (Eds.). (2013). *The business school in the twenty first century*. Cambridge University Press.

10

Coaching for Leadership

Bob Thomson

In an increasingly volatile, uncertain, complex, and ambiguous (VUCA) world, the ability of groups of co-workers to operate as an effective team in pursuit of the organisation's objectives is vital. As we have seen in previous chapters, crises require teamwork of a highly developed order. It is essential to be able to mobilise effectively in response to ambiguous and rapidly changing challenges which bring pressure and perhaps even fear. Adopting a coaching approach offers leaders a way of developing this capability within their teams and organisations. Coaching is a practical approach that can be used with all levels of staff to improve performance, to develop people, to build teams, and to enhance organisational resilience.

> **This chapter asks questions that encourage you to reflect on your own practise, including:**
>
> - What is coaching?
> - What are the skills needed for effective coaching conversations?
> - How might a manager use a coaching approach to enhance the performance and development of individuals who work for them?
> - How might you coach yourself?
> - How can you coach the team that you lead?
> - How can you develop a coaching culture within your organisation?

J. Colley, D. Spyridonidis, *Unprecedented Leadership*, Palgrave Executive Essentials, https://doi.org/10.1007/978-3-030-93486-6_10

What Is Coaching?

Any thesaurus is likely to offer some or all of the following suggestions for the noun '*coach*': *trainer, teacher, instructor, tutor, football coach*—all of these suggest that a coach knows what needs to be done and can tell the other person what to do and how to do it. This is probably what is in the mind of most managers when they talk about coaching their team; they draw on their knowledge, skills, and experience to advise and guide subordinates.

In this chapter, however, we'll be exploring a different view of coaching—a technique I have refined over more than twenty years and for which each term has been carefully defined.

> Coaching is a relationship of rapport and trust in which the coach uses their ability to listen, to ask questions and to play back what the client has communicated in order to help the client to clarify what matters to them and to work out what to do to achieve their aspirations (Northose, 2007).

My approach to coaching is primarily non-directive. I use my listening and questioning skills to manage conversations, encouraging the other person to clarify their goals and to decide upon actions that will help them to achieve these. In this chapter, I'll assume that you already know how to tell people what to do—in part, because in your own career it's likely you yourself have been told what to do by someone higher up in your organisation.

Telling People What to Do

A manager—by definition—is someone who achieves results through other people rather than exclusively through their own efforts. Writing one hundred years ago, the French mining engineer and executive Henri Fayol set out a general theory of management or, in his term, Business Administration (from which the MBA degree takes its name). He was the first person to describe management as a top-down process based on planning and the organisation of people. He listed five functions which a manager needs to perform:

- Plan
- Organise
- Co-ordinate
- Command
- Control

Command and control is a widely accepted, often very effective view of management in organisations. In setting out an alternative, primarily non-directive view of coaching in this chapter, I want to make clear that I am not suggesting the conventional top-down view to be wrong or inappropriate, rather I wish to present a different approach to leadership and the role of coach in particularly challenging circumstances.

The Directive to Non-directive Spectrum

I find the idea of a spectrum of behaviours from directive to non-directive a useful framework to think clearly about the choices you make when engaged in conversation—as a manager, coach, consultant or teacher—with another.

At the directive end of the spectrum, you might give an instruction, offer advice or guidance or make a suggestion. You know, or may have a clear opinion of, what the other person needs to do; when you tell them this, you are looking to give them a solution.

At the non-directive end of the spectrum, on the other hand, you utilise the conversational skills set out in my definition of coaching—listening, questioning, and playing back—to help the other person think through their situation and, if appropriate, to set goals and make an action plan. You are looking to draw out the solution from the other person.

We continually have to make choices about what approach to take—both in an overall sense and in how we respond within a conversation. In choosing whether to be directive or non-directive, it's important to be clear in your own mind what approach you are taking and why you're taking it.

Case Study

Let me give an example: a new member of staff asks you how to work on the office photocopier. There is a clear answer to this question, and you yourself know it. It makes sense and saves time to simply to tell them what to do. Some months later, that same member of staff asks you if they should accept a job offer in another department within your organisation. You could tell them what you think—or you could engage in a coaching conversation to help them work out what is the best choice for them. In terms of career development, they may live with the consequences of their decision for many years. The choice may be finely balanced, with pros and cons, and what matters to them in their career may be very different from what matters to you. It may be much more useful to listen and ask questions to help them clarify their thinking than to tell them what you think.

In my experience of helping managers learn how to coach, I find that they often struggle with the idea that there is a powerful alternative to telling people what to do. They are so used to telling, that it's difficult to restrain themselves from giving advice or making suggestions.

Reflection: How Directive are You?

- When one of your team—or a colleague or friend—comes to you with a problem, how likely are you to respond from the directive end of the spectrum with instructions, advice, guidance or suggestions?
- How often do you respond from the non-directive end by listening and asking questions?

Awareness and Responsibility

In 1992, John Whitmore published *Coaching for Performance*, now a classic and hugely influential text in coaching circles in the UK and beyond. In his book, Whitmore argues that the essence of what you are trying to do as a coach, or a manager using a coaching approach, is to raise the other person's AWARENESS and encourage them to take RESPONSIBILITY for action. He summarised this in the following equation:

$$Awareness + Responsibility = Performance$$

In other words, someone who knows what needs to be done (and who is capable of doing it) and who also takes responsibility for doing it will perform—whatever, performance means in the context. It may be completing a report, making a sales call, hitting a golf ball, or managing a team.

Whitmore adds that *Awareness without Responsibility is just Whingeing*. Someone who's very clear on what's needed but doesn't actually *do* anything is simply moaning.

For a manager taking a coaching approach (in the sense that we're discussing), the challenge is, first, to help your people to be clear about what they need to do and, second, to give them responsibility for taking action. With awareness and responsibility, they will perform.

The Skills of Coaching: Listening

My definition of coaching includes the three key conversational skills: listening, questioning, and playing back. Let's look at these in turn.

Listening is the fundamental skill needed to coach well. Everything you say or do in a coaching conversation follows listening in an effort to understand the other person. The questions that you ask, and the summaries that you play back, flow from what you've understood. And even if you want to move to the directive end of the spectrum and offer, say, a suggestion or advice, this will be more relevant when it's based on a good understanding of the other person and their situation.

There are different levels of listening, which you might imagine as a ladder:

- The lowest level is simply **not listening** to what the other person is saying.
- Then there's **listening, waiting to speak**—this is when your focus is on what you're going to say when they stop talking, and is likely to mean you've stopped listening.
- Further up comes **listening to disagree**—this is when you have a strong point of view that you hope will prevail, you therefore listen very selectively to the other person for weaknesses in their perspective. Listening to disagree is about winning or losing an argument. In some situations, this is really important, but not in coaching.
- Finally, **listening to understand** is the quality of listening that you need to bring to a coaching conversation. You are listening with empathy to appreciate the other person's position. You may also be paying attention to their non-verbal communication, picking up clues from their body language, facial expression or tone of voice. This can be particularly important when they're talking about something personal with a high emotional content.

Reflection: How Do You Listen?

Over the next few weeks or months, check in with yourself as to how you're listening. Notice which of the four levels of listening you're using.
  You might also look for any patterns in your level of listening.

- Who do you listen to, and who do you not listen to?
- When do you listen to disagree?
- In what contexts do you really listen in order to understand?

As well as appreciating more fully the other person's perspective, there is a further really important advantage in listening to understand another person. Recall that my definition begins *Coaching is a relationship*: as a manager, you have a relationship with each of the people who works for you. It may be a close or a distant relationship, but it's a relationship. Listening to understand—and playing back reasonably accurately your understanding—shows the other person that they've been listened to and, hopefully, understood. This helps to deepen the relationship between you.

In her book *Turning to One Another* (2002) there is a quote from Margaret J. Wheatley which captures the power of this:

> Why is being heard so healing? I don't know the full answer to that question, but I do know that is has something to do with the fact that listening creates relationship.

The Skills of Coaching: Questioning

A second vital skill in coaching conversations is questioning. You can use questions not merely to gain information but, more importantly in a coaching context to focus the thinking of the other person. Your questions can help to raise their awareness and/or encourage them to take responsibility for action.

It's useful to distinguish between closed and open questions. A closed question can be answered *Yes* or *No*, or a similarly short answer. For example:

1. Is this an interesting chapter?
2. Do you think you will use the above ideas on listening as a manager?
3. Should all managers be able to coach?

In a conversation, closed questions not only gather little information but, more importantly, seldom stimulate much thought in the other person.

Generally, an open question will be more useful. You will gain more information, and the other person will be prompted to think. Here is a rewording of the above closed questions:

1. What is interesting in this chapter?
2. How might you use the above ideas on listening as a manager?
3. In what situations would a manager find it useful to be able to coach?

I encourage you to practise asking open rather than closed questions in your conversations and meetings.

Occasionally, a closed question is appropriate. As an illustration, you might have used a coaching approach to help someone think through the pros and cons of a job opportunity. It may now be time to encourage them to make a decision, and you might, for example, ask, *so, are you going to apply for this job?*

It's also useful to ask short rather than long or complicated questions, and to ask one at a time rather than multiple questions. In her book, *Coaching Skills: A Handbook* (2004), Jenny Rogers writes:

> As a coach, when you ask long questions, you are at risk of turning the spotlight of the coaching onto yourself. Long questions normally come out of uncertainty [...] As a coach, you cannot afford the luxury of doing your thinking out loud.

One common, but not particularly helpful in coaching, is a leading question, that is, one which already contains or heavily suggests an answer. For example, those beginning *Do you think it would be a good idea to...* which is more of a statement or suggestion than a question. I encourage you, if you want to make a suggestion, to do this cleanly and clearly. In the example, you might say, *I think it would be a good idea to do ... What do you think?* Don't dress up your suggestions or advice as questions.

Questions to be sparing with in coaching are those that begin with *Why?* Although technically an open question, it may put the other person on the defensive, feeling that they have to justify themselves or their actions. A rewording and softening of a *Why?* question might be:

- *I'm wondering what led you to do that.*
- *What do you think that this will achieve?*

Reflection: What Kinds of Questions Do You Ask?

Over the next few days, pay attention to the questions you yourself ask in meetings or one-to-one conversations. Notice when you:

- Ask closed questions.
- Ask simple, open questions.
- Ask leading questions which contain advice or a suggestion.
- Ask multiple, complicated questions.

When you are tempted to ask a leading or complicated question, pause for a few seconds and frame a crisp question that focuses on what you *really* want to know. Notice how few words you actually need.

The Skills of Coaching: Playing Back

Some coaching textbooks focus on listening and questioning as the key conversational skills in coaching. Reflecting on my own practice as a coach, I realised that I often used a third skill in coaching conversations—playing back to the client what they'd told me. This is a powerful way of showing that you've been listening, which helps to build the relationship. It's also very useful in managing and structuring a session and can provide a useful segue from one part of the conversation to the next.

I use three forms of playing back. First, I might summarise an extended piece of conversation. Second, I might paraphrase what someone's said, changing their words into a different expression; this might be helpful but runs the risk of getting the meaning of what they've said wrong. An additional way therefore is when I play back using the exact words of the client—I call this 'reflecting back'. Sometimes, there is a real power in the precise word or metaphor that the other person has used. I might simply repeat their words with an inquisitive tone, or I might say, *Tell me more about [their exact words]*.

Although I use summary a lot in coaching conversation, I invariably leave it to the client to make the final summary. I might end a conversation by saying something like, *As we draw to a close, tell me what you're taking from today's session*. Or perhaps, *summarise what you're going to do as a result of today's conversation*. Note that the focus of these two summaries is different, with the latter emphasising action; this might not be appropriate if the client didn't reach this point in the discussion. I'm sometimes surprised that what they summarise as important, wouldn't have been what I'd have picked out. My belief is that what they're taking from a session is more important than what I think.

Challenges for a Manager-Coach

The question of how directive or non-directive you wish to be is particularly important if you are a manager. You have legitimate objectives to achieve and need to satisfy the demands of your own superiors. Helping a subordinate to achieve their personal objectives might conflict with this. Another challenge for a manager-coach is regarding confidentiality—the person may have good cause to be guarded in what they share with you. And it can be that the key issue they want help with is their relationship with you. For these reasons, it's often easier for an external coach to work with a client.

Jenny Rogers (2016) reflects these additional factors when she writes:

> As a boss, it is entirely probable that you are part of whatever problems your coachee has and this can be difficult to see let alone acknowledge. Also, it is always more difficult to promise confidentiality, encourage or expect complete disclosure, set aside your own considerations or remain detached from the possible outcomes. As a boss you have a stake in the outcome, whereas when you are purely a coach you do not.

The Coaching Dance

A useful way of looking at the challenge of balancing your objectives as a line manager within an organisation with the individual objectives of one of your team is the idea of the coaching dance. I first heard about this from David Hemery, who won the 400 metres hurdles in the 1968 Mexico Olympics and who later went on to help many managers learn how to coach.

Hemery suggests that it's important to distinguish clearly when you are **telling** someone what you want them to do and when you are **asking** them for their ideas. A simple example is that you might **tell** one of your team that you must have a report by Friday morning and then **ask** them what they need in order to complete the report by then. They will know better than you what else they have on this week, how they like to work, and where they are struggling. You can tap into their knowledge and ideas and help them identify a clear plan of action. And you might also ask what support they need from you.

It's called the coach dance because it's about moving skilfully and gracefully (and appropriately) between telling and asking. I encourage you to have this idea of the coaching dance in mind when you converse with the people who work for you. Be clear when it's appropriate to tell them what you want or what you think, and when it will be more useful to ask them what *they* want or think.

Another time when you might usefully move between telling and asking is in the area of feedback. Let's imagine that your employee did complete the report by Friday morning. You could give them feedback, telling them what you thought was good or poor in their report. Or you could ask them first what they thought they did well and what they could have done better. They might well cover all the points that you would have made—and, if they miss something important, you can go on to add this. Distinguish between **giving** feedback and **generating** feedback—in other words, dancing between asking and telling.

Performance and Development Reviews

Managers often think that they don't have time to spend on coaching conversations due to the pressures of their job. One situation which lends itself well to a coaching approach is the annual performance and development review meeting. I do hope you treat this as a valuable opportunity to engage in a rich and productive conversation, not just a time to fill in a form to keep the HR department happy!

You can use the idea of short, open questions to structure the conversation. Here are a few suggestions which you can adapt for your own context.

Performance

- How would you assess your performance over the last twelve months?
- What did you do well?
- Where could you have contributed more?
- What do you want to achieve over the coming year? (This is likely to call for the coaching dance—you and your organisation may have some clear views on what the person needs to achieve over the coming year.)
- How can I support you?

Development

- What are your development goals?
- What will you do to pursue these goals?
- How can I support you?

The GROW Model

In his book *Coaching for Performance*, John Whitmore popularised the GROW model, which is now a widely used way of structuring a coaching conversation to help someone explore an issue and then to decide what to do. In other words, to raise their AWARENESS and then to encourage them to take RESPONSIBILITY for action. A simplified version of the model, which creates the acronym GROW, is:

Goal	What are you trying to achieve?
Reality	What is currently going on?
Options	What might you do?
Will	What will you do?

Note that these are overview questions. The more detailed questions you ask will emerge from listening to the other person. It might be, for example, that you need to spend time clarifying the Goal and then the actions become obvious. Or, the Goal might be clear, but the constraints of the current Reality are large and need careful unpicking. Or, you might find that there are no practical Options to achieve the Goal and so you may need to return to modify (or perhaps abandon) the original version of the Goal. It's a framework to be used flexibly, not mechanically.

Case Study: Using the GROW Model to Coach Yourself

Think of an issue or problem that you yourself are currently facing, in either your working life or in your life outside work. It needs to be a real issue—something that matters to you and where you're not sure what to do.

Write down in a sentence what the issue is.

Then, ask yourself some crisp, open questions to think the issue through in a structured way using the four aspects of the GROW model. You might need to spend different amounts of time on different steps.

Here are some possible questions to expand on the four aspects:

Goal

- What do I want to achieve?
- Where would I like to be in twelve months' time?
- If I succeed in achieving this goal, what will that look like?

Reality

- What's going on now that makes this an issue?
- What are the constraints?
- What resources do I have?
- Who can assist me here?

Options

- What options do I have?
- What are the alternatives?
- If I were bold (or less fearful), what would I do?

Will

- Which of these options seems the most practical?
- Which option will I choose?
- What specifically will I do to carry out this option?
- What timetable will I set myself?
- How will I review my progress?

What is a Team?

Just because a group of people report to the same boss, or share the same office, it does not follow that they are—or that they need to be—a team. They might simply be a group of people who may have some things to communicate to each other, but they essentially do different things and have no requirement to be a team.

In their book, *The Wisdom of Teams* (1992), Jon Katzenbach and Douglas Smith offer a definition of a team that explains the difference between a group and a team:

> A team is a small number of people with complementary skills committed to a common purpose, performance goals and ways of working together for which they hold themselves mutually accountable.

What is Team Coaching?

Team coaching can be viewed as an intervention to help a team to:

- Clarify and achieve their collective goals.
- Communicate and interact with one another effectively.
- Constructively explore and resolve differences within the team
- Make wise decisions.
- Engage effectively with key stakeholders outside the team.

In her chapter on team coaching in the book *Excellence in Coaching: the Industry Guide* (2016), Kate Lanz writes that, 'In essence, teams are all about relationship'. She adds that, 'The quality of relationships enables the team to get to true clarity of purpose, develop effective use of resources and focus on delivering the task'.

As leader, you may wish to engage an external coach to work with your team. Team coaching is about much more than the facilitation of away days or strategy retreats. Rather, it's about enabling the team to manage itself. In his book *Coaching the Team at Work* (2007), David Clutterbuck crystallises the difference: '*facilitation is about external management of the dialogue whereas team coaching is about empowering the team to manage its own dialogue*.' The goal of the team coach is to help the team to become self-sufficient.

Alternatively, as the leader of the team, you might choose to adopt your own coaching approach. This has parallels with taking a coaching approach to managing an individual, which we discussed earlier. There will be times when you will be telling the team what is required—perhaps because you are following a wider organisational agenda—and times when you are consulting the team to gather their views and insights.

Goal	What are we trying to achieve? *It may be more difficult to get agreement on this with a group than with an individual, since different people may well have different views.*
Reality	What is the current reality? *Again, there might be very different perceptions and perspectives.*
Options	What options do we have? *There is an advantage in working with a team here as you can draw on and build upon the ideas of a number of people.*
Will	What will we do? *Again, making a collective decision might be more challenging, particularly if you are seeking consensus and commitment. It may be that you need to take the decision yourself as the team leader.*

Case Study: How Well Developed Is Your Team?

Each phrase in Katzenbach and Smith's definition of a team has been carefully crafted. Here are some questions to assess how well your team satisfies the elements of the definition.

- How many people are in your team? (In their research, Katzenbach and Smith found that most high-performing teams had less than ten members.)
- What is the purpose of the team? To what extent is this shared by everyone in the team?
- What are your key performance indicators? How committed are individuals to achieving these?
- What attitudes and behaviours characterise how your team work together? What could you do differently to collaborate more effectively?
- To what extent do people feel accountable to one another?

Creating a Coaching Culture

In their book, *Building and Sustaining a Coaching Culture*, David Clutterbuck, David Megginson, and Agnieszka Bajer note three key aspects of organisational culture:

- Culture is created over time through the interaction of people and their environment.
- Culture creates consistent patterns of meaning and behaviour that bind people together and make them unique as a group.
- Coaching is a combination of visible and invisible elements that exist on multiple levels.

In her book *The Coach's Coach*, Alison Hardingham explains that a coaching culture in an organisation is one 'where people coach each other all the time as a natural part of meetings, reviews and one-to-one discussions of all kinds'. She illustrates this with an example from one firm:

> The message 'coaching is a normal part of what successful people do around here' is communicated loud and clear. For anyone wanting to establish a coaching culture, that is the message that has to be got across. And it will be got across by actions, not words.

There is a saying sometimes found in literature concerning organisational culture that 'a fish rots from the head'. To create a coaching culture requires the active commitment from the person at the top of the organisation. While it may be possible to create an oasis within the organisation where coaching is used as a management style, there will inevitably be tensions when engaging with the rest of the organisation where the management style is more traditionally command and control.

Shifting the culture of an organisation takes time, potentially several years to establish. In pursuing this goal, as in many other aspects of leadership, actions speak louder than words. If you are sincere about wanting to establish a coaching culture in the organisation that you lead, recognise that this needs to work at all levels of the organisation, including among the top 'team'. It isn't something that only middle managers need.

Reflection: Establishing a Coaching Culture within Your Organisation

Here are some questions to consider if you are a leader seeking to establish a coaching culture within your organisation. As in the previous exercises in this chapter, these are short, open questions to focus your thinking. In terms of the GROW model, the questions explore reflect on Reality before looking at a possible Goal. This is often a more natural way to use the framework in conversations. The questions skip Options and go to Will.

Reality

- How committed are you to establishing a genuine coaching culture in your organisation?
- What do you see as the challenges in undertaking this?
- What resources or people can you draw upon to assist you in this?

Goal

- If you are successful in establishing a coaching culture, what would you see happening in your organisation?

Will

- What actions will you take to pursue this goal?
- What deadlines will you set?
- When and how will you review progress?

Summary of Key Learning Points

- In contrast to a directive, command and control style of management, a coaching approach operates primarily from the non-directive end of the spectrum to help someone clarify what matters to them, and to work out what to do to achieve their aspirations.
- The key conversational skills in coaching are listening to understand, asking open questions, and playing back your understanding.
- The questions you ask as a coach are designed to raise awareness in the other person and to encourage them to take responsibility for action: Awareness + Responsibility = Performance.

- As a line manager, you can apply the coaching dance to move skilfully between *telling* someone what to do and *asking* them for their ideas.
- You can use the GROW model to structure a coaching conversation or to coach yourself on an issue you are facing.
- You can apply the basic ideas of individual to team coaching, though this is inevitably more complicated.
- Creating a coaching culture in which people naturally coach each other demands the active commitment of the person at the top of the organisation and will take time to establish.

Further Reading

Arnold, J. (2016). *Coaching skills for leaders in the workplace*. Robinson.

Downey, M. (2014). *Effective modern coaching*. Texere.

Hardingham, A. (2004). *The coach's coach*. Chartered Institute of Personnel and Development.

Rogers, J. (2016). *Coaching skills: A handbook*. McGraw-Hill.

Rogers, J., Whittleworth, K., & Gilbert, A. (2012). *Manager as coach*. McGraw-Hill.

Thomson, B. (2020). *How to coach*. Sage.

Whitmore, J. (2017). *Coaching for performance*. Nicholas Brealey.

Part V

Conclusion

11

Conclusion: Unprecedented Leadership for Unprecedented Times

Considerable changes continue to cloud the horizons of future business. We must anticipate that climate change, technological development, and the truly unprecedented disruptors such as COVID-19, are risks and circumstances for which we should mitigate and prepare. These waves of crises, however rapid or great in magnitude, influence the nature of almost everything we do. In a business context, a leader may find traditional market channels constrict or disappear, whilst once reliable and secure business models are no longer viable. In this state of unpredictability, it is all too easy for management to deteriorate into a regime of the patched up and painted over, which inevitably precedes decline.

The intention of this book has not been to ruminate on all that has happened, nor make doom and gloom forecasts for the future but to equip you as a future leader with the skills to respond to crises. Learning from the case studies given, we hope it will have helped you to identify and diffuse potential problems at their earliest point. It has become increasingly evident over the past decade that how you might lead a team through crisis circumstances must now be built into any pragmatic leadership training.

The materials here compiled are a product of our ongoing interaction with executive students and colleagues over the course of many years; it is also the product of crises. With the gathering of long-term examples and the need for rapid action, this publication itself demonstrates the duality of a crisis response. All its advice originates from key issues which our students face in

© The Author(s), under exclusive license to Springer Nature Switzerland AG 2022   **237**
J. Colley, D. Spyridonidis, *Unprecedented Leadership*, Palgrave Executive Essentials,
https://doi.org/10.1007/978-3-030-93486-6_11

progressing their careers and leadership skills. The overall aim of its collected theories, lessons, and case studies is to influence leadership behaviour and performance, whilst recognising that all leaders have and develop their own styles and ways of doing things.

With this in mind, we have adopted a number of perspectives on leading in turbulent times. The diverse backgrounds of its contributors and the vivid examples they bring to the table are intended to prompt the reader to consider what they would do if facing a given set of circumstances. Those pursuing leadership goals who ask this question of themselves when watching crises unfold may find a more structured response here.

This pragmatic 'what would you do?' approach is the basis of the first, essentially practical section, written by a practitioner-turned-academic with extensive experience in the field. From exploring crisis leadership and decision making, this section addressed some of the most difficult situations to negotiate in a chapter on 'Ethics and Values: Negotiating a Complex Minefield'. Whilst any leadership training will stress the importance of upholding high ethical standards regardless of crisis situations, it is not often clear what constitutes these situations and how best to resolve them. This section generates situations similar to those commonly encountered by leaders in senior positions and that have transferable teachings and relevance.

*   *   *

Each section of this book operates on the basic principle of extracting the practical and appropriate responses to crisis that are often buried beneath business theory. Our guidance has concerned how to respond to a rapidly changing environment which presents leaders with unforeseen challenges, not simply more rapidly but necessitating more innovative and flexible approaches. Crisis response, like all emergency services and measures, is in ever greater demand, as is effective change management in the aftermath of difficult times. We have reviewed the relationship between the leader, their team, and organisational objectives, stressing the significance of cohesion and trust. We have also identified issues which have and will hold back many otherwise capable leaders; the responses we have addressed may motivate a leader to invest in their team now in order to achieve their full potential.

*   *   *

Section 1: Crisis from the Ground Up

The chapter 'Crises Global and Local: When Leadership Becomes Critical' concludes that experience and practice do help improve performance responses to crises. It is difficult to recreate training and development exercises that replicate the fear and prolonged pressure to which teams and their leaders are subjected when crises arise. It is these very circumstances which make crises so difficult to counter with an effective response, particularly whilst complex situations are continually evolving.

What is consistently evident is that the saviour of a crisis is as simple as a collaborative, cooperative team. Whilst the leader may be enmeshed in damage-limitation and conversations with concerned, often disadvantaged stakeholders, the quality and ability of the team to work together are tested to the limit. It is at this stage that weak links become apparent, and the inexperienced leader may regret not having addressed known weaknesses in the team previously.

In this, the significance of decision making comes to the fore. We contend that leadership critiques, studies, and publications often highlight stereotypical character-facets of good leadership such as emotional intelligence and charisma; here decision making is often overlooked and certainly undervalued. We addressed this common oversight here, alerting readers to personality traits such as hubris, narcissism, impulsivity, or risk aversion that can result in experienced leaders making poor decisions.

This led to a discussion of different organisational models: those that place responsibility for decision making solely at the leader's door, whilst others disperse the task amongst committees, thereby avoiding personal responsibility. We have seen how providing clarity of responsibility can bring a broader sense of perspective to the decision making process. We have also identified when opportunities for individual development may exist, but also where this exposure may not be appropriate for a team.

In the chapter 'Ethics and Values: Negotiating a Complex Minefield', we explored a series of case studies which place the leader in a difficult position, each requiring of the leader calm reflection in order to determine the actions that will prevent the situation persisting. As is often the case, some solutions may result in an immediate loss in value, at which point the inexperienced leader may well panic and react impulsively and unwisely. Regardless of circumstances, your team will only function well with confident leadership.

We also consider what clear practical steps are necessary to create an ethical organisation. Many organisations are quick to make clear their high moral standards, and publicising their policies prematurely before creating the environment in which those ethics can become reality. Therefore, we have considered what practical steps are necessary in creating a sustainably ethical organisation, outlined the warning signs of an unethical organisation and concluded with the message that any ethical organisation requires actions as well as words.

*   *   *

Section 2: Philosophical Underpinnings and New Directions

The second, more philosophical and thought-provoking section examined exactly what leaders are attempting to achieve and how. Here, we have set out some of the issues which should remain central in the minds of leaders, and how these are to be upheld in a challenging environment. Subsequently, this section provides higher level longer term guidance that explores how a leader might achieve responsible outcomes. These scenarios are particularly applicable to the ongoing issues of climate change and socio-economic change, as well as the need for strategic leadership in difficult environments.

We have shown how change management is more about people—their feelings, attitudes, and roles—who in difficult times need visible and confident leadership. If leaders lack conviction, then they will undoubtedly find it difficult to convince a team that implementing change is necessary and deserving of their effort and enthusiasm. The key is not process but leadership. The chapter explored the critical steps to leading major change initiatives, drawing on theory from a number of prominent writers on the subject who demonstrated that the key is not process but leadership.

Consumed by uncertain circumstances, organisations will need a responsible leadership strategy that places value on sustainability. In a climate of flux, some industries are rendered obsolete, and new, more innovative businesses are created in their place. The message here is that we ignore such transience at our peril. Instead, we encourage you to utilise this environment, in which new ideas and innovation can flourish as rules change and consumer demand moves.

Underlying this are more serious concerns in regard to investment. Fund managers and pension schemes are becoming much more selective and thinking more carefully about the implications of Environment, Social, and

Governance (ESG) when deciding which firms they choose to invest in. With this in mind, a closer consideration of strategic leadership encompasses the entire process of investment strategies before directing teams and organisations in their implementation. There are issues of values and culture here, as well as critical decisions surrounding how and with whom should be given central, focused roles.

*   *   *

Section 3: Communications, Education, and Coaching—Tools for Leading During Crisis

In our final section, our specialist contributors provided valuable insights into leadership communication, the role of executive education in developing crucial leadership skills, and how coaching can effectively contribute to team and leader development. This is all advice from, and directed to, emerging and aspiring leaders who are likely, at some stage in their career, to encounter similar scenarios.

The more thorough, practical consideration given to communication here explored the key facets of transmitting confidence, providing direction and motivating a team. In particular, it evidenced how the creation of a strategic narrative with authenticity at its heart is the cornerstone of great leadership. We have acknowledged the paradoxes in executive education with an astute look at the problems created by hierarchies and silos. Learning more about vertical organisation along functional or geographic lines highlighted how these might limit the flexibility of an organisation, especially at a time when businesses need to innovate and coordinate a reaction to rapid change. This section concludes with an exploration of how coaching techniques can be used to effectively develop teams and individuals in pursuit of organisational objectives.

This book is proof of how powerful stories can act to sell concepts and ideas, and generate motivation in a flagging team. In fact, this book itself is a metaphor for crisis management: it identified a crucial deficiency in leadership training, coordinated a rapid response founded on long-term experience but hastened into print by the short-term response to the pandemic crisis. This demanded all the skills we have discussed—agreeing on core objectives and contacting potential contributors before beginning the challenge of manuscript drafts and overarching narratives.

If this book has taught you anything, it will be that communication and teamwork are key, and we must take this opportunity to acknowledge the motivated and supportive toing and froing of drafts across many miles and in many emails. We have all learnt something from this process, and we hope you, with aspirations to lead, will have too.

Index

A

Academia, 188
Adaptation, from uncertainty, 98–99
Adaptive, 125
Agility, 124, 125, 130
Ambiguity, 26, 28, 29
Anatomy of crisis, 29–30
Art of listening, 178
Asking Questions, 59–61
Authentic communication, 175–177
Authenticity, 141, 168, 175, 176, 183
Avoiding corporate speak, 178–179
Awareness and responsibility, 222

B

Bedrock of leadership, 11–15
Beliefs
    What Do You Really Believe?, 104
    'Whys'?, 104
Bribery, 68, 71
Business
    as unusual, 97–98
    as usual, 97–98

C

Case studies, 68–69
    discussion, 70–75, 83–84
    whistle blowers, 76–77
    white-collar crime, 77–78
Change
    change efforts, failure of, 100
    motivation, 102–103
    poor decisions, 44
    support for, 52
    transformation, 100–101
Coaching, 219–234
    culture, 232–233
    dance, 227
    tool for leading during
        crisis, 241–242
Communication, 28, 34, 39, 101–103,
        106, 163–183, 241–242
    communicate continuously, 106
    effective leadership
        communication, 174–175
    strategies, 171–174
    tool for leading during
        crisis, 241–242

© The Author(s), under exclusive license to Springer Nature Switzerland AG 2022
J. Colley, D. Spyridonidis, *Unprecedented Leadership*, Palgrave Executive Essentials,
https://doi.org/10.1007/978-3-030-93486-6

Consistency, 180–181
Context of strategic leadership, 124–127
    digitisation, 124–125
    reflection, 126
Corporate change, 107–115
    case study, globalisation, 108–110
    commentary and analysis, 110–111
    Kotter's eight-step change
        model, 111–113
COVID-19, 3, 5
Crises/crisis, 5, 15, 16, 237–239
    from ground up, 239–240
    opportunities and silver-
        linings in, 38
    tools for leading during
        crisis, 241–242
Critical test of leadership
    capability, 4–5

D

Decision making, 41–46, 48–51,
        58–63, 238, 239
    bad decision, 45–50
    components of, 44–45
    hubris, 45
    narcissism, 46–47
    pride, 47
    risk aversion, 47
    self and friends, 48
Delegation, 11–14
    how do you go about
        delegating?, 12–14
    so why is delegation so hard?,
        11–12
Digital media skills, 181–182
Development, 41, 42, 50–52, 55, 62,
        185–216, 219, 221, 227–228
Directive to non-directive
    spectrum, 221–222
Driven culture, ethics and values
    in, 81–84
Dynamics, of organisational
    communication, 169–171

E

Education, tool for leading during
    crisis, 241–242
Ethical culture, 84–86
    discussion, 88–90
    ethical hazard zones, 85–86
    product recalls, 86–90
    unethical culture, 86
Ethics, 65–91
    in driven culture, 81–84
Executive Education
    Introduction to, 186–189
    Changing Nature, 186–187
    Returns on, 187–188

F

Fear, 26–31, 38

G

GROW model, 228–230

H

Hierarchy, 186, 196–198, 202,
        204, 216
How to Pick the Right
        People, 52
Human-centred change, 103
    expect casualties, 105
    motivates humans, 106–107
    power of networks, 105–106

I

Industry, 188
Ingredients of success, 113
    actionable first steps, 115
    effective rewards, 115–116
    leadership and vision,
        114–115
    pressure for change, 114
    skills and resources, 115–116

J

Judgment, 44, 53

K

Key leadership skills
  curiosity, 132
  know which battles to fight, 131
  navigating complexity and
    unpredictability, 129
  purpose, 128
  restlessness, 130–131
  sharing learning, 132–133
  strategic leaders, 127–136

L

Leadership, 4, 9, 95–99, 101, 102,
    104, 107, 110–112, 114–115
  communication, 164–166
  ethics, 66–69
  relationship between self, teams, and
    organisations, 6–7, 9–10
  translating theory, 7–9
    learning from other leaders, 7–8
Leading organisations, 34–37
  crisis, 99–100
  learn and recover, 37
  make decisions, 36
  truth, 34–35
  values, 35–36
  visibility, 36–37
Leading self, 30, 96–97
  anxieties, 96
  assumptions, 96
  self-awareness, 96
Leading teams, 30–34
  challenge culture, 33
  clear communication, 34
  clear objectives, 31–32
  collaborative planning, 32
  connected system, 30–31
  decision making, 32–33
  facts, not fear, 31

risks, 32–33
  teamwork, 33
Legacy of our decisions, 42–43
Learning, 186–191, 193–194,
    196–198, 200, 201, 204,
    209–211, 213–216
Learning points, 38–39, 62,
    183, 233–234
Lessons, 91
Listening, 220–226, 228, 233

M

Making decisions, in volatile and
    uncertain world, 41–62
  hubris, 45–46
Manager-coach, challenges for, 226
Models
  GROW model, 228–229
  Kotter's, 111–113
  responsible leadership, 150–153
  system leadership, 153–154

N

Narrative, 165–172, 174, 183
Negative emotion, 101–102
Networks, 164, 168–172, 174,
    182, 183
Non-directive, 220–222, 226, 233

O

Organisation, 65–70, 75–77, 86, 91
  reality, 166–169

P

Pandemic, 4
Paradox, 185–216
Paradox 2
  hierarchy, 196–201
  development, benefits of, 200–201
  leaders in isolation, 198–199

Paradox 3
  context, 205
  fixation with leadership, 202–206
  meaning and purpose, 204
  new leadership paradigm, 205
Paradox 4
  certainty and answers, 207–210
  executive development, 213–215
  fashions and fads, 207
  implications for leadership, 210
  value of business schools, 209
Paradox mindset, 133–136
  fast and slow, 134
  leaders without answers, 135–136
  of purpose, 135
  of self *vs.* community, 136
  of today and tomorrow, 134–135
Performance and development
     reviews, 227–228
Personality, 44, 46, 53
Philosophical underpinnings and new
     directions, 240–241
Power of stories, 179–180
Practice, 239
  responsibility, accountability, and
     power, 14–15
Pressure, 26–32, 34, 36, 38, 39

Questioning, 220–222, 224–225

Reputation, 145, 155, 157
Resilience, 125–127, 131
Responsibility, 10–12, 14–15, 17
Responsible leadership
  in business world, 149–150
  case study, Lush and AIB, 146
  case study, pacific gas and
     electric, 149

Central Banks, role of, 147–148
challenges of, 148–149
corporate social
     responsibility, 144–145
personal leadership, 143
sustainable change, 154–158
vision, values, purpose, 142–143

Shareholder theory, 79–81
Skills of coaching
  listening, 222–224
  playing back, 225–226
  questioning, 224–225
Stakeholders, 139, 143–154, 156
Stakeholder theory, 79–81
Stewardship theory, 79–81
Strategic, 119–136
Strategic leadership, 119–124
  pound stores *vs.* John
     Lewis, 120–124
Strategy, crises, and people, 52–53
  potential risks of 'new blood,' 56–58
  team, internal or external, 53–56
Sustainability, 139–158
  and leadership, 19

Team, 41, 42, 44, 48–63
  alignment and motivation, 51
  coaching, 230–232
  consultation of, 50–58
  decision making,
     involvement, 49–50
  open-mindednesshow, 51–52
  self-interest, 49
  delegation, 51
  development, 50
  expertise, 50
  time, 50

Teamwork, 242
Telling People What to Do,
        220–221
Transformation, 99–102, 115
Trust, 11, 13

U

Unethical cultures, 65, 86, 91
Unprecedented leadership, 15–21
    capacity for strategic
        leadership, 18–19
    coaching for leadership, 21
    communication, purpose and power
        of, 19–20
    crises global and local, 15–16

ethics and values, 16–17
    key decisions, 16
    responsible leadership and
        sustainability, 19
    turbulent times, change in, 17
    for unprecedented times, 21
Unprecedented times, 3–21
Urgency, 112

V

Values, 65–91, 140–147, 149,
        152, 154–157
    in driven culture, 81–84
Vision, 104, 111–115, 122, 123, 127,
        128, 135

Ingram Content Group UK Ltd.
Milton Keynes UK
UKHW021817180423
420384UK00009B/328

9 783030 934859